WHAT'S RIGHT WITH THE TRINITY?

The doctrine of the Trinity poses a series of problems for feminist theology. At a basic level, the androcentric nature of trinitarian language serves to promote the male as more fully in the image of God and as the archetype of humanity, pushing women to the margins of personhood. It is no surprise then that feminist scholarship on this doctrine has often focused on what's wrong with the Trinity, setting out the problems raised by the use of traditional androcentric trinitarian language.

This book brings together a discussion of feminist theological methodology with a critical exploration of the doctrine of the Trinity. Focusing on what's right with the Trinity as opposed to what's wrong with the Trinity, it considers the usefulness of this doctrine for feminist theology today. It replaces a stress on trinitarian language with an emphasis on trinitarian thought, exploring how we might effectively think rather than speak God in light of feminist concerns. In particular, it asks how a trinitarian understanding of God might support, and be supported by, key values which underpin a feminist way of doing theology, specifically values which underpin the methodological use of women's experience in feminist theology. The central argument is that thinking God as Trinity need not serve to reinforce patriarchal values and ideals but may in fact promote the subjectivity and personhood of women.

ASHGATE NEW CRITICAL THINKING IN RELIGION, THEOLOGY AND BIBLICAL STUDIES

The *Ashgate New Critical Thinking in Religion, Theology and Biblical Studies* series brings high quality research monograph publishing back into focus for authors, international libraries, and student, academic and research readers. Headed by an international editorial advisory board of acclaimed scholars spanning the breadth of religious studies, theology and biblical studies, this open-ended monograph series presents cutting-edge research from both established and new authors in the field. With specialist focus yet clear contextual presentation of contemporary research, books in the series take research into important new directions and open the field to new critical debate within the discipline, in areas of related study, and in key areas for contemporary society.

Other Recently Published Titles in the Series:

Evagrius Ponticus
The Making of a Gnostic
Julia Konstantinovsky

The Identity of Christian Morality
Ann Marie Mealey

Phenomenology and Eschatology
Not Yet in the Now
Edited by Neal DeRoo and John Panteleimon Manoussakis

Jürgen Moltmann's Ethics of Hope
Eschatological Possibilities For Moral Action
Timothy Harvie

Reading Anselm's Proslogion
The History of Anselm's Argument and its Significance Today
Ian Logan

The Challenges of the Pentecostal, Charismatic and
Messianic Jewish Movements
The Tensions of the Spirit
Peter Hocken

Theosis *in the Theology of Thomas Torrance*
Myk Habets

What's Right with the Trinity?
Conversations in Feminist Theology

HANNAH BACON
University of Chester, UK

Routledge
Taylor & Francis Group
LONDON AND NEW YORK

First published 2009 by Ashgate Publishing

Published 2016 by Routledge
2 Park Square, Milton Park, Abingdon, Oxon OX14 4RN
711 Third Avenue, New York, NY 10017, USA

Routledge is an imprint of the Taylor & Francis Group, an informa business

British Library Cataloguing in Publication Data

Bacon, Hannah.

What's right with the Trinity? : conversations in feminist theology. — (Ashgate new critical thinking in religion, theology and biblical studies)

1. Feminist theology. 2. Trinity. 3. Bible—Feminist criticism.

I. Title II. Series

231'.044—dc22

Library of Congress Cataloging-in-Publication Data

Bacon, Hannah, 1978–

What's right with the Trinity? : conversations in feminist theology / Hannah Bacon.

p. cm. — (New critical thinking in religion, theology, and biblical studies)

Includes bibliographical references and index.

ISBN 978-0-7546-6673-8 (hardcover : alk. paper) 1. Trinity. 2. Feminist theology. I. Title.

BT111.3.B33 2009

231'.044—dc22

2009017752

ISBN 9780754666738 (hbk)

For Kate and in memory of Hilda Mary Freeman and Elizabeth Bacon

Contents

Acknowledgements

There are a number of people who have made this publication possible and who must be acknowledged here. Priority must be given to J'annine Jobling for her support during the length of time I studied under her supervision as a PhD student and for providing invaluable guidance on the manuscript in its first form as a PhD thesis. I would also like to thank the Department of Theology and Religious Studies at Liverpool Hope University for the gift of a bursary during the first two years of my doctoral studies and for enabling me to gain a wealth of teaching experience.

Thanks must also be given to colleagues and friends at the University of Chester for their support and interest in my work. To David Clough, Tom Greggs and Wayne Morris for being good enough to meet with me during my sabbatical and to all those who covered for me whilst on research leave. Special thanks to Ruth Ackroyd as Head of Department, for her constant support and for making my sabbatical possible. Thanks to Celia Deane-Drummond for reassurance and to past colleagues for their support – to Chris Partridge for reading material and Andrew Dawson for encouragement and true friendship. Special thanks to Wayne for reading a draft of this manuscript, for providing timely words of encouragement and for helping me through the difficult times. Your friendship and humour have kept me grounded and are of immeasurable value.

Thanks also to friends at All Saints Church in Hoole, for love and fellowship, and to all those who have put up with my absence whilst writing this work – particularly Nicki and Paul, Christie and Patrice. Special mention must be given here to Berni who has sustained me during the writing of this manuscript and who has endured a multiple of sins on my part, including my absence from cooking and cleaning duties! For being a prevailing source of strength and encouragement, and for your love, grace, care and forgiveness, thank you.

My final thanks, however, must go to my family for their overwhelming love, reassurance and faithfulness: to my parents, June and Roger for always supporting and listening, and to my elder sister Helen, for her genuine love and for always phoning. Thanks also to G, and to my wonderful niece, Olivia, who never fails to make me smile. This book, however, is dedicated to my twin sister, Kate, and to the loving memory of my two Nans, Elizabeth Bacon and Hilda Mary Freeman. Where Kate is concerned, I can never express my gratitude for the amount of help, comfort and guidance she has provided whilst writing this work. Thank you for being strict with me, for your wisdom, for your insight, your honesty and most of all, for your unconditional love. We will always journey together. I end, however, by acknowledging the lives of my two Nans; women who excelled in humour and personality, who always took an interest in my academic life and who always had time for me. This book is for them. You will never be forgotten and you are greatly missed.

Introduction
Thinking and Speaking Rightly about God

The doctrine of the Trinity is one of the most defining features of the Christian faith. According to the Nicene-Constantinopolitan Creed of 381, to believe in One God is to confess a trinitarian faith. 'We believe in One God', the creed exclaims; the 'Father Almighty', in 'One Lord Jesus Christ, the only begotten Son of God', and in 'the Holy Ghost, the Lord and Giver of life'. Rather than being one of a series of beliefs held by the Christian community, belief in the Trinity establishes the general setting for the central convictions of the Christian faith. This doctrine provides the *grammar* of Christian faith, a means of expression in relation to other areas of belief and, as such, is of prime importance to the identity of the Christian community.

This said, the Trinity has not always been seen in these terms.[1] Karl Rahner, in the opening to his seminal work, *The Trinity*, claims that despite the orthodox confession of the trinitarian God, most Christians live as 'mere "monotheists"' failing to work out the practical applications of this doctrine in their everyday lives. If the doctrine of the Trinity was ruled out as 'false', he contends, there would be little difference in the way Christians lived and the way God was understood.[2] Certainly historically, a number of theologians have considered the doctrine to be questionable in terms of its usefulness both for understanding God and living the Christian life. This is particularly true within feminist theological debate. Indeed, within the feminist arena, many may wish this doctrine was declared 'false' and ruled out by the Christian community on the basis that it serves to support the superiority of men and to establish patriarchal values as integral to the trinitarian being of God. Daphne Hampson, for example, argues that the doctrine cannot help but establish the maleness of God and the male as normative. Although feminist theologians have tried to rectify this through the use of more inclusive language, Hampson is clear that such pursuits are, in the end, fruitless. 'As long as one remains within a biblical and Christian tradition', she claims, 'the problem may be thought to be without solution.'[3]

Certainly, the main reason many feminist theologians have come to question the usefulness of the doctrine of the Trinity to date surrounds the use of androcentric, patriarchal God-*language* and the imagery this produces. 'Father-Son' language, it has been suggested, presents an exclusively male view of God which leads to an understanding of the Trinity as two males and a bird ('bird' here referring to the

---

[1] See the opening paragraph of Fred Sanders' article, 'Trinity Talk, Again', *Dialog: A Journal of Theology*, 44/3 (2005): 264–72.

[2] Karl Rahner, *The Trinity*, trans. J. Donceel (London, 1970), pp. 10–11.

[3] Daphne Hampson, *Theology and Feminism* (Oxford, 1990), p. 96.

winged animal, usually a dove, or the token presence of a stereotypically 'feminine' dimension),[4] or as two males and an amorphous third.[5] Unsurprisingly, such conceptualizations have been criticized by feminist theologians on the grounds that they present the male as the archetypal human subject and consequently legitimise the relegation of women to the margins of personhood.

As a result, many feminists insist that Christian God-talk must be radically revised if the doctrine of the Trinity is to remain useful within feminist theological discourse and is to inform Christian belief and praxis in ways that do not undermine the full humanity of women or their place within the *imago Dei*.[6] Elizabeth Johnson, for example, develops the trinitarian model of Spirit-*Sophia*, Jesus-*Sophia* and Mother-*Sophia* as an attempt to reclaim the Hebrew female personification of God as Wisdom/*Sophia* and to redirect trinitarian discourse away from an androcentric focus.[7] Sallie McFague presents the parallel models of Mother, Lover and Friend; Creator, Saviour (or Redeemer), Sustainer[8] as a means of signalling a more holistic understanding of the divine, specifically one which identifies the world as God's 'body' (rather than as wholly separate from God) and humankind as active, responsible agents in caring for it.[9]

As we might expect, attempts such as these have been both welcomed and questioned by feminist as well as other audiences. Daphne Hampson, although commending Sallie McFague for her 'impressive' model, queries its usefulness for the church today. She asks, how can this fit with the models the church already has for speaking about God? If the way God is spoken of in church and in the Bible conceives God in predominantly patriarchal terms through the use of predominantly patriarchal metaphors, then speaking God as Mother, Lover and Friend will not change this. Instead, this may lead to competing models, to what Hampson calls 'a different religion' which is unrecognisable within a Christian setting.[10]

Hampson may indeed have a point. The language the Christian community uses to speak about God is so incredibly vast, wide ranging and ingrained that revising the trinitarian formula can only ever constitute part of the solution. It is also perfectly possible to speak God in one way (say as 'Mother') whilst simultaneously

---

4 See Jane Williams, 'The Doctrine of the Trinity: A Way Forward for Feminists?', in Teresa Elwes (ed.), *Women's Voices: Essays in Contemporary Feminist Theology* (London, 1992), pp. 31–43, esp. p. 32.

5 Elizabeth Johnson, 'The Incomprehensibility of God and the Image of God Male and Female', *Theological Studies*, 45 (1984): 441–65, esp. p. 458.

6 See for example, Elizabeth Johnson, *She Who Is: The Mystery of God in Feminist Theological Discourse* (New York, 1992).

7 Ibid.

8 See Sallie McFague, *Models of God: Theology for an Ecological, Nuclear Age* (Philadelphia, 1987), pp. 78–180.

9 Ibid., pp. 72–4. Also see her more recent book, *A New Climate for Theology: God, the World, and Global Warming* (Minneapolis, 2008).

10 Hampson, p. 160.

thinking God in another (say as tyrannical, distant and aloof). Thus, the assumed view that the imagery produced by new trinitarian language will somehow replace or override imagery produced by traditional trinitarian language may be rather naïve. My anxiety is that the perceived change represented by such a shift towards more inclusive God-talk may give the impression that all is now well for women. Because a shift in speech has taken place, we may assume that women have been recognized as fully sharing in the image of God when in fact this may not be the case. In this sense, changes to traditional trinitarian God-talk may be little more than tokenistic and may not achieve what they appear to achieve on the surface. To the extent that problems surrounding thinking God run alongside problems surrounding speaking God, it is necessary to consider the former as well as the latter in feminist debate concerning the doctrine of the Trinity. This book, therefore, proposes a shift in emphasis away from a focus on *speaking* the Trinity to a consideration of trinitarian thought (or 'logic') and an emphasis on *thinking* the Trinity.

Of course, this is not to say that a straightforward distinction can be easily made between 'thinking' and 'speaking' about God or between trinitarian language and trinitarian thought for that matter. We do not stop thinking when we speak and we do not stop using language when we engage in thought. It is also true that feminist calls for more inclusive language are not simply calls to change the way we speak about God but calls to change the way we think by changing the way we outwardly speak. My argument, however, is that an emphasis on the threefold name of God need not be where feminist theological discussion must begin. By placing a stress on trinitarian 'logic', this book deliberately starts with a reflection on the triune operations rather than with the triune name. What this shift means in reality is discussed in more detail throughout the course of this book. However, in order to map this move away from inclusive language more thoroughly, we first need to acknowledge why speaking rightly about God is considered to be so important within feminist debate concerning the doctrine of the Trinity.

The Importance of Speaking Rightly about God

In the opening to her book, *Models of God*, Sallie McFague asserts that the old childhood taunt, 'sticks and stones may break my bones, but names can never hurt me' could not be more wrong. 'It is the "names" that hurt', she says; 'one would prefer the sticks and stones.'[11] Her point here, of course, is that language and naming do matter; that the language and names we use for God are not neutral but rather deeply loaded with potentially destructive meaning and power. Language, for McFague, is critical in informing how we think about the world and also about God. She thus sets about exploring new ways of speaking about God which are appropriate for an age on the brink of ecological deterioration and one experiencing

[11] McFague, *Models of God*, p. 3.

the threat of nuclear extinction.[12] Her reformulation of trinitarian discourse aims to communicate the inter-relationality of the cosmos and the need for humans to take responsibility in and for the world. Her hope is that such language may help change the way we think about God and consequently the way we behave in the world.

There are, however, other prominent voices who have heralded similar calls. In his book, *What Language Shall I Borrow*, Brian Wren argues that 'to separate language from action is false. Language change is an *essential part of action*'.[13] Thus, for him, there is no escaping the problems of sexist language within Christian worship and liturgy. If we are to challenge and change the sexist assumptions within the church, we must address the way the church uses and abuses language in speaking about God. Elizabeth Johnson also argues that exclusive male speech for God serves in a variety of ways to support a world that excludes and subordinates women.[14] Like Wren, she contends that if God-language is sexist, it will endorse and perpetuate sexist behaviour and thinking. Thus, if we speak about a tyrant God then the community of faith will be encouraged to show disrespect to one another.[15] 'Women have been robbed of the power of naming', Johnson says, 'of naming themselves, the world, and ultimately holy mystery, having instead to receive the names given by those who rule over them.'[16] She therefore constantly reminds us that the 'symbol of God *functions*'.[17] It does not lie dormant, it produces an effect and this, according to Johnson, serves all too easily to support a patriarchal world which excludes and subordinates women.[18] Following Paul Ricœur's axiom that symbols give rise to thought, she provides a thorough critique of male God-language. Specifically, she argues that the exclusive, literal and patriarchal use of male language gives rise to an understanding of God which flies in the face of the orthodox claim that God is incomprehensible and sexless.[19] Such language, Johnson argues, fails to speak rightly of God because it reduces divine mystery to a male idol. It also fails to speak rightly of women because it does not reflect women's dignity or full participation in the *imago Dei.* Inasmuch as this is the case, justice towards women, she maintains, is not to be seen as something separate from right speaking about God;[20] if our words are to speak truthfully of God then they must, at the same time, affirm women as fully human.

---

12 See Sallie McFague, *The Body of God: An Ecological Theology* (Minneapolis, 1993), p. 1.

13 Brian Wren, *What Language Shall I Borrow? God Talk in Worship: A Male Response to Feminist Theology* (London, 1989).

14 Johnson, *She Who Is*, p. 5.

15 Ibid., p. 4.

16 Ibid., p. 27.

17 Ibid., p. 5, emphasis mine.

18 Ibid., pp. 4–5.

19 Ibid., pp. 33–6.

20 Ibid., p. 12.

Of course, this is deeply commendable. It is true that women have been robbed of their power to name, both in relation to themselves and the divine, and that language shapes and creates the worlds in which we live. Using exclusively male and patriarchal language for God will then certainly serve to further endorse patriarchal structures of oppression; in this sense, the critique provided by Johnson (and others) is both credible and significant. However, is this the only way in which to view the relationship between speech and thought? What is the significance of *thinking* rightly about God?

The Importance of Thinking Rightly about God

Dedicating a renewed amount of space and time to *thinking* God as Trinity recognizes that the way we outwardly speak about God does not connote the full extent of the problem surrounding the Trinity. The Christian imagination is full of non-verbal images as well as names and descriptions we use to speak about God. Of course, all are immersed within language, with language sometimes giving rise to such imaginings. However, what goes on inside our heads (thought) can, and often does, have a seemingly separate existence to what comes out of our mouths (speech). I might, for example, privately think that my sister is terrible as a singer, but tell her that she sings perfectly well. In a similar way, I might privately imagine God as tyrannical whilst outwardly speaking of God as friend. In this sense, changing the verbal, outward language we use to speak about the trinitarian God need not always impact the private, inward ways we think about God and may not be the solution it first appears to be.

Thomas Scirghi shares this perspective. In his text, *An Examination of the Problems of Inclusive Language in the Trinitarian Formula of Baptism*, he suggests that there is insufficient evidence for the claim that language influences thought or action. Such a claim, he insists, is a 'dubious assumption which has yet to be proven'.[21] He draws on the words of Steven Pinker, professor for cognitive neuroscience and specialist in child language association, in order to make his point clear:

> Words are not thoughts. Despite the appeal of the theory that language determines thought, no cognitive scientist believes it. People coin new words, grapple for *le mot juste*, translate from other languages and ridicule or defend P.C. terms. None of this would be possible if the ideas expressed by words were identical to the words themselves.[22]

---

[21] For example Thomas J. Scirghi, *An Examination of the Problems of Inclusive Language in the Trinitarian Formula of Baptism* (New York, 2000), p. 202.

[22] Ibid., p. 202.

This does indeed seem to be the case. Often we can stand back from language enough to realize that what we're saying does not resonate with what we're *really* thinking, however, this is not to claim that we can think God outside of language. One of the greatest contributions of postmodern thought has been the proclamation that there is no 'beyond' in terms of language; no outside 'space' to which we might escape. Reality is structured in and through language, and not simply verbal language – through the cultural signifiers and symbol systems that surround us. Lyotard was right that knowledge cannot be separated from its linguistic context. According to him, we can never encounter bare physical objects or uninterpreted data. All objects are given meaning with reference to language and there can be no knowledge outside of this context.[23] What I am arguing then, more particularly, is that the language we use to structure our outward speech about God need not always reflect the language we use to organize our private thinking about God. Instead, the relationship between the two may be more complex than this. Speech may inform thought/action, but it also may not; thought may inform speech, but it also may not. As such, the relationship between the two is best seen as a dynamic, reflexive relationship of exchange. Rather than proposing a one-way flow from thought to speech, we consider the two as jointly constructing one another.

Within this setting, the role of trinitarian thought in speaking about God becomes just as important as the role of trinitarian speech in thinking about God. Male-centred, patriarchal trinitarian thought (what goes on in our heads) is seen as just as potentially culpable as male-centred trinitarian God-talk (what we speak) for contributing to the exclusion and marginalization of women. Of course, the two are related. However, not withholding that there are a number of serious problems and difficulties with Trinity-talk, my central remit in this book is not to remodel God through the use of more inclusive speech but to consider the usefulness of *thinking* God as Trinity for feminist theology today.

To be sure, feminist work which seeks to reconstruct trinitarian God-talk will not 'solve' problems surrounding this doctrine. Because the traditional language of 'Father', 'Son' and 'Spirit' is evident in the Bible and is used in creeds, liturgies, and everyday Christian discourse, it will take more than a number of feminist suggestions (whether radical or not) to undo such a length of history and tradition. We also have to remember that for many, even for some feminists (at least those who have the courage to admit it), the language of Father, Son and Spirit is to be treasured; not as the 'proper' name for God but as language which nevertheless communicates *something* meaningful and theologically significant about God and God's relationship with the rest of creation. Of course, this is not to say that feminist attempts at revising trinitarian language are unnecessary or unimportant. I am certainly not suggesting that because the task is hard, there is no point trying. Feminist efforts to revise trinitarian language are indeed invaluable and of great importance, however if problems surrounding the Trinity lie in the Christian

[23] Jean-François Lyotard, *The Postmodern Condition: A Report on Knowledge*, trans. Geoff Bennington and Brian Massumi (Manchester, 1984).

imagination, then we must admit that this runs far deeper than the way Christians *talk* about God.

It is also worth noting that thinking God as Trinity does not claim to comprehend the manifold greatness of God. Indeed, to understand God as triune requires that we adopt, at least in part, an *apophatic* stance, acknowledging that our trinitarian thought leaves more unsaid than it does said. Thinking God as Trinity is not a theological equation to complete; it does not represent some form of theological Rubik's cube which must be twisted and pulled until solved, but a *mystery* to behold. To think God as Trinity always means to think God in such a way that recognizes God's unknowability and the consequent and necessary partiality of all our thought. The task before us here then is grounded in Augustine's sobering words that: 'If you have fully grasped what you want to say, it isn't God. If you have been able to comprehend it, you have comprehended something else instead of God. If you think you have been able to comprehend, your thoughts have deceived you.'[24] And yet it is equally unhelpful to resign ourselves to silence about God. If God has made Godself known in the economy of salvation and in and through the person of Jesus Christ, then we must admit that there is *something* positive to say about what God is like – that God is relational and inclusive of difference. However, whatever we do think is always a thought about a God who is, by nature, unthinkable. Although we know, we only know in part and although we see, we only see in a mirror dimly (1 Corinthians 13.12).

Feminist Theological Methodology

In addition to this shift in focus from trinitarian speech to trinitarian thought, this book also proposes that we assess the doctrine of the Trinity on the basis of its ability to affirm the key principles and values underpinning a feminist theological method which takes women's experience as its starting point. In other words, it proposes a somewhat original dialogue between feminist theological method and what it means to think God as Trinity. This avoids an overly generalized discussion about how the Trinity might be useable within a feminist theological context by taking a fresh look at what it means to ground theology in women's experience in particular and by considering the ways in which a trinitarian understanding of God might cohere with this. By focusing on theological method we ask 'what does it mean to do theology from the basis of *women's* experience' and 'what key values characterize this distinct approach'? By exploring these kinds of questions we are able to identify central values which underpin a distinctly *feminist* approach to theology and it is these values which provide the criteria against which our thinking about the Trinity is then assessed.

---

[24] Augustine, *Sermons*, III, 51–94 on the New Testament, trans. Edmund Hill, ed. John E. Rostelle (New York, 1991), 52.16, p. 57.

Of course, much time has been spent articulating what it means to do theology from the starting point of women's experience. Rosemary Radford Ruether provides one of the most famous articulations of the role of women's experience to date, insisting that there can be no theology outside of experience. For her, human experience constitutes the beginning and ending point of the hermeneutical circle.[25] What have been seen as the 'universal' and 'objective' sources of theology – scripture and tradition – she insists, are actually nothing more than codified collective human experience, and more importantly, *male* experience.[26] The use of *women's* experience then within feminist theology, she argues, 'explodes as a critical force',[27] revealing the experiential nature of all theology and the exclusion of women's experience from the theological enterprise.

In a similar voice, Linda Hogan argues that the prioritization of women's experience in the doing of feminist theology has effected what she refers to as a 'methodological revolution', signaling a new departure in theology.[28] To do theology as a feminist, she argues, is to use women's experience as a central resource and criterion of evaluation.[29] However, she, like many other feminist theologians, is clear that such a category must not be approached uncritically. 'The category of women's experience', she says, 'is essentially a celebration of the plurality and diversity of women's lives, choices, values. It does not transcend class, racial or cultural differences but is intimately bound to them.'[30]

Indeed, in recent times much attention has been given to the diverse nature of women's experience and to the related need for identifying to which woman – or women – exactly this 'experience' belongs. Womanist theology, for example, emerges as a challenge to the white, Western, affluent, middle-class nature of feminist theology, exposing its presumption to speak for all women and its disregard for racial and class difference. The force of this critique should not be underestimated and many have added to its strength. Attention to 'difference' must lie at the heart of any discussion of women's experience and this book certainly makes a case for this. Indeed, my intention here is to work towards an understanding of 'woman' and 'women's experience' which takes difference between women seriously whilst nevertheless insisting on the meaningfulness and necessity of the category 'women's experience' as an important point of feminist theological departure. Through an investigation of this approach, I suggest that the central values inherent within this identify with the central values which characterize a

---

[25] Rosemary Radford Ruether, *Sexism and God-talk: Towards a Feminist Theology* (Boston, 1983), p. 12.

[26] Ibid., p. 12.

[27] Ibid., p. 13.

[28] Linda Hogan, *From Women's Experience to Feminist Theology* (Sheffield, 1995), p. 11.

[29] Ibid., p. 17.

[30] Ibid., p. 11.

specifically trinitarian understanding of God, exposing this doctrine as of extreme import for the Christian feminist community.

As such, this book seeks to address the doctrine of the Trinity from a different angle to many other feminist works in the area. Rather than focusing on what's *wrong* with the Trinity and working towards new ways of *speaking* the trinitarian God, this book explores what's *right* with the Trinity and considers how *thinking* God as triune might support and be supported by central values which underpin the use of women's experience in feminist theology. Essentially, it maintains that thinking God as Trinity provides a theological context in which women are able to fully identify with God as fully *imago Dei* and a theological logic by which the complexity, richness and diversity of women's experiences might be both acknowledged and celebrated. It is not simply that feminist values support a trinitarian understanding of God, but that a trinitarian understanding of God affirms feminist values. This book then sets about the task of demonstrating the former in order to establish a case for the latter. Because feminist values align with a trinitarian understanding of God and thinking God in this way requires that we think God as ontologically existing in this way in eternity, then the feminist values articulated here are exposed as Christian values also. They are identified as being theologically rooted in the trinitarian God and as, therefore, establishing a Christian as well as feminist mandate for liberative praxis which celebrates difference and acknowledges and affirms the subjectivity of all women.

Outline of Chapters

In plotting this course, the following work divides into three central sections. Part One sets about the task of thinking the Trinity, engaging with theological as well as feminist theological approaches to the doctrine as a means of working towards a clear trinitarian thesis of my own. Chapter 1 begins with the question, 'what's wrong with the Trinity?' and addresses current feminist contentions surrounding this doctrine. Locating the majority of feminist debate within calls for more inclusive God-talk, this chapter, whilst not denying the importance of this agenda, suggests that speech about God is not the only important factor when it comes to assessing the usability of this doctrine for feminist theology. Chapter 2 takes this argument forward by transferring attention away from speaking the Trinity toward thinking God as Trinity. This chapter dialogues with five thinkers significant in the development of trinitarian thought (Augustine, Gregory of Nazianzus, Karl Rahner, John Zizioulas and Jürgen Moltmann) and uses this discussion in order to clarify what it means to understand God as Trinity.

Part Two transfers attention from thinking the Trinity towards feminist theological method, exploring what it means to do theology from the point of view of women's experience. As such, it makes a case for the use of women's experience as 'source' and 'norm' and provides a justification for this. Chapter 3 begins this process by working towards what I call an 'orthodox-contextual' theological method. This engages the methodological approaches of Karl Barth and Friedrich Schleiermacher in order to establish context/experience as the logical starting point of all theology whilst simultaneously preserving the priority of God (as Trinity) in revelation. Chapter 4 then takes this grounding in context forward by thinking specifically about what it might mean to begin theological reflection with *women's* experience in particular. Avoiding an essentialist reading of 'woman' and a universal account of 'women's experience', this chapter argues that women's experience operates as a meaningful starting point for feminist theology so long as it is established on non-foundational grounds, is justified on methodological, ethical and pragmatic grounds, and draws on the experiences of women which are shared and critiqued within Christian *feminist* communities of resistance. Although there can be no shared 'feminist' standpoint, there can be a shared commitment to dialogue and liberative praxis. This chapter develops the notion of 'positionality' in order to identify women's subjectivity in relation to a series of influences (biological, social and discursive) and in order to locate the female body within phallocentric discourse, specifically in relation to its structural position as 'lack' in the symbolic order.

This structural and symbolic positioning is further interrogated in Chapter 5 as I expose the implications raised by woman's symbolic position within phallocentrism for a theological method which seeks to take women's experience as its starting point. If woman has no language of her own within the symbolic and subsequently no subjectivity of her own, then it follows that she also has no *experience* of her own and women's experience becomes a contentious starting point. Engaging with Irigaray and her theoretical strategy of *parler-femme*, this chapter finalizes my discussion of feminist theological method by uniting feminist appeals to women's experience with women's attainment of subjectivity. To begin with women's experience, it is argued, demands that women occupy their *own* positions as subjects and this requires the tactical use of *mimesis* as a strategic tool of resistance.

Part Three places Part One and Part Two in creative dialogue within one another, addressing how thinking God as Trinity might support and be supported by the central values which underpin feminist appeals to women's experience. Overall, it is argued that feminist theology need not require the demise of the doctrine of the Trinity. On the contrary, it can claim that thinking God as Trinity stands in contradistinction to phallocentrism and serves to support rather than undermine the subjectivity of women. Using Chapters 4 and 5 as points of reference, Chapter 6 therefore identifies 'difference' and 'subjectivity' as two broad fundamental values which underpin the use of women's experience in feminist theology. By interrogating the particular, nuanced meaning of these values, this chapter establishes these as the criteria against which to assess the usefulness of thinking God as Trinity for feminist theology today. Understood as diversity in communion, as the very life and livingness of God, the Trinity, it is suggested, provides a powerful logic by which phallocentric accounts of difference and subjectivity might be resisted and subverted and a theological context in which the diversity of women's experiences might be acknowledged, welcomed and celebrated.

PART ONE
Thinking the Trinity

Chapter 1
What's Wrong with the Trinity? A Feminist Critique

> Batter my heart, three-personed God, for you
> As yet but knock, breathe, shine and seek to mend;
> That I may rise and stand, o'erthrow me and bend
> Your force to break, blow, burn and make me new ...
> Divorce me, unite, or break that knot again,
> Take me to you, imprison me, for I,
> Except you enthral me, never shall be free,
> Not ever chaste except you ravish me.[1]

What then is wrong with the Trinity according to feminist theological debate? This question is not an easy one to answer. Feminist discussion surrounding the Trinity reveals a range of views and perspectives. Indeed, what is clear is that feminist theologians do not all agree on where the problems lie, consequently leading to a diversity of suggestions as to how such difficulties might be overcome.

At its most basic, however, the feminist critique surrounding the Trinity tends to identify two main areas of contention. First, it highlights how the obvious androcentric nature of trinitarian language serves to reinforce men as more fully in the image of God and as the archetype of humanity, pushing women to the margins of the *imago Dei* and of human personhood itself. Second, it highlights how the imagery such language depicts serves to sacralize the patriarchal values of power, rule, authority and self-sufficiency, carrying with it violent overtones[2] which tend to depict God as a coercive, and controlling monarch who both justifies and supports abusive relationships. Such overtones are indeed evident from the sonnet by John Donne cited at the outset of this chapter.

In addressing these interlinked concerns, relatively few feminist theologians have provided sustained, full-length studies of the doctrine in its entirety. Although feminists such as Elizabeth Johnson, Sallie McFague and Catherine LaCugna offer detailed examinations, the majority of feminist literature tends to focus on one particular 'person' or *hypostasis* within the trinitarian community; either on God the Father, God the Son or God the Holy Spirit. In seeking to survey feminist theological

---

[1] John Donne, 'To the Trinity' cited in Mary Grey, 'The Core of Our Desire: Re-imaging the Trinity', *Theology*, 93 (1990): 362–72, esp. p. 365.

[2] See Mary Daly, *Beyond God the Father: Towards a Philosophy of Women's Liberation* (London, 1991).

approaches and responses, this chapter therefore organizes feminist perspectives in relation to the three individual titles of the trinitarian name.[3] Such a categorization does not intend to imply that each *hypostasis* can be viewed separately from the others – as will become apparent in our discussion in the next chapter – but instead, serves to break down feminist contentions so as to present a more manageable account of feminist debate. The chapter begins with an outline of the main areas of difficulty identified by feminist theologians surrounding this doctrine and then moves on to address and critically assess feminist responses. The chapter ends by clarifying my own suggestions in relation to how best to speak the Christian God.

God the Father

Feminist concerns surrounding understanding God as 'Father' tend to focus around three main points of criticism:

1. that this serves to reinforce the maleness of God;
2. that this justifies and reinforces patriarchal values and ideals; and
3. that taken together, both of the above serve to perpetuate an unhealthy understanding of divine transcendence.

The Maleness of God

The language of God as 'Father' has perhaps come under the most intense scrutiny from feminist theologians to date. At one level, the critique says that such language perpetuates the idea that God is male, or at least the idea that God is more *like* men than women. Thus, in her text, *Beyond God the Father*, Mary Daly famously asserts that 'If God is male, then the male is God',[4] drawing attention to the way in which the exclusive symbolization of God as male serves to compromise women's humanity and divinize the male. Such language, she claims, stands to both affirm and justify patriarchy because it highlights the male as both dominant and normative for understandings of what it means to be human. She therefore concludes that the signifier of God the Father can only ever serve to diminish women and must, therefore, be abandoned.

The Reinforcement of Patriarchal Ideals

At a second level, the language and image of God as 'Father' has been criticized for reinforcing and promoting the patriarchal ideals of hierarchy, violence,

[3] For a further summary of feminist contentions surrounding the Trinity see Hannah Bacon, 'What's Right with the Trinity? Thinking the Trinity in Relation to Irigaray's Notions of Self-love and Wonder', *Feminist Theology*, 15/2 (2007): 220–35.

[4] Daly, p. 19.

dominance, rule and control. Again Daly remarks: 'If God in "his" heaven is a father ruling "his" people, then it is in the "nature" of things and according to divine plan and the order of the universe that society be male-dominated.'[5] In other words, if God is both male and sovereign, male domination is placed safely within the will of God, ordained as holy and right. Within this context, maleness and rule come to be knitted together to form an inseparable bond which inevitably carries disastrous implications for women. Indeed Daly argues that the image of God the Father justifies all systems serving to oppress and 'castrate' women and other minority groups.[6]

In a similar vein, Rosemary Radford Ruether argues that the over-reliance of Christianity on the model of God as 'Father' often tends to present God as a 'neurotic parent who does not want his children to grow up'.[7] Such a model, she says, suggests a permanent parent-child relationship between God and humankind in which human subjects are encouraged to remain in an infantile, dependent relationship with God. In this context, autonomy and personal responsibility are represented as the gravest of sins.[8] Such a model, she claims, reinvests patriarchal power with divine credence and enables men to claim authority *over* women and children.

Understanding Divine Transcendence

Taken together then, such an emphasis on the maleness of God and the sacralization of patriarchal values and ideals can be seen as contributing to a particular patriarchal understanding of divine transcendence. Within this understanding, God is depicted as absolute, almighty, all-powerful, controlling, self-sufficient, immutable, impassable, infinite and sovereign. In short, God is understood to be totally 'other' and infinitely different – 'he' has *all* the power leaving us with none.[9]

For Sallie McFague, such an emphasis on the distance and otherness of God may serve to polarize God and world, God and humanity, so that God the Father is seen as all-powerful, absolute and timeless, rendering human subjects passive, temporal and dependent. Indeed, as Father, God may be understood as 'set apart' from the world, a notion clearly central to the doctrine of creation *ex nihilo.* For McFague, this is indeed the dominant understanding of God. 'His' kingdom is not of this world and to reach it we have to depart from this earthly existence. Such an understanding, she claims, is deeply problematic in an age threatened by

---

[5] Ibid., p. 13.

[6] Ibid., p. 10.

[7] Rosemary Radford Ruether, *Sexism and God-Talk: Toward a Feminist Theology* (Boston, 1983), p. 69.

[8] Ibid., p. 69.

[9] McFague voices this critique in relation to God in general. See Sallie McFague, *Models of God: Theology for an Ecological Nuclear Age* (Philadelphia, 1987), pp. 9–19.

ecological deterioration and nuclear extinction since it encourages Christians to treat the world as a hotel rather than a home.[10]

This understanding of divine transcendence, however, may be more far reaching than this. Rather than simply serving to polarize God and world or God and humanity, this understanding may also serve the ideological agenda of polarizing males and females. If God is aligned with traditional and stereotypical understandings of the male-masculine, then the world is similarly aligned with traditional and stereotypical understandings of the female-feminine. Hence the following dichotomies come to be constructed:

God	**World**
Male	Female
Transcendent	Immanent
Powerful/active	Passive
Spirit	Body/flesh

Of course, such identifications are not exhaustive – the list is potentially far more extensive yet the dualisms mentioned here are arguably the most significant. Where God is male, the world is female; where God is transcendent, the world is immanent; where God is powerful and active, the world is controlled and dependent; where God is spiritual, the world is bodily.

The main difficulties with this particular understanding of the Father's transcendence, however, are that it conveniently serves to justify male domination, portrays an oppositional relationship between women and God, and reinforces harmful stereotypes of femininity. Just as God the Father rules *over* the world and is above and beyond it, so the male is justified as ruling *over* the female, being above and beyond her in power and influence. Since the world is anti-God then women are likewise depicted as anti-God and are once again pushed to the margins of imaging the divine. Since the world is seen in opposition to God as female, immanent, passive, and bodily, patriarchal stereotypes are once more reinforced, identifying women with bodiliness, sin (the 'flesh'), and passivity.[11]

However, crucially, the relationship between God and world is not only presented here as oppositional, but more importantly, as hierarchical. Whereas God is symbolized as holy, the world is symbolized as sinful. Thus, all qualities associated with God – namely maleness, transcendence, power and spirit (or mind) – are not only symbolized here as being different to femaleness, immanence, passivity, and the body/flesh, but also as being superior to them. In this sense, the

10 Sallie McFague, *The Body of God: An Ecological Theology* (London, 1993), pp. 100–129.

11 See Loren Wilkinson, '"Post-Christian" Feminism and the Fatherhood of God,' in Maxine Hancock (ed.), *Christian Perspectives on Gender, Sexuality and Community* (Vancouver, British Columbia, 2003), pp. 103–26, esp. p. 110.

male is represented as being 'set apart' from the female just as God is seen as being 'set apart' from the world.[12]

Given such associations, feminist theologians often criticize the image of God the Father for projecting patriarchal ideals and oppressive stereotypes, for it is through such projectionism, many claim, that such ideals and stereotypes come to be affirmed and sacralized. Elizabeth Johnson thus states:

> Is not the transcendent, omnipotent, impassible symbol of God the quintessential embodiment of the solitary ruling male ego, above the fray, perfectly happy in himself, filled with power in the face of the obstreperousness of others? Is this not man according to the patriarchal ideal?[13]

Indeed, for radical feminists like Mary Daly, God the Father amounts to nothing more than this. For Daly, the male has named God in relation to himself, deifying himself, pushing women to the margins of humanity. 'To exist humanly' she says, 'is to name the self, the world, and God.'[14] Hence she argues that it is the right to name, and more specifically, the right to name God that women must claim. Using their own experiences as source, women must set about this task in such a way as to affirm their full humanity. This therefore, according to Daly, demands a shift in imaging God and necessarily requires 'the death of God the Father'.[15]

God the Son

Difficulties surrounding the language and imagery of God the 'Son' tend to be organized around three main concerns:

---

[12] This conception of God has close associations with the so-called 'God of philosophy'. Like the God of philosophy, God the Father is imaged as immutable, impassible, and self-sufficient, being intrinsically connected to the mind, spirit, reason, and activity. 'He' is imaged in exclusively male terms as absolute being or pure act. Imaged as such, God the Father, like the God of philosophy, cannot suffer and cannot change. He is the supreme monarch who escapes all associations with the world 'below'. For related information see Elizabeth Johnson, 'The Incomprehensibility of God and the Image of God Male and Female', *Theological Studies*, 45 (1984): 441–65, esp. p. 442; Carl E. Braaten, 'The Problem of God Language Today', in Carl E. Braaten (ed.), *Our Naming of God: Problems and Prospects of God-Talk Today* (Minneapolis, 1989), pp. 11–33, esp. pp. 16–18; McFague, *The Body of God*, esp. Chapter 5, pp. 131ff.; and Robert Hannaford, 'Gender and the Person God Is', in Robert Hannaford and J'annine Jobling (eds), *Theology and the Body: Gender, Text and Ideology* (Leominster, 1999), pp. 30–46.

[13] Elizabeth A. Johnson, *She Who Is: The Mystery of God in Feminist Theological Discourse* (New York, 1992), p. 21.

[14] Daly, p. 8.

[15] Ibid., p. 13.

1. that this serves to reinforce rather than challenge the maleness of God;
2. that this tends to present Jesus as the unique manifestation of God, thereby affirming the male as more fitting for divine revelation and as more theologically significant; and
3. that this often depicts the Son's death as a requirement of God the Father, thereby modelling male violence and glamorising sacrifice and suffering.

The Maleness of Jesus

Of course, the maleness of God becomes more apparent when faced with the historical person of Jesus of Nazareth. Confessed as the *logos*, God incarnate, Jesus brings together maleness and divinity in such a way that makes it difficult to separate the two. That Jesus is male furthers the difficulties already encountered in relation to God the Father, seemingly identifying men as not only more theomorphic (that is, like God) than women, but also as significantly more Christomorphic (that is, like Christ). Mary Daly therefore argues that Christology amounts to nothing short of idolatry, idolising the male sex at the expense of the female. She renames Christology, 'Christolatry', rejecting any claims that Jesus might offer or achieve salvation for women:[16] She says:

> ... the idea of a unique male savior may be seen as one more legitimation of male superiority ... The image itself is one-sided as far as sexual identity is concerned, and it is precisely on the wrong side, since it fails to counter sexism and functions to glorify maleness.[17]

Of course, the issue of salvation is of great import. If we are to agree with Gregory of Nazianzus that only that which Christ assumes is saved then this arguably raises far reaching difficulties for women. We are indeed forced to ask with Ruether whether a male saviour can save women.[18] Since Jesus only assumes *male* flesh, the implication is that women cannot be represented, and therefore saved, by a male saviour. Also, if we admit that Christ can only save that which Christ assumes, then we must also acknowledge that all bodies other than the body of Christ are seemingly unredeemable. Indeed, we are forced to claim that because of Jesus' particular embodiment, he can only affirm and save Galileans, Jews, the able bodied and so on. This undermines the inclusivity of Christ and so rightly problematizes the centralizing of Jesus' maleness.[19]

---

[16] Ibid., p. 96.

[17] Ibid., p. 72.

[18] See Ruether, *Sexism*, p. 116ff.

[19] For more on this point and for a detailed discussion of incarnation and its relevance for affirming female embodiment see Hannah Bacon, 'A Very Particular Body: Assessing the Doctrine of Incarnation for Affirming the Sacramentality of Female Embodiment', in

For some, however, the significance of Jesus' maleness cannot be escaped. Daphne Hampson, for example, maintains that God's choice to reveal Godself in a patriarchal time through the male Jesus appears to indicate that God favours male humanity, viewing it as more fitting for God's revelation. Indeed, for her, patriarchy and maleness both come to be sacralized and divinized in such a way that it becomes impossible to glean anything liberating from this.[20] Of course Hampson's critique is important, for if the incarnation endorses that the male is closer to God, then this signals a hierarchical structure of relations which runs from Christ (at the top) to man and finally to woman (at the bottom), reinforcing Augustine's view that woman can only image God by first imaging man.[21]

The Particularity of Christ

Jesus' maleness, however, does not exhaust feminist contentions with the language and imagery of God the 'Son'. A major concern in addition to this has been the claim that Jesus, as male, constitutes the *only*, the unique and the particular revelation of God. Hampson, for example, states:

> It is not a question of whether feminists have something against 'men'. Whether or not that is the case, the problem here is not that Jesus was a man, but that this man has been considered unique, symbolic of God, God Himself – or whatever else may be the case within Christianity.[22]

For Hampson, belief in the uniqueness of Jesus demands a break in the causal nexus of nature and history and this, she argues, is deeply illogical. That Jesus constitutes the once and for all revelation of God does, for her, seem unfeasible within a contemporary scientific world-view. Hampson, however, notes that without such a claim of uniqueness, Christianity loses its Christology and as such, fails to be Christian.[23] The Christian, she says, 'must say of Jesus of Nazareth, that there was a revelation of God through him in a way in which this is not true of you or me'.[24] She therefore claims to dismiss Christianity on intellectual, as opposed to specifically feminist, grounds.

The 'scandal' of the particularity of Christ, as it has come to be known, has been taken up by a range of feminist theologians. Besides Hampson, Mary Daly, Rosemary Radford Ruether, Sallie McFague and Elisabeth Schüssler Fiorenza are

---

J'annine Jobling and Gillian Howie (eds), *Women and the Divine: Touching Transcendence* (Palgrave, 2009), pp. 227–52.

[20] Daphne Hampson, *Theology and Feminism* (Oxford, 1990), p. 51.

[21] Augustine, *On the Trinity*, trans. Rev. Arthur West Hadden, B.D. (Edinburgh, 1873), pp. 292–3.

[22] Hampson, p. 51.

[23] Ibid., p. 50.

[24] Ibid., p. 8.

among the many who have discussed this problem. Daly, for example, argues that it is nonsensical to think that God would become manifest in only one individual. Instead, she says 'the creative presence of the Verb can be revealed at every historical moment, in every person and culture'.[25] In a slightly more conservative voice, Rosemary Radford Ruether argues that Christ continues to reveal himself in the world today through men and women alike. For Ruether, Jesus the man does not constitute the last word on revelation, so 'Christ' is presented as an inclusive symbol which is ascribed cosmic significance, reaching beyond, whilst at the same time including, the historical person of Jesus.[26]

Sallie McFague presents a more unconventional Christology. In her two publications, *Models of God* and *The Body of God*, she argues that the exclusivity, uniqueness and particularity of Jesus are deeply problematic since they encourage an apathetic attitude towards the world. Jesus saves and so all we need do is sit back and let salvation run its course. We rely on this man for everything and as such, are free to become totally irresponsible ourselves. Consequently, McFague images the entire universe as the incarnation of God. In this sense, the body of Christ is truly the world around us rather than being exclusively limited to the male Jesus.[27]

The Cross as Glamorization of Suffering and Male Violence

Imagery surrounding God the Son has also become problematic for many feminist theologians because of its seeming endorsement of male violence. Although this concerns the subject of atonement, it is still pertinent here because the perceived dominance of God the Father *over* the obedient, self-sacrificing Son, appears to replicate patriarchy, presenting male violence as appropriate within this setting.

Delores Williams, a contemporary womanist theologian, argues that substitutionary sacrifice theologies of atonement serve to sacralize black women's experiences of surrogacy. Within this setting, Jesus, she claims, comes to be seen as 'the ultimate surrogate figure'[28] whose body functions as surrogate or substitute for the sin of humankind. This is wholly unhelpful for black women, she argues, because it justifies their exploitation. For her, God did not intend the death of Jesus and so does not intend the surrogacy roles black women are often forced to perform.[29] She consequently rejects any substitutionary understandings of the cross and claims that it is Jesus' ministerial vision of life (rather than his death or blood) which redeem humankind.[30]

---

[25] Daly, p. 71. 'The Verb' constitutes Daly's designation of the divine.

[26] See Ruether, *Sexism*, pp. 116–38.

[27] McFague, *The Body of God*, pp. 179 and 183.

[28] Delores Williams, *Sisters in the Wilderness: The Challenge of Womanist God-Talk* (Maryknoll, New York, 1993), p. 162.

[29] Ibid., p. 166.

[30] Ibid., p. 167. For more on Williams' understanding of atonement see her chapter 'Black Women's Surrogacy Experience and the Christian Notion of Redemption', in

Indeed, for many feminist theologians, the concern is that through such an understanding of atonement, Jesus comes to model suffering with God the Father subsequently modelling oppressive, tyrannical and violent parental demands. This, according to Ruether, conveniently leads to the view that 'We become Christ-like by enduring suffering like Christ, who, though innocent, suffered for our sins'.[31] The suffering of Jesus, she claims, becomes a powerful tool for justifying domestic violence and for advising women to endure it without complaint.[32] Indeed, it seems that if Jesus' death is sanctioned and required by God, then God the Father becomes a divine child abuser who must punish in order for redemption to take place. This affirms suffering as redemptive and may consequently encourage those who suffer (both men and women) to see their suffering as inherently good.[33]

God the Holy Spirit

The Christian confession of God as 'Holy Spirit' produces less obvious difficulties than those associated with the language and imagery of 'Father' and 'Son' on the grounds that this does not necessarily imply a male God. However, despite this, current feminist debate tends to identify three general points of difficulty:

1. that the under-acknowledgement of the Spirit as feminine often reflects a patriarchal reading of God;
2. that the subordination of the Spirit within Western theology may reflect the marginalization of women within Christian history; and
3. that the amorphous nature of the Spirit may serve to reinforce women within the realm of abstraction and non-being.

The Under-acknowledgement of the Spirit as Feminine

Traditionally, the Holy Spirit has been understood as the love or kiss between Father and Son.[34] In the Bible, the Spirit is often depicted as personal, creative,

---

Marit Trelstad (ed.), *Cross Examinations: Readings on the Meaning of the Cross Today* (Minneapolis, 2006), pp. 19–32.

31 Rosemary Radford Ruether, *Introducing Redemption in Christian Feminism* (Ohio, 2000), p. 98.

32 Ibid., p. 100.

33 See Joanne Carlson Brown, Rebecca Parker, 'For God so Loved the World?' in J. Carlson Brown and C.R. Bohn (eds), *Christianity, Patriarchy and Abuse* (New York, 1989), pp. 1–30.

34 Denise Carmody, *Christian Feminist Theology* (Oxford, 1996), p. 199. Irenaeus, for example, depicted the Spirit as a drink given by the Father to the Son and to the world. For more on this see Yves Congar, *I Believe in the Holy Spirit*, trans. D. Smith (3 vols, New York, London, 1983), vol. 3, p. 145.

instructing, guiding and as helping those in need. Gen. 1.2, for example, identifies the Spirit as brooding over the earth to bring forth life in creation. In the New Testament the Spirit is designated the comforter who comes to heal, restore and make things new. Such opinion has been articulated by scholars like Jay Williams[35] and Yves Congar,[36] both claiming that the Holy Spirit can be viewed as the 'maternal' function of God.

However, such opinion does not go very far towards solving the androcentric nature of the trinitarian model. Indeed many feminists claim that even if the Spirit introduces so-called 'feminine' characteristics into the divine, the Holy Spirit still continues to be imaged as male. The Holy Spirit may be maternal, but *he* gives birth and broods over creation,[37] (more attention will be given to the 'feminine' aspects of the Spirit later on). To be sure, such a notion of 'femininity' can itself be seen as a patriarchal construct, confining women and men to particular sets of pre-defined characteristics which themselves serve to support male dominance and female subjugation. When tied to the Holy Spirit, such a model serves to reinforce, rather than dismantle, harmful gender stereotypes which tie women once more to the body and their reproductive capacity.

Feminist debate has also drawn attention to the grammatically feminine nature of the Hebrew word *ruach* used for the Spirit in the Old Testament. Here it is argued that such an observation means that there are explicitly no grounds on which to establish the maleness of the Spirit.[38] On the contrary, since the term itself is feminine and the function of the Spirit a maternal one, the third *hypostasis* should be spoken of using specifically female pronouns.[39]

The Subordination of the Spirit

Running parallel to this critique is a recognition that the Holy Spirit has traditionally suffered from an inferior status within Western trinitarian theology.[40] Indeed, it is important to note that it was not until the Council of Constantinople in 381 CE that the Holy Spirit was clearly identified as co-equal to God the Father and God the Son.[41] As the last 'person' of the Trinity to gain affirmation as fully

---

35 Jay G. Williams, 'Yahweh, Women and the Trinity', *Theology Today*, 32/3 (1975): 234–42.

36 Congar, p. 157.

37 Donald Bloesch is one example of such a scholar. See his book, *The Battle for the Trinity: The Debate Over Inclusive Language* (Michigan, 1985), p. 47.

38 Rebecca Oxford-Carpenter, 'Gender and the Trinity,' *Theology Today*, 41/1 (April 1984): 7–25, esp. p. 11.

39 See Congar for example.

40 See Nicola Slee, 'The Holy Spirit and Spirituality', in Susan Frank Parsons (ed.), *The Cambridge Companion to Feminist Theology* (Cambridge, 2002), pp. 171–89, esp. p. 171.

41 Oxford-Carpenter, 'Gender and the Trinity', p. 8. Also see Williams, 'Yahweh, Women and the Trinity', pp. 238–40.

divine, the Spirit has often been viewed as an appendage within Western thought. Arthur Wainwright, for example, points out that the Spirit 'seems to have been included in the doctrine of God almost as an afterthought about which men had no strong feelings, either favourable or hostile'.[42] The inferiority of the Spirit then conveniently aligns with the pronouncement of the Holy Spirit as feminine. If the feminine is traditionally understood as inferior to the masculine, then it is not surprising that the Spirit, understood as the *feminine* dimension of God (and so as maternal, nurturing, immanent, caring, compassionate and so on) has been, and sometimes continues to be, viewed as a trivial and auxiliary member of the Christian Godhead.

The Abstraction of the Holy Spirit

Taken together with the previous two difficulties, this final area of concern highlights how the amorphous character of the Spirit conveniently serves to reinforce women within the realm of abstraction and non-identity.[43] Unlike Father and Son, the Spirit is most obviously conceived as being sexless. Common associations are with wind, fire, movement, breath and so on, positing the Spirit as vague and 'faceless'.[44] While the Son has appeared in human form and we can at least make a mental image of the Father, the Spirit escapes all attempts of definition and classification. As such, one concern within feminist debate has been that the Trinity tends to be imaged as two males and one amorphous third,[45] often referred to as an 'it' or a 'thing' rather than as a co-equal 'person'. That the Spirit is linked to femininity, some therefore maintain, conveniently serves to reinforce women within the realm of abstraction and objectivity.[46]

Assessing the Critique

From the above discussion then it should be clear that the androcentric language of the trinitarian name and the related patriarchal imagery which this often connotes have been rendered problematic by many feminist theologians for a variety of reasons and to a variety of degrees. It is not surprising then that a plethora of

---

42 Arthur W. Wainwright, *The Trinity in the New Testament* (London, 1962), p. 199.

43 See Slee, 'The Holy Spirit', pp. 171–89.

44 See Johnson, 'The Incomprehensibility of God', p. 158 and Congar, p. 144.

45 Johnson, 'The Incomprehensibility of God', p. 458.

46 This has caused theologians such as Yves Congar to argue that the subjectivity of women depends on the reaffirmation of the Holy Spirit (as feminine) as a co-equal member of the Trinity (Congar, p. 160). It is also important to note that the Spirit is traditionally understood by the West as proceeding from both Father *and* Son (hence the *filioque* controversy) and so is often literally interpreted as the 'third' person, constituting the last stop in the trinitarian Godhead.

responses have been presented by feminist theologians seeking to engage with such difficulties. Some, for example, have moved towards reimaging the divine as 'Goddess' on the grounds that this provides a more healthy understanding of God free from the overtones of male dominance. Carol Christ, for instance, proposes a shift away from an imaging of the divine as 'God-He' towards 'God-She' on the basis that this has positive psychological implications for women.[47] Others, however, have been more concerned with trying to reform Christian discourses on the divine so as to retain some degree of relationship with the Christian tradition. Within this camp, some have drawn attention to the usability of traditional trinitarian language by looking afresh at biblical expression and assessing how such language might be helpful for women, whereas others have sought to reconstruct the trinitarian name in light of the issues highlighted above. It is these latter two directions which are of interest here as I seek to address how a trinitarian understanding of God might challenge rather than reinforce patriarchy. In order to understand these general directions, however, we first need to understand how God-talk operates, whether as a literal naming or a non-literal symbol.

The Function of Trinitarian Language

Trinitarian language as literal: The 'proper' name for God The first option here is to understand trinitarian language as literal and as the proper name for God.[48] Within this approach, trinitarian language and the trinitarian God are considered to be inseparable to such an extent that the titles of Father, Son, and Holy Spirit are seen as self-expressions of the ontological being of God. Hence scholars like Donald Bloesch, Alvin Kimel, Carl Braaten, Roland Frye, Geoffrey Wainwright, Robert Jenson, Colin Gunton and Elizabeth Achtiemer insist that replacing the traditional trinitarian name with more inclusive formulations risks replacing the Christian God with a convenient construction of our own making. Elizabeth Achtiemer, for example, writes: 'By attempting to change the biblical language used of the deity, the feminists have in reality exchanged the true God for those

---

[47] Carol P. Christ, 'Theological and Political Implications of Reimaging the Divine as Female', *Political Theology*, 8/2 (2007): 157–70.

[48] See Christian J. Barrigar, 'Protecting God: The Lexical Formation of Trinitarian Language', *Modern Theology*, 7/4 (July 1991): 299–310 where he refers to this as the 'name-theory view' (p. 304). According to this perspective, Fatherhood and Sonship are viewed as leading qualities of God which say something particular as opposed to general about the divine. Unlike 'indefinite descriptions', 'proper names' and 'definite descriptions' refer to the singular and the unique as opposed to a particular 'type'. Hence, whereas 'red shoe' would constitute a proper name, the general descriptor 'shoes' would constitute an indefinite description. Whereas the former gives complete information and is, therefore, nominal, the latter demands additional information and further explanation in order for the intended referent to be correctly identified (see pp. 300–301).

which are "no gods".'[49] In a similar voice, Donald Bloesch warns his readers against opting for inclusive language on the grounds that it makes Christianity pander to the demands of feminist ideologies.[50] Alvin Kimel also remarks that God is a God who likes his name, so much so that one cannot be Christian without speaking the trinitarian language. 'To replace or alter the triune formula' he argues, 'is to repudiate the creed, church, God of our baptism.'[51] Of course, the difficulty with views such as these is that if the trinitarian name of God the Father, Son and Holy Spirit *is* the proper name for God, then maleness is also in some sense 'proper' to God. Given this, feminist theologians tend to adopt a non-literal understanding of trinitarian language.

Trinitarian language as non-literal Understanding trinitarian language as non-literal means to refuse a straight forward association between trinitarian language and the trinitarian God. According to this view, the androcentric and patriarchal nature of God language reflects and borrows from the patriarchal structures within which such language was formulated. Rosemary Radford Ruether thus argues that male monotheism – which images God solely through one gender – models God after the patriarchal ruling class and thus privileges men as the responsible partners of God's covenant.[52]

Specifically, it is argued that to collapse the Trinity into trinitarian language is to reduce the ineffable God to a linguistic formula, claiming direct access to the incomprehensible being of God. As such, most feminists understand language as a 'gateway' into knowledge of God rather than as something which is directly identifiable with the divine.[53] Within this view, our images, symbols, metaphors and names are not considered to be identical with that to which they point. Trinitarian language loses its literal status and is understood instead in either metaphorical or analogical terms.

Indeed, for many feminist theologians, to render the trinitarian name as the literal, proper name of God is to fall into idolatry. Ruether thus claims that taking

---

49 Elizabeth Achtiemer, 'Exchanging God for "no Gods": A Discussion of Female Language for God', in Alvin F. Kimel (ed.), *Speaking the Christian God: The Holy Trinity and the Challenge of Feminism* (Grand Rapids, Michigan & Leominster, 1992), pp. 1–16, esp. p. 3.

50 Interestingly, Bloesch never conceives that the trinitarian name itself may have been formulated in relation to patriarchal ideology, supporting (either consciously or unconsciously) male superiority and privilege.

51 Alvin Kimel, 'The God Who Likes His Name: Holy Trinity, Feminism and the Language of Faith', in Alvin F. Kimel (ed.), *Speaking the Christian God: The Holy Trinity and the Challenge of Feminism* (Grand Rapids, Michigan & Leominster, 1992), pp. 188–208, esp. p. 194. For similar perspectives see Roland M. Frye, *Language for God and Feminist Language* (Edinburgh, 1988), and Geoffrey Wainwright, 'A Language in Which we Speak of God', *Worship*, 57 (1983): 309–21.

52 Ruether, *Sexism*, p. 53.

53 Such a position is expressed well by Letty Russell in her book, *Human Liberation in a Feminist Perspective – A Theology* (Philadelphia, 1974).

the human male language for God literally is idolatrous[54] since it reduces the reality of God to the male sex. Similarly, Johnson argues that a literal understanding of 'He' language (such as 'Father' and 'Son') undermines the primary claim of Christianity that God is mystery, incomprehensible and unfathomable, implying that such male language represents the whole of the divine reality and that this reality can be reduced to the male sex.[55]

Feminists however disagree on how exactly trinitarian language operates – whether analogically or metaphorically. It is the approach of Janet Soskice however that I find the most compelling in this debate and which I expand in more detail here.[56] According to Soskice, trinitarian language operates metaphorically and so cannot claim direct access to the divine being. It can, however, claim some sort of correspondence with it,[57] for it is not metaphorical *language* that is true, but the *meaning* behind such language. It is not that Jesus *is* literally a lamb or a shepherd but that he is integral to the work of salvation and cares for humanity.[58] Soskice therefore claims that metaphor 'is a kind of language use and not a kind of truth'.[59] Such a view is useful because it seeks to establish a midway point between the two extremes of a) collapsing God into language and b) alienating God from language altogether. Her identification of 'theological realism' as an approach to theological language is attractive because it recognizes the inability of language to encapsulate God, whilst simultaneously accepting that there *are* divine realities 'out there' that theologians are nevertheless trying to lay hold of.[60] This avoids the theological relativism inherent within McFague's articulation of metaphor since it does not reduce trinitarian language to mere theological play.[61] Unlike McFague, Soskice is not arguing that trinitarian language fails to say anything informative about the trinitarian God. Instead, she argues that even though the divine being is

---

54 Ruether, *Sexism*, p. 69.

55 Johnson, *She Who Is*, pp. 39–40.

56 Janet Martin Soskice, 'Theological Realism', in William J. Abraham and Steven W. Holtzer (eds), *The Rationality of Religious Belief* (Oxford, 1987), pp. 105–20. Also see her monograph, *Metaphor and Religious Language* (Oxford, 1985).

57 Soskice, 'Theological Realism', p. 105.

58 These are examples provided by Soskice. Ibid., p. 106.

59 Ibid., p. 107.

60 Ibid., p. 108.

61 According to McFague, Metaphorical theology takes metaphors from our time and relates them to the God-world relationship, encouraging non-traditional, imaginative and unconventional ways of expressing God. Metaphorical theology is also heuristic, exposing our concepts of God as *our* concepts rather than constituting God per se. Finally, metaphorical theology is pluralistic: since no metaphor can capture God we must image God through a diversity of metaphors, realising that the 'is not' of metaphor is far greater than the 'is'. However, this is not to say that we are free to image God as we like, for although McFague forcefully presents language as theological 'play' she also argues that it must image God in ways relevant to the ecological concerns of our time. See *Models of God*, pp. 34–46.

in the end impenetrable, theology is still about the business of speaking God in ways that highlight glimpses of the divine, even if they are only glimpses.[62]

Soskice then goes on to identify metaphor with 'models' of God, asserting that as models, metaphors should not simply amount to convenient fictions which serve to order the world around us, but should instead provide access to states that exist independently of our theorizing about them. To understand trinitarian language as metaphor then means that such language cannot carry literal or ontological significance in the sense that it is essentially tied to the *being* of God. Instead, it is to be interpreted as *pointing towards* divine reality, corresponding to the God who is beyond words and beyond all imagery. In this sense, all models of the Trinity are recognized as contextual, limited and partial, whether traditional or otherwise. Because such models serve as a way of naming experience of the divine, they can be understood as signally *something* about divine reality, but never *everything*. The language of Father, Son and Holy Spirit can never claim exclusivity and must always be accompanied by non-patriarchal alternatives so as to draw attention to the inadequacy of such language as well as reaffirming the incomprehensibility of God.[63]

Responding to the Problems

Now that we have established the metaphorical nature of trinitarian language, let us explore and weigh up how various feminist theologians have responded to the difficulties outlined at the start of this chapter.

Feminist responses to the Trinity tend to adopt one of two strategies, either a 'reformist' approach or a 'revolutionist' approach.[64] Whereas the former seeks to work at various levels within the Christian tradition, the latter seeks to break from this so as to present an alternative tradition 'free' from patriarchal associations. Reformist dealings with the Trinity therefore maintain a trinitarian understanding of God but are committed to rethinking and re-imaging the Trinity at various levels in light of feminist concerns. Revolutionist dealings, on the other hand, tend to reject the doctrine of the Trinity outright as irredeemably sexist and misogynist, and consequently look towards constructing the divine afresh in relation to a more radical feminist agenda. Inasmuch as the latter fails to deal with the Trinity, it is the reformist strategy that is outlined below.

---

62 Ibid. She distinguishes this approach from 'theological instrumentalism' which insists that theological language cannot correspond with such an ontological, transcendent reality.

63 For more on metaphor and analogy see Gail Ramshaw, 'De Divinis Nominibus: The Gender of God', *Worship*, 56 (1982): 117–36 and DiNoia, J.A., 'Knowing and Naming the Triune God: The Grammar of Trinitarian Confession', in Alvin F. Kimel (ed.), *Speaking the Christian God: The Holy Trinity and the Challenge of Feminism* (Grand Rapids, Michigan and Leominster, 1992), pp. 162–87.

64 Such categories are used by Carol Christ to characterise the two main strands within feminist thought. See Carol P. Christ, 'The New Feminist Theology: A Review of the Literature', *Religious Studies Review*, 3 (1977): 203–12.

Within this framework, feminist responses tend to pursue one or more of the following five directions:

1. promoting a defence of the traditional trinitarian language;
2. emphasising biblical imagery which depicts God as either female or in feminine terms;
3. using specifically female metaphors to refer to the *fullness* of the Trinity;
4. de-personalizing trinitarian language; or
5. de-sexing trinitarian language.

The defence of traditional trinitarian language This initial measure represents the most conservative end of the reformist agenda. Feminists who seek to preserve traditional trinitarian language tend to either highlight how the original meaning has been overtaken and undermined by a patriarchal world-view, or seek to expose the potential original language holds for us today. Both interlink, tackling trinitarian language from the position of feminist hermeneutics, aiming to bring to light interpretations which might challenge and expose patriarchy.

Seeking to reinforce the original meaning of trinitarian language, many feminists argue that the term 'Father' should not be understood as connoting sexual identity. That God is imaged as Father throughout the Bible, it is suggested, does not mean that God was understood as male, but that God communicated intimately with God's people, especially with the person of Jesus Christ. Mary Hayter, for example, notes how the term 'Father' is used very rarely of God in the Hebrew Scriptures (15 times) in an attempt to avoid pagan connections with a generative God.[65] She cites Hosea 11.9, 'For I am God, and not man', claiming that divine Fatherhood was intended to convey divine otherness and transcendence as opposed to sexuality.[66] It depicts Yahweh's love and intimacy as well as Yahweh's sovereignty and holiness.

In the New Testament, however, God as 'Father' appears rather more frequently and now, at this point, on the lips of Jesus himself. Matthew notes that God is our heavenly Father[67] and that God's Fatherhood is unparalleled on earth;[68] Luke understands God's Fatherhood in terms of otherness, transcendence, kingly majesty, mercy and compassion; Mark, like Matthew, refers to God as 'your father in heaven', and John understands divine Fatherhood as being Christologically

---

65 Mary Hayter, *The New Eve in Christ* (London, 1987), p. 27. Indeed, she argues that the Old Testament is hostile towards Goddess and fertility religions precisely because Yahweh was always understood to be supra-sexual see pp. 13–18.

66 Such a view is also emphasized by Colin Gunton in his chapter, 'Proteus and Procrustes: A Study in the Dialectic of Language in Disagreement with Sallie McFague', in Alvin F. Kimel (ed.), *The Triune God and the Challenge of Feminism* (Grand Rapids, Michigan and Leominster, 1992), pp. 65–80, esp. p. 79.

67 For example, Matt. 5.45, 6.32, 7.21, 12.50, 18.10.

68 For example, Matt. 23.9.

revealed, only making sense through association to Jesus the Son.[69] Feminists wishing to recover the language of God as 'Father' then often note that examples such as these do not communicate God's maleness. Indeed, Mary Hayter, for example, argues that nowhere in either the Old or New Testament does divine Fatherhood connote sexuality.

Jesus' use of the term *Abba* has also been heavily evaluated by a number of scholars, feminist and otherwise. It is suggested that Jesus' use of the word 'Father' points towards an intimate and close relationship between Christ and God rather than suggesting that God is somehow male.[70] Many in fact argue that the term only carries meaning in the context of this relationship, hence the meaning of 'Father' can only be determined in specific relation to the 'Son'.[71] By referring to God as 'Father', human beings identify their participation in the intimate relationship Jesus enjoyed with God. In this sense, the image does not signify God's maleness but God's closeness to us. It is an image of intimacy and trust, and as such, constitutes a direct attack on patriarchal notions of divinity.

For some feminist theologians then, the image of God the Father criticized by feminists like Daly is not the image presented in the Bible.[72] Diane Tennis, for example, draws attention to the way in which most feminist reactions to God the Father tend to link divine wrath with divine Fatherhood. Tennis, however, urges her readers to exert caution since not all characteristics of God can be associated with Fatherhood. 'Parenting symbols' she says, 'cannot be identified with any or all of the vast dimensions of Yahweh's character willy-nilly.'[73] God the Father implies something specific and according to Tennis this constitutes divine reliability. 'God as Father does not abandon and does not destroy … He does not reject the children through abandonment or death. Instead, he is present to them and with them. He is a Father who really fathers.'[74]

---

69 For example, Luke 10.21, 11.13, 15.11–32, 22.29, Mark 11.25, John 1.18, 5.20, 6.46.

70 Gordon Kaufman demonstrates how the tetragrammaton came to be overtaken by 'Lord' (*kyrios)* and 'Creator' in the Old Testament and 'Father' in the New Testament. None of these images, he argues, are intended to connote God as sexually male but instead point towards God as transcendent and personal. See *In Face of Mystery: A Constructive Theology* (Cambridge, Massachusetts, London, 1995), pp. 301–21.

71 A point made by various theologians. See particularly Wainwright, *The Trinity in the New Testament*, pp. 44–50 and Garrett Green, 'The Gender of God and the Theology of Metaphor', in Alvin F. Kimel (ed.), *Speaking the Christian God: The Holy Trinity and the Challenge of Feminism* (Grand Rapids, Michigan & Leominster, 1992), pp. 44–64, esp. p. 59.

72 See for example Janet Soskice, 'Trinity and Feminism', in Susan Frank Parsons (ed.), *The Cambridge Companion to Feminist Theology* (Cambridge, 2002), pp. 135–50, esp. p.139; Carl Braaten, 'The Problem of God-Language Today', p. 27; Claude Geffré, '"Father" as the Proper Name of God', in Johannes-Baptist Metz and Edward Schillebeeckx (eds), *God as Father?* (Edinburgh, New York, 1981), pp. 43–50.

73 Diane Tennis, *Is God the Only Reliable Father?* (Philadelphia, 1985), p. 11.

74 Ibid., p. 13.

To this extent, Tennis argues that God the Father constitutes a direct attack on the patriarchal father, for here God is not distant but involved, not solitary but in relationship with God's people, not totally transcendent exerting power *over*, but immanently sharing God's own being with humanity.[75] Whereas the patriarchal father is typified by absence, God the Father is present and reliable.[76] Thus, Tennis strongly argues that the image of God the Father *must* be kept precisely because we have scant experience of a reliable man. If God the Father is reliable then God stands in judgement of all fathers who are not. In this understanding, Tennis suggests that God the Father calls men not to dominate, control or suppress women, but to be present, reliable, trustworthy and loving. Indeed, she argues, as does Rosemary Radford Ruether, that if God is the only Father then human beings are all brothers and sisters together. To be in relationship with Abba God through Jesus Christ means to enter into a new relationship with others – a relationship of mutual service as opposed to mastery and servitude. 'Because God is our parent', says Ruether, 'we are liberated from dependence on patriarchal authority.' The biblical tradition, she argues, reverses the symbolic relation between divine fatherhood and sovereignty and challenges the sacralization of patriarchy.[77] The image of God as Father, for Ruether, need not promote a patriarchal order in which women are encouraged to remain dependent and subordinate.[78]

Indeed, the image of God the Father need not be interpreted as hopelessly patriarchal but may in fact shed some degree of light on the full humanity of women. If the traditional belief in God as incomprehensible spirit is to be maintained, it does indeed follow that God cannot *be* male. Hence, talk of God as 'Father' cannot signify the sex of God as this would contradict the numerous warnings against idolatry in the Old Testament (for example, Exodus 20.4–5) and the Arians would have got it right! Ruether's view that such an image may offer a critique of male dominance is, therefore, compelling. If God is Father then we are all children, independent of sex. This understanding of God's fatherhood allows little room for the establishment of patriarchal relations of dominance and subservience between individuals. However, despite such insights, difficulties still remain. Tennis, by aligning God the Father with human fathers seems to maximize rather than minimize the significance of God's maleness. If God as Father provides some kind of role model for human fathers then a clear connection is made between God as Father and the male as father, seemingly reinforcing rather than subverting the claim that God is male. Indeed, it still appears that the image of God the Father

[75] Ibid., p. 90.

[76] According to Tennis, the patriarchal father is absent in at least five ways: either he has gone because of work patterns, he is absent through abandonment or occasional presence, he is absent as an anticipated presence, he is emotionally absent, or finally, he is physically present but dangerous. Ibid., pp. 35–49.

[77] Ruether, *Sexism*, p. 65.

[78] Despite this, Ruether continues to maintain that the image is problematic because it serves to encourage humans to remain child-like in relation to God (see p. 4).

continues to distance God from female embodiment, implying that God is closer to the male than to the female. Employing Soskice's understanding of metaphor, however, may help us here since it requires us to admit that whilst the language of God as 'Father' may say *something* about God, it cannot say *everything*. If Father language does not *belong* to God as already proposed, then it can be retained, however, it must be complemented by other metaphors. What this might involve will be discussed later in this chapter.

Many feminists have similarly sought to defend the title of Jesus as the Son of God on the grounds that it is not Jesus' maleness that is significant but his relationship with God. This constitutes an attempt to minimize the maleness of Christ. Elizabeth Johnson, for example, in her book, *Consider Jesus*, accuses Christian theology of understanding the sex of Christ as an ontological necessity rather than as an historical option. According to her, the Word could have been made female flesh; that Jesus was male says nothing about God's nature or being.[79] The problem, as she sees it, is that Christ has been interpreted within a patriarchal framework so that the good news of the gospel has become the bad news of masculine privilege.[80] Jesus' maleness has been linked to his divinity in such a way that the female has become marginalized from imaging Christ. Johnson therefore argues that Jesus' sex is no more important than his race, his Galilean roots or his age.[81] 'To make the maleness of Jesus Christ a christological principle' she argues, 'is to deny the universality of salvation.'[82] This is unacceptable for Johnson since it denies the inclusivity of Christ.

Feminist attempts to minimize the maleness of Jesus have also stressed the so-called 'feminine' traits of Christ, the aim here being to present Jesus as an androgynous individual, encompassing the best characteristics of both sexes in one ideal human state. Jesus is the woman who searches for the lost coin, the one who offers his tears upon finding Lazarus dead, the one who listens, shows compassion, is tender and kind; the one who offers forgiveness.[83] Emphasis has also been placed on Jesus' actions and function as the great liberator. Feminist liberation theologians particularly emphasize the liberating qualities of Jesus' life and ministry for the oppressed, hence Rosemary Radford Ruether highlights how Jesus went against the conventions of his time, having table fellowship with sinners and marginalized people, talking to women and encouraging them to

---

[79] See Elizabeth Johnson, *Consider Jesus: Waves of Renewal in Christology* (London, 1990), p. 107.

[80] Elizabeth Johnson, 'Redeeming The Name of Christ: Christology', in Catherine Mowry LaCugna (ed.), *Freeing Theology: The Essential Theology in Feminist Perspective* (San Francisco, 1993), pp. 115–27, esp. p. 118.

[81] Ibid., p. 119.

[82] Johnson, *She Who Is*, p. 73.

[83] See María Pilar Aquino, *Our Cry for Life: Feminist Theology From Latin America* (Maryknoll, New York, 1993), pp. 135–6.

follow him.[84] Elisabeth Schüssler Fiorenza also argues that Jesus never uttered misogynist comments despite this being normative at the time. Within this context, Christ is presented as a liberating symbol who serves to empower women and other oppressed groups to claim their place within the *imago Dei*. Here, Jesus' maleness is not overlooked, but his significance is not considered to be caught up with his sex.

The understanding of Jesus as 'liberator' is also key to other non-Western women's theologies. Within womanist theology, for example, Jesus is depicted as one who identifies with black women and their oppression, as one who affirms the basic humanity of black women, and as one who inspires hope through his resurrection.[85] African women's theologies also often emphasize Jesus as the brother or kin who frees women from the domination of inhuman husbands; as one who knew suffering, hunger, thirst and who was oppressed by the culture of his own people. 'Jesus the liberator', says Mercy Oduyoye, 'is a paradigm for the critique of culture that most African women theologians do.'[86] For her, Jesus sets women free from sexism, oppression, and marginalization through his death and resurrection; Jesus, gives voice to the voiceless and so reverses cultural norms which expect women to remain mute and accept oppression.[87]

However, all of these options are problematic to some degree. Attempting to play down Jesus' maleness as insignificant or irrelevant tends to ignore the force this already carries in the church and in Western Christian consciousness in general. It also underestimates the value of the incarnation and risks losing sight of the wonder of God becoming human. Stressing the feminine side of Jesus reinforces rather than challenges harmful stereotypes of masculinity and femininity keeping the two essentially apart. Emphasizing the liberating praxis of Jesus does not overcome the fact that Jesus, despite all his significance, continues to remain male.[88]

Given this, some feminists replace the desire to minimize Jesus' maleness with a desire to demonstrate the ways in which his maleness might hold significance for women and, ultimately, for the demise of patriarchy. The two most central emphases within this option are to stress the servanthood of Jesus and his suffering on the cross. Beginning with the former, Mercy Amba Oduyoye, for example, argues that 'if Jesus is the God who has become weakness in our context, in his identity as God-Man, Jesus takes on the condition of the African woman'.[89] In other words, if God has become weak through the incarnation, then Jesus as

---

84 Ruether, *Sexism*, esp. pp. 116ff.

85 Jacqueline Grant, 'The Challenge of the Darker Sister', in Janet Martin Soskice and Diana Lipton (eds), *Feminism and Theology* (Oxford, 2003), pp. 302–11, esp. p. 307.

86 Mercy Amba Oduyoye, 'Jesus Christ', in Susan Frank Parsons (ed.), *The Cambridge Companion to Feminist Theology* (Cambridge, 2002), pp. 151–70, esp. p. 152.

87 Ibid., p. 157.

88 For more on these options and the difficulties with them see Tennis, pp. 96–103.

89 Oduyoye, 'Jesus Christ', p. 160.

God incarnate identifies with all African women who are weak and oppressed. Indeed, many feminist theologians suggest that Jesus, as the God-man-servant, challenges patriarchal notions both of divinity and of male humanity.[90] Such imagery identifies that God is *present* with us not absent, outside the world or ruling from a distance as in the traditional patriarchal model identified by Daly. Gail Ramshaw thus remarks: 'Christology brings God out of the clouds, and outside my imagination. God has feet, not on a footstool in the sky, not on my neck, but dirty with the dust of the earth.'[91] For some feminist theologians then, God is not the power hungry dominant male criticized by Daly but the one who comes to sacrifice God's own privilege for the sake of love. Jesus Christ does not seek equality with God, but instead comes to serve and to fellowship with sinners (cf. Philippians 2.5–8). Diane Tennis thus notes that God becoming manifest both as a servant and as a male means that patriarchal notions of power and privilege are exploded. She says:

> Unlike women, he [Jesus] did not have to be a servant. He had power and access to power. But he gave it up! Jesus thereby modelled in his own being the dramatic assault on male privilege. Who but a man could credibly teach and model such a revolution in relationships by giving up power? Only a man could do that, because only men had power. Jesus' maleness is neither a weakness in the story nor is it irrelevant. The maleness of Jesus is a strong point in the story of giving up power and becoming a servant, joining the underclass of women and other servants in order to abolish servitude altogether.[92]

For feminists like Tennis then, Jesus' maleness carries great significance for the undermining of traditional patriarchal expectations of male behaviour.[93]

In addition to this, many feminists also draw attention to the ways in which the cross of Christ might challenge rather than reinforce or glamorize patriarchal structures of oppression. Rosemary Radford Ruether, for example, famously interprets the cross as the *kenosis* of patriarchy, as the 'emptying out' of male privilege and power.[94] For her, the crucifixion signals the end of male domination, revealing a new order marked by a new humanity in which all are equal and all are one. Similarly, for Julie Hopkins, the death of Jesus is not necessary to satisfy God's honour. Instead, the cross, she contends, reveals a God who is personally

---

90 See Gail Ramshaw, 'Naming the Trinity: Orthodoxy and Inclusivity', *Worship*, 60/6 (1986): 491–8 and Russell, *Human Liberation*, p. 100.

91 Gail Ramshaw, *Under the Tree of Life: The Religion of a Feminist Christian* (New York, 1998), p. 82.

92 Tennis, pp. 103–4.

93 See Karen Bloomquist, '"Let God be God": The Theological Necessity of Depatriarchalizing God', in Carl E. Braaten (ed.), *Our Naming of God: Problems and Prospects of God-Talk Today* (Minneapolis, 1989), pp. 45–60, esp. p. 59.

94 Ruether, *Sexism*, p. 135. Also see Bloomquist, 'Let God be God', p. 59.

present in loving solidarity, vulnerability and suffering with those who are oppressed.[95] The cross, put simply, enables the sufferings of women (and other oppressed groups) to find expression and theological voice.

But does this simply encourage women to persevere with their sufferings rather than challenge them? For many, emphasis is at this point again brought back to the notion of Jesus as liberator. Jesus, many argue, does not simply identify with those who are oppressed, but also shows, through his life, death and resurrection, that liberation is possible and indeed, desirable. Mercy Oduyoye, for example, writes: 'The emphasis of women, however is not that we emulate the suffering but that it becomes the source of our liberation. We do not only admire Jesus, but we are caught in the net of liberation which we believe will bring us into fullness of life.'[96] In a similar tone, Karen Baker-Fletcher argues that, for womanist theologians, the sacrifice of Jesus does not endorse violent practices towards indigenous peoples, the poor or any other subject or group, as this would be to deny that Jesus has overcome evil and violence through the cross. Instead she says: 'To overcome the cross by taking up one's cross is to claim divine and personal power over all crosses. It is the power that turns the cross into two pieces of wood instead of a tool of destruction … It is the path of resistance against evil.'[97] That God suffers through Jesus need not endorse suffering but may in fact empower those who suffer. If Christ has overcome evil and death, then resurrection faith is the source of power to oppose evil and injustice.[98]

Talk of God the 'Son' then may be deemed meaningful and appropriate when viewed through the lens of Soskice's understanding of metaphor. If Father-Son language does not belong to God but says *something* about what God is like, it can be retained. However, insofar as such language can never say *everything* about God, it can and must be complemented by other metaphors (I will return to this at the end of this chapter). However, the question still remains as to how we might effectively understand the significance of Jesus' maleness.

In responding to this, I propose that it is the doctrine of incarnation which holds the greatest potential for subverting and resisting associations between God and maleness and for challenging an exclusive relationship between Jesus the 'Son' and male humanity. Indeed, insisting on Jesus as the unique manifestation of God – as God incarnate – does not have to equate to a patriarchal endorsement of the maleness of God or the divinization of the male. If Jesus' historical embodiment includes more than his maleness then we have to ask why his maleness is seen as being more theologically significant than say his able-bodiedness. Because such an exclusive focus on Jesus' sex seems both problematic and rather dubious on

95 Julie Hopkins, *Towards a Feminist Christology: Jesus of Nazareth, European Women and the Christological Crisis* (Grand Rapids, 1995), p. 62.

96 Oduyoye, 'Jesus Christ', p. 162.

97 Karen Baker-Fletcher, *Dancing with God: The Trinity from a Womanist Perspective* (St Louis, Missouri, 2006), p. 150.

98 Ibid.

these terms, I suggest we see 'particularity' rather than maleness as the central characteristic of incarnation.[99] It is not that God becomes *man* that is the point of incarnation but that God becomes particular through the taking on of embodiment itself. It is not through sharing in the same particularities as Jesus that we are able to identify with Christ, but through being particular bodies in the first place. Within this setting, *all* bodies are affirmed as sacramental on the basis of their own individual particularized embodiments rather than on the basis of their alignment with the male sex.

As God incarnate, Jesus transgresses the classical metaphysical distinction between Creator and creature, divinity and humanity.[100] The body of Christ is thus an 'extendable body',[101] not limited by historical or geographical location. The historical embodiment of Jesus, although constituting the starting point of incarnation, is not where incarnation (or redemption) ends. Instead, the particular manifestation of God in Jesus Christ provides the ontological basis upon which the incarnational and sacramental value of material things is established in the world. What this means is that the particular incarnation of God in the historical Jesus constitutes the grounds upon which the 'cosmic' principles of incarnation and sacrament are secured. We cannot have the latter without first confirming the former. The particular, embodied situation of Jesus establishes the general principle that God is the kind of God who is made known through the particularity of bodies and through material things. That Jesus is God incarnate – the 'primordial sacrament'[102] of God – then enables other bodies to incarnate God. Also, because Jesus is the eternal *logos*, the second *hypostasis* of the eternal Trinity, incarnation is exposed as being integral to the eternal identity of God. Within this setting, the *logos asarkos* (the *logos* 'without the flesh') cannot be meaningfully separated from the *logos ensarkos* (the *logos* 'within the flesh'), hence there can be no meaningful talk of God without talk of incarnation.

This clearly avoids difficulties surrounding Jesus' maleness and uniqueness, for although Jesus is male, this is not considered to be important to the incarnation. Although Jesus is the unique manifestation of God in history, this provides the basis upon which other bodies might communicate something of God in the world, hence the principle of incarnation is extended beyond the confines of Jesus' own particular embodiment. It is also true, however, that if Jesus is the eternal *logos*

---

99 This argument has been developed in more detail elsewhere. See my chapter, 'A Very Particular Body'.

100 Sarah Coakley makes this point in her essay, 'The Trinity and Gender Reconsidered' in Miroslav Volf and Michael Welker (eds), *God's Life in Trinity* (Minneapolis, 2006), pp. 133–42, esp. p. 141.

101 I borrow this term from Graham Ward. See 'Bodies: The Displaced Body of Jesus', in J. Milbank, C. Pickstock and G. Ward (eds), *Radical Orthodoxy: A New Theology* (London, 1999), pp. 163–81, esp. p. 167.

102 Edward Schillebeeckx, *Christ the Sacrament of the Encounter with God* (Maryland, 1963), p. 15.

then 'Christ' cannot be easily reduced to maleness. Womanist theologian, Karen Baker-Fletcher, makes this point insisting that although the historical Jesus had a gender, Jesus as Word and as the living Christ transcends gender.[103] The earthly Jesus is *hypostatically* joined to the Word, the second person of the Trinity. Christ then includes but reaches beyond the earthly Jesus and as such cannot be reduced to maleness. This is not to ignore or overlook Jesus' maleness but to say with the likes of Johnson that his significance is not tied up with his sex. Such a proposed Christological focus then need not constitute an androcentric one, since emphasis on Jesus' historical particularity coupled with Jesus' eternal identity as the Word-made-flesh means that 'Christ' cannot be reduced to maleness.

Reference to the Holy Spirit is perhaps most comfortable out of the three trinitarian persons within a feminist environment. Considering the amorphous and abstract nature of this image, feminists have found it considerably easier to affirm the supra-sexuality of God within this context. Given that the Hebrew term *ruach* is grammatically feminine and that the Spirit is often ascribed traits which are stereotypically feminine, some claim that reasserting the Holy Spirit as fully divine may considerably redirect attention away from the maleness of God and further towards the full humanity of women. The Spirit comforts as a loving mother, is gentle, kind, and wise.[104] She is the presence that creates the world and the breath that breathes life into the world.[105] She is characterized by fecundity, giving birth and sustaining life. Some feminists therefore argue that the Holy Spirit constitutes the feminine side of God and as such stands to affirm rather than deny the personhood of women.

There are obvious problems with this perspective, however. Most obviously, it identifies women more readily with reproduction, care, nurture and compassion and thus serves to polarize masculinity and femininity. This is just as unhelpful for men as it is for women since it places limits on both women and men in relation to their gender roles. I will return to this critique in more detail in the next section.

Female imagery and the feminine side of God Aware of the sexist and patriarchal tendencies within traditional trinitarian language, this second alternative seeks to append female imagery or feminine traits to the masculine trinitarian image. According to this second approach, traditional trinitarian language is not exclusive. God is not only Father, Son and Holy Spirit, but can also be imaged in female or feminine ways, affirming women as well as men as theomorphic.

Female imagery for God although not dominant within the Bible, is by no means absent. God is imaged as midwife (Ps. 22.9), mother (Is. 49.13–15, Is. 66.13, Ps. 131.2, Is. 42.14–15) and as giving birth (Is. 42.14, Jer. 31.20, Is. 14.1, Ps. 77.10, Ps. 79.8). Many feminists then set about emphasising such imagery in

---

103 Baker-Fletcher, p. 61. Also see pp. 119–20.

104 See Aquino, p. 136.

105 Ibid., p. 135.

order to combat the androcentric image of God that prevails within contemporary Christian trinitarian thought.

Imaging God as Mother is often not intended to replace the image of God the Father, but instead to complement it. Within this context, reference is frequently made to Julian of Norwich, a medieval mystic who famously presents the metaphor of Jesus as Mother.[106] According to Julian, Mother Jesus constitutes the wisdom of God,[107] carrying, restoring, sustaining and remaking his children. Aligning the two together, she firmly identifies Christ with suffering, giving birth and new life. Indeed, she sees in the person of Jesus a broken, bleeding and suffering body; a body which sustains and carries us like that of a mother. Hence she comments:

> We know that all our mothers bear us to pain and to dying; a strange thing that! But our true Mother Jesus, he alone bareth us to joy and to endless living; blessed may he be! Thus he sustaineth us within him, in love and in travail unto the full time in which he willed to suffer the sharpest throes and most grievous pains that ever were, or ever shall be; and he died at last.[108]

As such, she claims that Jesus alone can properly be called 'Mother'.[109]

In addition to this, some feminists posit a feminine dimension in the divine. Here, God is not only understood in female terms, but also as having specifically feminine traits. God is loving, caring, compassionate, faithful, nurturing, kind, sympathetic, merciful, and forgiving. God may be Father, but God is what Jürgen Moltmann terms a 'motherly Father',[110] ruling with compassion, tenderness and love.

The most dominant understanding within this approach posits the Holy Spirit as the feminine dimension of God. In Genesis the Spirit is noted as brooding to bring forth life in creation (Gn. 1.2), and in the New Testament the Spirit is designated the comforter who comes to heal, restore and make things new. Jay Williams, for example, refers to the Spirit as the divine mother of Jesus: since Mary is made pregnant by the Holy Spirit, the Spirit can be imaged in feminine terms as giving birth and bringing forth life.[111] Yves Congar presents a similar opinion asserting that within the Christian tradition, the feminine character of God is ultimately attributed to the Holy Spirit.[112] As Spirit, God reveals God's maternal function.

---

106 Julian of Norwich, *The Revelations of Divine Love*, trans. J. Walsh, S.J. (Tenbury Wells, 1961), p. 161.

107 Ibid., p. 159.

108 Ibid., p. 163.

109 Ibid., p. 164.

110 See Jürgen Moltmann, 'The Motherly Father: Is Trinitarian Patripassionism Replacing Theological Patriarchalism?', in Johannes-Baptist Metz and Edward Schillebeeckx (eds), *God as Father?* (Edinburgh, New York, 1981), pp. 51–6.

111 See Williams, 'Yahweh, Women, and the Trinity'.

112 Congar, p. 157.

However, both strategies are problematic. Imaging God as female or with a feminine side threatens to reinforce harmful patriarchal stereotypes which link women 'essentially' with the maternal feminine, defining them primarily in relation to their reproductive function and the related characteristics of compassion and love.[113] The image of God as 'Mother' can present motherhood as the ultimate fulfilment of womanhood, ignoring the suffering of many mothers and the fact that motherhood is for many, not a matter of choice.[114] Although a more accurate understanding of the Holy Spirit may identify the Spirit, not as passive or dormant, but as actively stirring creation towards life-enhancing ends,[115] the image continues to carry predominantly maternal associations and maintains its exclusive connection with stereotypically feminine traits. Such characteristics do not exhaust female embodiment, since women do not *just* give birth, nurture, show compassion, mercy and love, but also demonstrate anger and judgement. Not all women mother, not all women are maternal. It is therefore right that we exert caution before embracing such an essentialist reading. Indeed, it remains to be seen why such characteristics are specifically 'feminine' in the first place.[116]

Linking the sex of God then to particular character traits may cause more problems than it potentially seeks to solve, conveniently trapping women and men within harmful gender roles. For example, relating God's feminine side to maternity, relationship, love and compassion not only confines women to the stereotypical roles of parenting and relationships, but also alienates men from such roles. This obviously supports a view of sexual difference in which women are not expected to exert power nor men expected to nurture. Within this setting, women and men can only identify with God insofar as they fit the mould already carved out for them by patriarchy. If we are to affirm the *full* humanity of women and men however, this would mean affirming masculinity in relation to love, nurture and compassion, as well as in relation to more traditional characteristics, and femininity in relation to power and strength alongside other traditional characteristics.

At a second level it is also apparent that despite exhibiting female or feminine characteristics, God, although including feminine traits, continues to remain male.[117] For example, despite depicting Jesus as Mother, Julian of Norwich continues to

---

113 See Hannaford, 'Gender and the Person God Is', p. 38.

114 Mary Grey, *Introducing Feminist Images of God* (Sheffield, 2001), p. 27.

115 Indeed, for Williams, to conceive of woman in the image of the Spirit is to considerably revise what we believe woman to be. 'In the divine economy, it is not the feminine Person who remains hidden and at home. She is God in the world; moving, stirring up, revealing, interceding. It is she who calls out, sanctifies, and animates the church. Hers is the water of the one baptism. The debt of sin is wiped away by her. She is the life-giver who raises men [*sic*] from the dead with the life of the coming age. Jesus himself left the earth so that she, the intercessor, might come.' See 'Yahweh, Women, and the Trinity', p. 240.

116 See Johnson, *She Who Is*, p. 49.

117 This is a view expressed clearly by Ruether in *Sexism* when she says, '[w]e need to go beyond the idea of a "feminine-side" of God, whether to be identified with the Spirit or

refer to God as male. This measure has therefore been rightfully criticized for subsuming the feminine within the masculine and the female within the male, reinforcing the patriarchal ideology that 'man' is both generic and inclusive.

The fundamental assumption within both these suggestions then is that since women have been left out of imaging God, the answer is to simply 'add women and stir'. By recovering female imagery or making appeal to a feminine dimension in God, women are able to identify with God to the same degree as men. This conclusion, however, assumes a model of gender complementarity which takes for granted a patriarchal view of gender relations. Although masculine and feminine dimensions may be seen as complementary features in the divine, they are not equally valued. God may be imaged through both male and female metaphors, however it is often obvious that in the end, God is still considered to be male. Although, for example, God may be *like* a Mother, Sister or Wife, 'he' is often ultimately understood *as* Father and Son. Such a model of complementarity then is problematic because it allows male imagery to claim dominance *over* female imagery under the pretence of balance.

In response to this, many feminists have sought to dispose of the notion of complementarity on the grounds that it serves an ideological agenda of subordinating and diminishing women. Indeed, it reinforces the notion of the generic male and simultaneously confines women to stereotypical accounts of the feminine so that the *fullness* of their humanity fails to be represented. It is this central criticism then that causes many feminists to entertain a third option: that of using specifically female imagery to refer to the *fullness* of the trinitarian God.

Using female imagery to refer to the fullness of the trinitarian God This third option begins from the central premise that it is not enough to simply add women to the 'recipe' of imaging God. Adding a feminine dimension to the trinitarian God or speaking of God in female terms, say as Mother, Sister, Wife and so on, only has limited value. It points towards a feminine or female 'aspect' within God as opposed to representing the fullness of divine reality in female form. To this extent, feminists like Elizabeth Johnson argue that such measures fail to promote women as either fully human or fully *imago Dei*.

In her book *She Who Is*, Elizabeth Johnson proposes that the fullness of divine power be shown in female imagery so as to challenge traditional stereotypes of femininity *and* masculinity, demonstrating that women as well as men can *fully* represent the trinitarian Godhead. Women should not only signify an aspect of the divine, but should instead image the entirety of the trinitarian God. She writes:

> Only if the full reality of women as well as men enters into the symbolization of God along with symbols from the natural world, can the idolatrous fixation

---

even with the *Sophia*-Spirit together, and question the assumption that the highest symbol of divine sovereignty still remains exclusively male' (p. 61).

> on one image be broken and the truth of the mystery of God, in tandem with the liberation of all human beings, and the whole earth, emerge for our time.[118]

Johnson's point then is not to suggest that God *is* female but that God is mystery. It is her view that if both male and female imagery is used to refer to the *entirety* of God then this will perform the dual function of affirming women as *fully* theomorphic, while simultaneously exposing both male and female as equally inadequate for imaging the divine. She therefore presents the entire trinitarian formula through the use of exclusively female terms. Within this context God's power, strength and transcendence are all imaged as female, hence challenging patriarchal notions of femininity.

Johnson's trinitarian formula pivots around the central metaphor of wisdom (*Sophia*). She notes that in the Hebrew scriptures, wisdom constitutes the most developed personification of God's presence and activity, depicting God as female whilst at the same time transcendent, powerful, and active within the world.[119] Female wisdom speaks on her own authority, seeking justice, truth and life. She can do all things and as such shares the same characteristics traditionally associated with Yahweh: she is omniscient, omnipotent, omnipresent, active in creation and intervening in history to bring about salvation. Johnson also notes how the book of Wisdom draws a correlation between wisdom and the Spirit – wisdom is people-loving, filling the earth with her presence and guiding people in the path of righteousness. Finally, Johnson identifies overlap between Jesus and wisdom. He, like her, is the image of the invisible God, the firstborn of all creation, the one through whom all things are made; he is the one in whom rest is found, who calls aloud in public places preaching the good news of God's intended reign of shalom.[120] Jesus is Sophia incarnate, the daughter of God: the power and wisdom of God (cf. 1 Cor. 1.22–24). He is the human being Sophia became and so cannot simply be viewed in exclusively male terms.[121]

Johnson thus goes on to present her trinitarian formula of Spirit-*Sophia*, Jesus-*Sophia* and Mother-*Sophia*. As Spirit-*Sophia*, God is experienced in day to day situations from the rising of the sun to the sharing of love between people; from feelings of hope to those of trouble, toil and brokenness.[122] The Spirit, says Johnson, is both present and absent, drawing near and passing by in liberating power in the midst of struggle and suffering.[123] Constituting the mystery of God immanent within the world, she is the one in whom we have our life and being, for Johnson claims that existence itself is a gift from her.[124] She is the one in whom all things are held

118 Johnson, *She Who Is*, p. 56.

119 Ibid., p. 87.

120 Ibid., p. 95ff.

121 Ibid., p. 99.

122 Ibid., pp. 125–6.

123 Ibid., p. 127.

124 Ibid., p. 134.

together, for the Spirit sustains the world and moves it towards liberation, bringing healing and justice in the midst of suffering.[125] According to Johnson then, where there is brokenness and pain, the Spirit works to redeem and restore. In short, she makes the world liberation-bound, challenging and transforming structures of oppression, providing a hope against all hope that all will be well.[126] As such, Johnson argues that the Spirit stands in opposition to sexism, dwelling instead among those who gather together in mutual love.[127] Encouraging mutuality and reciprocity, the Spirit makes us friends with God drawing people into communion with one another and with the divine.[128] Promoting life and aliveness, the Spirit stands in judgement of all that threatens to extinguish this and as such, cannot be aligned with patriarchy.

Spirit-*Sophia*, however, is only one way in which God is God. As Jesus-*Sophia*, God's Spirit becomes manifest and dwells among the people. Johnson comments on the maleness of Christ stating that this should not be taken out of its proper context. As a human, Jesus inevitably takes on human sexuality as either male or female. She is also quick to identify that embodiment does not simply incorporate sex but also takes into account all other aspects of an individual's particularity.[129] Jesus is not *just* a man as this is not the *only* aspect of his embodiment.[130]

Johnson then goes on to argue that Jesus-*Sophia* sets about re-establishing the right order of creation, calling for new relationships between individuals.[131] Making friends with sinners, outcasts and those who were downtrodden, inviting women to join his discipleship and opening his table fellowship to all such minority groups, Jesus-*Sophia* reveals the friendship of God in the context of a new order of relationships in which the first are last and the last, first. Here, Jesus-*Sophia* contradicts social expectations revealing a God who delights in meeting the unprivileged, dwelling among those who are oppressed. While the cross reveals Jesus-*Sophia's* solidarity with all who suffer, the resurrection displays God's ability to empower and restore all that appears to be broken.[132] As such, she claims that the Christ event offers hope for those who suffer. All is not lost because Jesus

---

125 Ibid.

126 Ibid., pp. 137–8.

127 Ibid., pp. 141–3.

128 Ibid., p. 145. Consequently, Johnson describes Spirit-*Sophia* as Love, Gift and Friend.

129 Ibid., pp. 155–6.

130 For Johnson then, the term 'Christ' points beyond the maleness of the man Jesus to the risen Christ who now hides in the glory of God. Christ is also present, not through his physical body, but through his body, the Church, in whom we are all invited to participate. As such, Johnson claims that Jesus should not be reduced to maleness but should instead be viewed within the context of the 'whole Christ'. Ibid., p. 163. For a similar view see Gavin D'Costa, *Sexing the Trinity: Gender, Culture and the Divine* (London, 1991), pp. 300–301.

131 Johnson, *She Who Is*, pp. 157–8.

132 Ibid., pp. 158–9.

has revealed the future as being liberation bound. Such a message, Johnson argues, affirms women as both fully human and fully *imago Dei*.

The third way Johnson claims that God is God is as Mother-*Sophia*. As Mother, Johnson argues that God is properly understood as ineffable mystery.[133] Mother-*Sophia* is the unoriginate creator of all that is.[134] Birth-giving, nurturing, playing and delighting in the other, protective, compassionate, loving, forgiving, courageous and serviceable, she is not passive but actively involved with the world she creates.[135]

Imaging God as Mother, however, Johnson argues, should not be seen as an attempt to idealize motherhood. It is true, she says, that not all women are mothers and so she warns against any universalising tendencies which threaten to reduce women to this capacity alone.[136] Yet, she also recognizes the importance of affirming the specifically female function of giving birth. As such, she presents the analogy of Mother-*Sophia* as a daring attempt to image the transcendence and ineffability of God in a specifically female way.[137] As Mother, God is not simply caring and nurturing but also powerful and transcendent, giving life and sustaining it, always encouraging growth and development.[138] She carries the world just as a mother carries a child, nurturing and protecting it, having at heart the well being of the *entire* universe. As Mother, *Sophia* desires *all* of creation to flourish, judging anything that threatens to prevent this.[139]

Johnson's use of specifically female imagery then constitutes an attempt both to expose the androcentric nature of patriarchal trinitarian language and to promote the full humanity of women by establishing a separate space for them within the *imago Dei*. Indeed, for Johnson, the Trinity offers tremendous promise for feminist hermeneutics, flying in the face of patriarchal systems of domination and subordination. 'At its most basic' she remarks, 'the symbol of the Trinity evokes a livingness in God, a dynamic coming and going with the world that points to an inner divine circling around in unimaginable relation.'[140] Since the original language carries overtones of hierarchy and dominion, imaging the entire Trinity in the female affirms the value of women whilst at the same time pointing towards a God who promotes life, mutuality, equality and liberation. Such metaphors, she claims, are therefore both faithful to the Christian tradition whilst also operating in line with feminist concerns.

---

133 Ibid., p. 170.

134 Ibid., p. 171.

135 Ibid., pp. 174–5.

136 Ibid., pp. 176–7.

137 Ibid., p. 179.

138 Ibid.

139 Ibid., pp. 179–85 and pp. 229–35.

140 Ibid., p. 192.

To this extent, Johnson's model is entirely commendable.[141] To be sure, the excellence of Johnson's proposal is found in her ability to navigate the line between orthodoxy and creativity. Her argument exhibits an unquenchable conviction with regard to the full humanity of women and women's place within the *imago Dei* which is to be celebrated and applauded, whilst at the same time firmly establishing God's solidarity with all who struggle against sexism.[142] Unlike the other approaches mentioned, this approach communicates the full divinity of the three *hypostases* alongside the full humanity of women. Indeed, if women are *fully* in the image of God, then it follows that female metaphors can be used to refer to the fullness of God. This is a tremendous achievement by Johnson and one which marks a serious departure from a stress on the feminine dimension of God. Indeed, this approach undermines the binary logic of the masculine-feminine dichotomy by imaging God as female in such a way that does not repeat stereotypical accounts of womanhood. Her rendering of the Trinity is true to tradition whilst taking the experiences of women as adult equals seriously.

De-sexing trinitarian language For those who wish to avoid all associations with sexuality, a fourth strategy is followed which seeks to de-sex trinitarian language altogether. This approach presents personal yet neutral metaphors for the divine, imaging God in ways that can relate to both male and female, or neither in particular. Karen Baker-Fletcher, for example, refers to the first person of the Trinity as 'Parent'. 'God the parent', she says, 'is divine author or artist. This first, dynamic relation of God is also Provider/Nurturer.'[143] She thus considers the gender neutral term 'Parent' to be equivalent to the traditional language of 'Father' and proposes that it be used alongside this. Brian Wren also adopts such a strategy, recommending that the Trinity be imaged as Lover, Beloved and Mutual Friend.[144] Wren, like other theologians, takes his lead from Sallie McFague's articulation of God as Mother, Loved, Friend/Creator, Redeemer, Sustainer. Indeed, McFague

141 Ultimately, Johnson presents the metaphor of 'SHE WHO IS' so as to reinforce the fact that in the end, God surpasses all human models and images. This phrase obviously reflects the self-disclosure of God to Moses as 'I AM' in Exodus 3.14, understanding God as the ground of existence, ineffable mystery and the very essence of life itself. Ibid., pp. 224–5.

142 Alongside Johnson, there are other theologians who promote similar measures. Brian Wren, for example, claims that since God is *not* human, God is just as adequately or inadequately represented by women as by men. See the first stanza of his hymn, 'Who is She?' in *What Language Shall I Borrow? God-Talk in Worship: A Male Response to Feminist Theology* (London, 1989) pp. 141–2). Like Johnson, he calls his readers to name the *whole* being of God in the female gender, providing a plethora of suggestions including God as Mother, Sister, Midwife, and perhaps most potently, Bag Lady (pp. 160–70). Ultimately Wren argues that imaging God in ways such as these challenges Christianity's preoccupation with patriarchal notions of divinity, affirming women as equally adequate for imaging the *totality* of the trinitarian reality.

143 Baker-Fletcher, p. 60.

144 Wren, pp. 208–14.

provides possibly the most important contribution to this approach so it will be useful for us to spend some time outlining her proposal.

The central aim of her two publications, *Models of God* and *The Body of God* is to conceptualize God within a more holistic and organic paradigm. She therefore presents the metaphor of the world as God's 'body', suggesting that all things interconnect and interrelate within this body. It is therefore within this framework that her trinitarian theology develops. Articulating God as Mother first and foremost reinforces this concept. As Mother, God is imaged as containing the world within herself and as bringing forth life in her image. This confirms that the world is not Godless, nor is God worldless. Indeed, for McFague, God is not outside the world nor is the world created *ex nihilo*. Everything that 'is' exists within the body of God and as such within the Mother. She is the source of life and the one in whom all things have their being. Thus, God is also not anti-body, nor is the body anti-God. God has a body and this body is to be respected as good, sacred and holy.

As Mother then, God is first understood as Creator.[145] Within this capacity, the love of God is characterized by agape,[146] a wholly interested (as opposed to disinterested) love that wills life and existence at every level. As such, God is on the side of *all* life, wishing *all* life to flourish and grow. Agape then is inclusive, and as such contradicts any human claims to superiority. God seeks the good of the *entire* universe, and as such judges any who thwart the well-being and fulfilment of her body.[147]

The second metaphor of God as Lover is unsexed. It depicts God as being deeply passionate about the world. Like Wren after her, she argues that the relationship between lovers is primarily marked by *value* as opposed to sex or lust, and thus images God as one who affirms the world as valuable, not despite sin but as it is.[148] Consequently, she argues that God loves the world so much that she actually needs the world, finding the world attractive, desirable and even necessary. Just as two lovers value and need one another, so God values and needs the world. Understood this way, God's love is imaged primarily in terms of Eros[149] – a love which, according to McFague, prevails no matter what. Such a passionate and zealous love depicts God as being totally concerned and involved. Indeed, McFague argues that as Lover, God feels the pain of the beloved immediately. Because the world is so close to God, anything which harms the world necessarily harms God. To ignore the invitation to love creation then is sinful, replacing love of God with love of self.

---

145 McFague, *Models of God*, p. 101ff.

146 Ibid.

147 Ibid., p. 116.

148 Ibid., p. 128.

149 Ibid., p. 129ff.

Whereas God the Mother is Creator, God the Lover is Saviour or Redeemer.[150] As has already been noted, McFague argues that Jesus is not the only person responsible for salvation, but instead demonstrates the potential of all human beings to work alongside the divine in order to bring about healing and restoration within the world. The world itself is the incarnation of God, and so in this sense, God as Lover becomes incarnate in all who respond to God by caring for the world.[151] For McFague then, the world constitutes the 'Cosmic Christ', embodying the presence of God in concrete form. Hence within McFague's view, women are also constitutive of the Cosmic Christ and as such, are fully reinforced as *imago Dei*.

The final metaphor of God as Friend is also unsexed. Out of all three metaphors, McFague suggests that it is God as Friend that is the most inclusive and the most free.[152] We choose our friends she says, and friendship potentially strikes across barriers such as age, race, class, sexual difference and so on. Marked by a common interest as opposed to shared physical attributes or social situations,[153] friendship is characterized by interdependence and interrelatedness and a desire to take responsibility.[154] A friend, she says, holds the well-being of another with high regard. Thus, as Friend, God is imaged as being deeply concerned for the world and everything in it. It is, therefore, by sharing in this common interest that McFague believes we become friends of God.[155] Here, McFague identifies divine love as Philia,[156] arguing that God not only loves us but also *likes* us, *choosing* us as friends. As Friend, God sustains the universe,[157] unifying all things and directing the world towards salvation.

Although both of McFague's trinitarian models do, on the whole, avoid difficulties surrounding the sexuality of God by imaging the Trinity in predominantly neutral terms, there are fundamental inconsistencies and difficulties with them. Imaging the world as the body of God whilst simultaneously upholding it as the offspring of God technically means that God gives birth to her own body, which is difficult to comprehend.[158] Imaging God as inseparable from the world may also run the risk of pantheism, collapsing divine reality into the reality of the world itself. However, that the metaphor of God's body is in fact ambiguous may in fact serve to defend McFague, for if God as Mother gives birth to the world then the world is not strictly identical with her, but is instead released from God and potentially given its own space to evolve. McFague does indeed argue that

---

150 Ibid., p. 143ff.

151 Ibid., p. 136.

152 Ibid., p. 160.

153 Ibid., pp. 163–4.

154 Ibid., p. 165.

155 Ibid.

156 Ibid., p. 160.

157 Ibid., p. 167.

158 However, it may be argued that the traditional understanding of God creating *ex nihilo* is equally bogus and problematic.

although the world is found entirely within the being of God, the being of God is not found entirely within the world; God surpasses the world whereas the world does not surpass God. Hence she allows for some level of distinction.

Christology is also problematic, for if the world constitutes the incarnation of God then the particularity of Jesus as the Word-made-flesh is undermined and overtaken by the collective 'body' of God. To this extent, McFague's trinitarian model fails to be sufficiently 'Christian' because Jesus loses his unique significance as God incarnate. Indeed, for McFague, it is humankind who are the ultimate healers and saviours of the world. Although this commendably encourages human responsibility, it dangerously loses sight of the significance of Christ within the trinitarian community. Whilst understanding the world as God's body is inventive as a metaphor, replacing Christ as the actual embodiment of God with the world as the body of Christ should be questioned in regard to its adequacy as an acceptable 'Christian' solution to the problems posed by the doctrine of the Trinity for feminist theology.[159]

Finally, it is also the case that McFague's attempts at de-sexing the Trinity tend to dangerously abstract personhood from sexual embodiment. It is undeniable that within human experience the lover and friend are all embodied and as such, always sexed. De-sexing such terms therefore implies that bodily transcendence may in fact be possible or at least alludes to the possibility of a generic bodiliness. Given this, de-sexing the Trinity eventually returns to the same question encountered by the previous three strategies: namely, if God is personal then which personal pronouns are to be used?

De-personalizing trinitarian language This brings me to the final approach within the reformist strategy, that of depersonalizing God. For many feminist theologians, the only way to really avoid issues surrounding the gender of trinitarian language and as such the gender of the trinitarian God, is to de-personalize God-language altogether. Ruth Duck, for example, argues that the traditional language of Father, Son and Spirit is not the only name into which Christians may be baptized. She thus presents the trinitarian formula of 'Fountain, Offspring and Wellspring'[160] seeing this as a preferable option to McFague's seemingly modalist suggestion of Creator, Redeemer, Sustainer. The reference to water and its link with baptism are clear here. Duck certainly wishes to communicate baptism as a conversion to

---

[159] Indeed, David Scott argues that the problem with McFague is that she ascribes to the world everything that traditional Christianity associates with Christ, thus deifying the world and compromising the significance of Jesus. God births the earth, bringing it forth from her very being, communicating herself through it. The world therefore carries the marks of God's being and is inseparable from her. According to Scott, this dangerously amounts to the 'christification' of creation. See 'Creation as Christ: A Problematic Theme in Some Feminist Theology', in Alvin F. Kimel (ed.), *Speaking the Christian God: The Holy Trinity and the Challenge of Feminism* (Grand Rapids, Michigan & Leominster, 1992), pp. 237–57.

[160] Ruth Duck, *Gender and the Name of God: The Trinitarian Baptismal Formula* (New York, 1991).

new life in the egalitarian community of the body of Christ, and for this she is to be commended.

Indeed, nature imagery is not new to trinitarian thinking. The Bible, for example, associates the Spirit with a dove (Matt. 6.16, Luke 3.22, John 1.32) and with fire (Matt. 3.11, Luke 3.16). Tertullian also often used nature imagery to refer to the Trinity, imaging God as ice, liquid, and steam; sun, ray, and light.[161] However, as with McFague, such measures tend to run the risk of slipping into pantheism or animism, associating God too closely with nature and creation.

De-personalizing the Trinity through abstraction is the second alternative. Mary Daly, for example, adopts this strategy. Following Paul Tillich and his understanding of God as the Ground of Being or Being Itself, she refers to God as the 'Verb' and as 'Be-ing'. She says, 'Why indeed must "God" be a noun? Why not a verb – the most attractive and dynamic of all? Hasn't the naming of "God" as a noun been an act of murdering that dynamic Verb? And isn't this Verb infinitely more personal than a mere static noun?'[162] As Be-ing, God is the very ground of existence itself, encouraging all things in the direction of life and fullness. As such, Daly argues that women have their being in Be-ing, finding in God the encouragement to grow and become outside the confines of sex-role socializations. Since women participate in Be-ing as they become, individually and collectively claiming their own subjectivity, so God also becomes and unfolds.[163] Hence Daly claims that Be-ing is not a static noun like Father, but is always becoming in the face of human subjectivity. As women push and break through sex-role stereotypes, so God is gradually revealed.

Of course, de-personalizing the Trinity, like de-sexing the Trinity, avoids difficulties concerning God's gender. Metaphors like wind, fire, dove, or Be-ing do indeed move God imagery substantially away from anthropomorphic associations, and so to this extent, reflect the Christian conviction that God is without sex. However, it is not specifically Christian to argue that God is impersonal. In fact, it is arguably the personal character of God which lies at the very heart of the Christian trinitarian God in the first place. As Trinity, God is first and foremost understood to be relational. Within this context, God is not a disinterested 'thing' but a personal community of love. Although metaphors like this are helpful, they do, in the end, fail to communicate a personal God and, as such, fail to image the Trinity in a sufficiently 'Christian' way. If God is personal then language about God will always be connected to issues of gender. One cannot be a person without being sexed since personhood is always embodied. Thus, as Robert Hannaford rightly points out: 'A personal God cannot be spoken of other than in images and language drawn directly from human experience … Gender terms are inevitably part of the logical grammar of a personal God.'[164]

---

161 Oxford-Carpenter, 'Gender and the Trinity', p. 22.

162 Daly, p. 33.

163 Ibid.

164 Hannaford, 'Gender and the Person God Is', p. 36.

Conclusion: Speaking the Christian God

What then can we conclude about how best to *speak* the Trinity? Of course, there are different merits and disadvantages associated with different feminist approaches, however the critical investigation of central trends within feminist theology presented here identifies that certain recommendations can be made.

First, to speak God as Trinity means to speak metaphorically about God. Trinitarian language does not speak literally about God nor does it connote the *proper* name for God. It does not contain the ontological reality of God nor is it necessarily tied to this. Such language does, nevertheless, say *something* meaningful about God. Following Janet Soskice, understanding trinitarian language as metaphorical allows the traditional language of Father, Son and Spirit to be retained on the grounds that it says *something*, although not *everything*, about what God is like. Importantly, metaphor identifies a tension between the 'is' and 'is not' of trinitarian language and it is this tension which must be preserved in our speaking about God. Indeed, trinitarian language operates between the two extremes of 'reticence' and 'exuberance';[165] between total silence and total knowledge, between total ignorance and total understanding. It is not that the triune name makes God available for our knowing, for God is, in the end, always incomprehensible. As Augustine puts it, 'the formula three persons was coined not in order to give a complete explanation by means of it, but in order that we might not be obliged to remain silent.'[166]

Of course, we are not obliged to stay silent because God has made Godself known. We assert this on the basis of the biblical revelation and on the basis that the hidden God *has* been made manifest in and through the person of Jesus of Nazareth.[167] To be sure, if God has made Godself known through the person of Jesus Christ, then our theological language need not amount to our clutching at straws; it need not be *entirely* vacuous or reduced to the kind of 'theological play' Sallie McFague proposes.[168] However, to the extent that revelation always takes place within a historical and cultural setting, the language we use to speak about God is always contextual, limited and incomplete and so cannot claim to reveal *everything* about the divine.

Traditional trinitarian language then does not connote the proper name for God and only provides a partial glimpse of what God is like. 'Father', for example, may signal a deeply intimate and personal relationship between Jesus and God. It

---

[165] This idea is taken from Franklin Sherman's chapter entitled 'Reticence and Exuberance in Speaking of God', in Carl E. Braaten (ed.), *Our Naming of God: Problems and Prospects of God-Talk Today* (Minneapolis, 1989), pp. 35–43.

[166] Johnson, *She Who Is*, p. 203.

[167] See Ronald F. Thiemann, 'Beyond Exclusivism and Absolutism: A Trinitarian Theology of the Cross', in Miroslav Volf and Michael Walker (eds), *God's Life in Trinity* (Minneapolis, 2006), pp. 118–29.

[168] McFague, *Models of God.*

may connote God as loving, faithful, trustworthy, relational and personal. 'Son' may point towards Jesus' own experience of closeness and intimacy with God and, as such, may signal inter-relationality within the Godhead. This language may speak of a personal relationship of love and commitment between Jesus and God the Father and places Jesus in a special and unique position in relation to the divine. 'Spirit' may signal God's amorphous, powerful, redemptive presence. It may communicate movement, energy, vitality, liveliness, and certainly avoids literal associations with the human body and human gender. This language may identify the Spirit as dynamic and as moving in creation to heal, encourage, make new and empower; indeed, it is by the Spirit that Christ, the Messiah, speaks (Lk. 4.16–21).

Such language, however, is problematic because it serves to legitimise patriarchy. Although such language may have positive connotations there are serious limitations with seeking to identify the 'intended' meaning of these terms. Indeed, insofar it is impossible to separate meaning in the past from meaning in the present, feminist theologians can never ignore the sexist and patriarchal connotations such language has. To this extent, traditional language must be supplemented with alternatives. If God is beyond human comprehension then our naming must reflect this through its diversity, creativity, and inclusivity. As Brian Wren rightly exclaims, we must 'bring many names' for the divine:

> Bring many names, beautiful and good;
> celebrate, in parable and story,
> holiness in glory, living, loving God.[169]

This, however, is not to say that female metaphors run alongside the traditional language offering a feminine 'dimension' or female 'side' of God. Agreeing with Johnson, I think the best approach is to image the *fullness* of God through reference to distinctly female metaphors. Johnson's trinitarian formula of Spirit-*Sophia*, Mother-*Sophia* and Jesus-*Sophia* is the most commendable out of the examples cited here because it most effectively challenges patriarchal stereotypes whilst retaining continuity with the Christian tradition. It successfully recognizes the significance of Jesus as the historical manifestation of God without limiting Christ to an earthly existence (and so to maleness), and also confirms the full humanity of women through reference to God as *Sophia*.

It should be clear, however, from this discussion that feminist theology has tended to focus its attention on trinitarian language, addressing the ways in which this and the imagery it depicts serve to sacralize patriarchy and theologically endorse the non-identity of women. In light of this, the next chapter marks a shift in approach, focusing attention on how we *think* rather than *speak* the Christian God. Technically, this signals a move away from a stress on trinitarian *language* towards a stress on trinitarian *logic*. The impetus for such a shift is the central claim that understanding the trinitarian relations (or operations) may in fact

---

169 Wren, p. 143.

point towards new and exciting horizons for feminist theology which have been previously insufficiently realized due to a preoccupation with the search for more inclusive trinitarian discourse.

Chapter 2
Thinking God as Trinity

What does it mean to think God as Trinity? This is the overarching question with which we are concerned here. Of course, there is no simple answer we can provide in response. The vast and complex debate which has historically surrounded this question and the controversy which has often accompanied it speak all too clearly of a doctrine which understandably baffles the best of theologians! Christian history is indeed peppered with a seamless spread of theologians who have sought to espouse this doctrine and to set out its perimeters and technical complexity. That this debate still takes place today further evidences the difficulties theologians continue to face when seeking to articulate the Trinity in clear terms.

This doctrine is hard to commit to paper, puzzling to conceptualize and difficult to express in words. Indeed, there is quite rightly, I think, a sense in which anything we do say about who the Ttrinitarian God is and how this God operates must automatically be consigned to the realm of partiality. If God is unfathomable and beyond human grasp, then it is appropriate that we should struggle as we seek to map out our limited theologies. We should be joyful about their partiality and content with the little we are able to say, excited about the freedom this allows us. It is also the case that although we may detect traces of the Trinity or a trinitarian pattern within the Bible, this doctrine is certainly not formalized or systematized in scripture. Although we may speak about the motifs of Wisdom, Word and Spirit in the Old Testament or make reference to New Testament passages such as Matthew 3.16–17, 28.19, 1 John 5. 7–8 which seem to identify a threefold concept of God as Father, Son and Holy Spirit, these kinds of examples do not set forth a *doctrine* of God as Trinity.[1] Instead what we have in the Bible is an indication that the early Christian believers had come to know and worship God in Jesus Christ. It is certainly the case that Jesus was worshipped before the church had managed to rectify how Christian monotheism could be resolved with belief in Jesus Christ as *homoousios* or as one person with two distinct natures! In this sense the roots of the Trinity are more appropriately rooted in doxology.

---

[1] See also Kevin Giles, *Jesus and the Father* (Grand Rapids, Michigan, 2006). For more on the biblical basis of the Trinity see Arthur W. Wainwright, *The Trinity in the New Testament* (London, 1962), esp. pp. 15–41 and Alasdair Heron, 'The Biblical Basis for the Trinity', in Alasdair Heron (ed.), *The Forgotten Trinity: A Selection of Papers presented to the BCC Study Commission on Trinitarian Doctrine Today* (London: BCC/CCB, 1991): 15–41.

Doxology, Language and the Beginnings of Divergence

Trinitarian theology then first found expression within a liturgical and doxological setting.[2] In worship, the first generations of Christians recognized Jesus as divine yet this was not an assertion based on abstract metaphysical claims about the being or substance of God or on speculation concerning the nature of God. Instead, it was grounded in the activities of Christ which had come to be aligned with activities traditionally associated with the one God of Israel.[3] In Paul's letter to the Philippians, for example, we see that Jesus Christ takes on the role of Yahweh as *Kyrios* (Lord), as judge and saviour of the world. Philippians 2.10–11 proclaims that 'at the name of Jesus every knee should bend, in heaven and on earth and under the earth, and every tongue should confess that Jesus Christ is Lord, to the glory of God the Father'. This resonates with Isaiah 45.23 where Yahweh says, 'To me every knee shall bow, every tongue shall swear'.

The first Christians had, therefore, come to know God in Jesus and their worship reflected this. Christians prayed to Jesus and were dependent on him for their salvation.[4] Understandably, however, there was a reluctance to call Jesus 'God'. The Jewish tradition firmly identified God as one ultimate Being (for example Deuteronomy 6.4; Isaiah 45.14b) and the early Christian community were committed to retaining such monotheism. New Testament worship therefore grew to be trinitarian by directing praise to the Father, *through* the Son, *in* the Holy Spirit.[5] The first Christians were not concerned with explaining *how* it might be possible to retain Jewish monotheism alongside belief in Jesus as Lord and saviour, they had simply experienced this to be the case and their worship followed as a result.[6] In this respect, the Bible does not develop or propose an explanation of the

---

2 See Geoffrey Wainwright, 'Trinitarian Worship', in Alvin F. Kimel (ed.), *Speaking the Christian God: The Holy Trinity and the Challenge of Feminism* (Grand Rapids, Michigan, 1992), pp. 209–21, esp. p. 211.

3 Wainwright, *The Trinity in the New Testament*, pp. 6 and 10; Gordon D. Fee, 'Paul and the Trinity: The Experience of Christ and the Spirit for Paul's Understanding of God', in Stephen Davis, Daniel Kendall, Gerald O'Collins (eds), *The Trinity: An Interdisciplinary Symposium on the Trinity* (Oxford, 1999), pp. 49–72, esp. p. 60. Also see Gordon D. Kaufman, *In Face of Mystery: A Constructive Theology* (Cambridge, Massachusetts, London, 1995), pp. 302–21 for a full and thorough account of how the Tetragrammaton came to be synonymous with *Kyrios* and later on with Father.

4 See William C. Placher, 'Believing in the Triune God: Three in One', *Christian Century* (17 April 2007): 28–32, esp. p. 30.

5 Wainwright, *Trinity and the New Testament*, p. 7. Also see Wainwright, 'Trinitarian Worship', p. 213.

6 C.C. Pecknold asserts that the apostles held 'dogmas', but these were '"rough and ready" dogmas developed in the service of mission and witness' as opposed to systematic articulations of belief. See his article, 'How Augustine used the Trinity: Functionalism and the Development of Doctrine', *Anglican Theological Review*, 85/1 (Winter 2003): 127–41. Catherine LaCugna is also firm in asserting that the relationship between doxology and

threeness and oneness of God; this would evolve over several centuries and be the topic of intense debate within early Christian, as well as subsequent, thought.

It is, however, difficult to say when exactly a theological 'doctrine' of the Trinity first emerged. The term *triad* first appeared in the liturgical writings of Thophilus of Antioch around 180 CE[7] but it is Tertullian who is most famous for his utilization of trinitarian language, using the Latin word *trinitas* in the late second century CE.[8] He also introduced the two central concepts of *substantia* (being) and *persona* (person) in order to clarify the meaning of the triune mystery.[9] Trinitarian language, however, became problematic due to the lack of consistency between Greek and Latin terms.[10] In Greek (Eastern) philosophy, the term 'person' (*prosopon*) tended to be associated with Greek drama and to the act of wearing masks.[11] This implied that God simply 'appeared' in different disguises, for the word was void of any ontological meaning, saying nothing about God in Godself, God's substance or God's essence. The alternative term, *hypostasis*, referred to substance and nature and so the two stood in opposition to one another.[12] On the other hand, Latin (Western) thought used the term *persona* to refer to the threefold nature of God and *substantia* to refer to the essence and unity of God.[13] Thus, there was no agreement as to which terms should be used for the unity and diversity of God. However, the breakthrough came when the Greek terms *hypostasis* and *prosopon* were united so that the former came to include the meaning of the latter. As such, the Latin *persona* came to be finally synonymous with the Greek *hypostasis* – both referring to the triune person of God.[14] However, misunderstanding still prevailed as the East continued to use *hypostasis* in its original ontological context exposing itself to charges of tritheism. Because the natural equivalent of *hypostasis* in Western thought was *substantia* (which itself was connected to *ousia*, that is being) the West encountered problems in articulating the exact meaning of this term.

Of course this draws attention to the unavoidable problems encountered when trying to speak meaningfully about the Trinity. Since the early Christian community were speaking both Greek and Latin it was to be expected that this would lead to

---

theology is a one-way dynamic. She distinguishes between what she calls 'primary' and 'secondary' theology stating that the first constitutes the birth place of theology in Christian worship and therefore provides the basis for the development of secondary theology in dogma and doctrine. See 'Returning from "The Far Country": Thesis for a Contemporary Trinitarian Theology', *Scottish Journal of Theology*, 41/2 (1988): 191–215.

7 Wainwright, *The Trinity in the New Testament*, p. 4.

8 Ibid.

9 George Newlands, *God in Christian Perspective* (Edinburgh, 1994), p. 132.

10 Ibid.

11 John D. Zizioulas, *Being as Communion* (New York, 1993), p. 32.

12 Ibid., p. 33.

13 Leonardo Boff, *Trinity and Society*, trans. Paul Burns (Eugene, Oregon, 1998), p. 60.

14 Zizioulas, *Being as Communion*, p. 37.

differences in the ways in which the trinitarian God was articulated.[15] Whether this equates to fundamental differences in theology, however, is questionable as we have already noted and as we will see in the discussion that follows.[16] The council of Nicaea in 325 led to the formalization of the doctrine making use of both Eastern and Western terminology. Against Arius, the Son was affirmed as fully divine and as consubstantial (*homoousios*) with the Father.[17] The Son was 'God from God', 'begotten not made' undermining Arius' claim that the *logos* was begotten and so must have had a beginning in time.

However, it was only at the second ecumenical Council held at Constantinople in 381 that the co-equality of the Spirit as divine was affirmed. This was in part a response to the Macedonian or Pneumatomachian heresy, which denied the divinity of the Holy Spirit, for it was felt that if the Spirit was the Spirit of the Father and of Christ then the Spirit must in fact have to proceed from both, being consubstantial with them. This, however, demonstrated a fundamental point of disagreement between East and West. Because the Eastern Church stressed the unity of God in the person of the Father and therefore defined the Father in terms of *archē* (beginning) and *aitia* (cause), it could not say that the Holy Spirit proceeded from the Father *and the Son* (*filioque*) as this would suggest two originates and two causes, thus compromising the unity of God.

Despite such perceived differences, however, it is clear that many theologians from both East and West were equally dedicated to upholding the orthodoxy established and formalized at Constantinople. Although differences in expression and approach can be identified, there are many points of overlap, making a straightforward division between East and West problematic.

Disputed Questions: Debating the Unity and Diversity of God

Indeed, there is a growing trend within contemporary trinitarian theology to avoid a straightforward split between East and West approaches to understanding the Trinity. It is certainly true that twentieth-century theology inferred a chasm between Eastern and Western approaches with Eastern (Greek) theology being perceived as starting from the threeness of God only then going on to establish the unity of God, and Western (Latin) theology being seen as beginning from the

---

15 This point is made by Paul Fiddes in his book, *Participating in God: A Pastoral Doctrine of the Trinity* (London, 2000), p. 14.

16 See Najeeb G. Awad, 'Between Subordination and Koinonia: Toward a New Reading of the Cappadocian Theology', *Modern Theology* (2007): 181–204 for en example of this point of view.

17 Catherine Mowry LaCugna, 'God in Communion with Us – The Trinity', in Catherine Mowry LaCugna (ed.), *Freeing Theology: The Essentials of Theology in Feminist Perspective* (New York, 1993), pp. 83–114, esp. p. 85.

unity of God only then moving to establish the threeness or diversity of God.[18] Karl Rahner provides a good example of this assumption. In his book, *The Trinity*, he argues that the two treatises, 'On the One God' and 'On the Triune God' have been separated with the former being explained in advance of the latter. Rahner blames this specifically on the 'Augustinian-Western' notion of the Trinity which, according to him, 'begins with the one God, the one divine essence as a whole, and only afterwards does it see God as three in persons'.[19] According to Rahner, this theological 'flow' from one to three is totally different from what the Bible and Greek theology teaches, both of which, according to him, begin with the unoriginate God; God the Father.[20]

The extent to which such a view can be maintained, however, is debatable and the discussion of trinitarian thought provided here should go some way to demonstrating this. Augustine, for example, although often associated with a stress on the unity and oneness of God, was, in reality, in no way hostile towards Cappadocian lines of thought[21] in the East. He was neither alarmed nor surprised that the Greeks interpreted the Trinity in a different way. Believing that God could be conceived more than expressed, Augustine was not so concerned that the Trinity be explained in terms of one essence, three substances (typical of Eastern terminology) or one substance, three persons (typical of Western terminology). What mattered was that the Trinity be preserved as a mystery and, therefore, as something never capable of being expressed fully.[22]

It is important then that we do not begin this discussion of trinitarian thought with an assumption that Greek theology differed fundamentally from Latin understandings of the triune God. Indeed, Lewis Ayres in his relatively recent work, *Nicaea and It's Legacy: An Approach to Fourth-Century Trinitarian Theology*, argues that Greek, Latin and Syriac speakers shared a number of fundamental strategies in their trinitarian theologies.[23] Amongst these was a commitment to uphold the unity of God and the irreducibility of the three persons. Although a range of language was used to express this basic distinction between the unity

---

18 Sarah Coakley notes this in her article 'Introduction: Disputed Questions in Patristic Trinitarianism', *Harvard Theological Review*, 100/2 (2007): 125–38, esp. p. 131.

19 Karl Rahner, *The Trinity*, trans. J. Donceel (London and New York, 1970), p. 17.

20 Ibid. For a further example of this see Tarmo Toom, *Classical Trinitarian Thought: A Textbook* (London, New York, 2007), pp. 49–51.

21 I use this phrase to refer to the theology of the Cappadocian Fathers, namely Basil of Caesarea (330–379), Gregory of Nyssa (331/40–c.395) and Gregory of Nazianzus (330–390), all of whom were born in Cappadocia, now central Turkey.

22 G.L. Prestige, *God in Patristic Thought* (London, 1964), p. 237.

23 Lewis Ayres, *Nicaea and Its Legacy: An Approach to Fourth-Century Trinitarian Theology* (Oxford, 2004), p. 16. Also see Lewis Ayers, 'Nicaea and Its Legacy: An Introduction', *Harvard Theological Review*, 100/2 (2007): 141–44. Also see his article, '"Remember That You are Catholic" (ser. 52.2): Augustine on the Unity of the Triune God', *Journal of Early Christian Studies*, 8/1 (2000): 39–82.

and diversity of God, pro-Nicenes[24] (whether Latin, Syriac or Greek) all defended this principle. Ayres therefore maintains that a distinction between Greek and Latin, Eastern and Western trinitarian thought is far less significant than has been shown to be the case within much previous theological discussion.[25] Indeed, he charges recent trinitarian theology with engaging the legacy of Nicaea 'at a fairly shallow level, frequently relying on assumptions about Nicene theology that are historically indefensible and overlooking the wider theological matrices within which particular theological terminologies were situated'.[26]

What the remainder of this chapter will hopefully show then is that Christian thinking has always wrestled with a tension between the unity and diversity of God and this is true of East and West alike. This is demonstrable historically as well as within current trinitarian theology. This said, however, there is still a sense in which the language used to articulate this doctrine by Eastern and Western theologians (and by those influenced by them) leads at points to a compromising of the diversity or unity of God. Rather than setting this up as a key distinction between East and West, however, it is presented here as an unavoidable consequence of trying to think the Trinity in the first place. If God is unfathomable then such limitations are to be expected and need not translate as fundamental differences in belief.

A Round-Table Discussion with Five Trinitarian Thinkers

In addressing what it means to think God as Trinity then my concern here is to articulate what I consider to be the central hallmarks of this doctrine. These are identified through a dialogue with five influential trinitarian thinkers: Augustine, Gregory of Nazianzus, Karl Rahner, John Zizioulas and Jürgen Moltmann. Because of space, discussion here is restricted to these voices alone.

I begin with Augustine and Gregory of Nazianzus; two patristic thinkers who constitute key players in the forming of early Latin and Greek trinitarian theology respectively. They are chosen here, not simply because of their unquestionable influence on trinitarian thought (past and present), but because they continue to be seen by many as representing the very chasm between Eastern and Western understandings of the Trinity previously mentioned. Following this, I turn to Karl Rahner, a twentieth-century Roman Catholic theologian renowned for placing the doctrine of the Trinity back on the theological map. For Rahner, there is no distinction between the economic and immanent Trinity and this raises important as well as interesting implications for what it means to think God as Trinity.

---

24 Ayres defines this category as referring to those theologians between the 360s to the 380s which formed the basis of Nicene Christian belief in the 380s. Such theologians presented argument *for* Nicaea, articulating in different yet compatible ways, how the Nicene creed should be understood (hence the term *pro*-Nicene).

25 Ayres, *Nicaea and It's Legacy*, p. 6.

26 Ibid., p. 1.

John Zizioulas, a contemporary Greek Orthodox theologian, is then invited into the conversation. Zizioulas is chosen here, not only because he is one of the main contributors to contemporary Orthodox trinitarian theology but also because his thought is often celebrated for reinstalling a connection between the 'person' and 'being' of God. He is called upon specifically as one who develops what I refer to as an 'ethical-pastoral' model of the Trinity – a social model which images the Trinity in terms of community and relationality and a model which is common within trinitarian theology today. I end with a discussion of Jürgen Moltmann, a contemporary German Protestant theologian who is most famous for challenging the apathetic understanding of God[27] common within classical understandings of the divine. Although presenting a social doctrine of the Trinity like Zizioulas, he is called upon here because of his specific discussion of the Trinity in terms of suffering.

Augustine

Augustine is a key contributor to Western trinitarian theology. Although commonly accused of starting with the oneness of the divine essence, and thus compromising the threeness of God, this charge may be unwarranted.[28] Drayton Brenner, for example, argues that Augustine does not 'begin' in any literal sense with the oneness of God; instead, Augustine begins with the scriptures and Nicene orthodoxy, using these as tools by which, and through which, to understand the Trinity. He argues, 'Given that neither the scripture nor Nicene orthodoxy logically privilege the one over the three, Augustine does not do so either'. [29] In a similar way, Lewis Ayres warns that the view that Augustine 'begins' with the unity of God is deeply problematic. For him, this amounts to nothing more than 'a persistent but strongly erroneous perception'.[30]

---

[27] That is, that understanding which posits God as unchangeable, unaffected by external influences and thus as unable to suffer. See Moltmann's discussion of divine *apatheia* in his essay, 'The Crucified God', *Theology Today*, 31/1 (1974): 6–18.

[28] For more see Lewis Ayres, 'The Fundamental Grammar of Augustine's Trinitarian Theology', in Robert Dodaro and George Lawless (eds), *Augustine and His Critics* (New York, 2000), p. 68.

[29] Drayton C. Brenner, 'Augustine and Karl Rahner on the Relationship between the Immanent Trinity and the Economic Trinity', *International Journal of Systematic Theology*, 9/1 (2007): 24–38, esp. p. 28.

[30] Ayres, 'Remember That You Are Catholic', p. 39. Colin Gunton also supports such a reading of Augustine maintaining that Augustine's emphasis on the unity of God stems from neoplatonic philosophy of the mind, specifically from the neoplatonic conception of God as 'One'. He then contrasts this with Greek thought which, according to him, begins from an emphasis on the three persons of the Trinity, and thus from an emphasis on the divine economy as opposed to the abstract oneness of God. See *The Promise of Trinitarian Theology* (Edinburgh, 1997), pp. 42–3. Also see Matthew Drever's comments on this in his article, 'The Self Before God? Rethinking Augustine's Trinitarian Thought', *Harvard Theological Review*, 100/2 (2007): 233–42.

It is true, however, that Augustine spends most of his time defending the equality of the triune relations and the inseparability of the triune operations. He is therefore a lot more susceptible to charges of modalism (where Father, Son and Holy Spirit are seen as different 'modes' of the one God) than he is to charges of tritheism (the view that there are three gods) or subordinationism (the view that God the Son and God the Holy Spirit are subordinate to God the Father); charges traditionally levelled at 'Eastern' approaches. Thus, Augustine argues that Father, Son and Holy Spirit, despite being in relation to one another, all share in one divine essence. There is only one divine substance, he says, and since all three share in this, all three are equally God.[31] 'The Father is God, and the Son is God, and the Holy Spirit is God', he says.[32] It is not one thing to 'be' and another to be God, since for God, to be is to subsist in the divine essence;[33] substance and being are therefore united. However, this raises the question that if God is three, then does this not imply that there are three separate substances within the godhead and therefore three gods?

Unsurprisingly, Augustine forcefully denies such a claim. There is, he says, 'one God, not three gods',[34] arguing that to be is said in respect to Godself (the substance of God) whereas the three persons of God are said relatively. It is not that each person is a single monad standing in respect to themselves, but that each person stands in respect to the other two.[35] This paints a picture of loving communion and inter-relationality. This may, however, also imply that to *be* is to be *one* for God. Suggesting that the three persons subsist within the oneness of divine being seems to suggest that divine being is itself locatable outside the triune relations and thus, to point towards the existence of a fourth 'other' outside the community of Father, Son and Holy Spirit. Since he refers to the three as subsistent relations within the Godhead he implies that the three constitute a threefold expression of the one God.[36] The danger then is that 'God' is seen as something separate from Father, Son and Holy Spirit and that the inherent distinctiveness of the three is overshadowed.

Two things are important to note at this stage however. First, that such a view is heartily rejected by Augustine. Indeed, he cautions against viewing the substance of God as a fourth person outside the trinitarian community. For Augustine, to speak of God is to speak of the Trinity. God is not something separate from the

---

[31] Augustine, *On the Trinity*, ed. M. Dods, trans. Arthur West Hadden (Edinburgh, 1873), p. 189.

[32] Augustine, 'Answer to the Arian Sermon', in John E. Rotelle (ed.), *Arianism and Other Heresies*, I/18, trans. Roland Teske (New York, 1995), 15, p. 153.

[33] Ibid., p. 194.

[34] Augustine, *Sermons*, III, 51–94 on the New Testament, trans. Edmund Hill, ed. John E. Rostelle (New York, 1991), 52.2, p. 51.

[35] Ibid., p. 195.

[36] J. O'Donnell, *Trinity and Temporality: The Christian Doctrine of God in the Light of Process Theology and the Theology of Hope* (Oxford, 1983), p. 43.

trinitarian relations, hence he writes: 'It remains, then, that we should believe that the Trinity is of one substance in the sense that the essence itself is not other than the Trinity.'[37] Augustine is also quick to point out that just because Father, Son and Holy Spirit are each God, this does not mean that the Father is the Son, the Son the Holy Spirit and the Holy Spirit the Father; although all are God, 'the Son is not the Father, and the Holy Spirit is neither the Father nor the Son'.[38] In a similar vein he claims that it is incorrect to suggest that all three triune persons were born of the Virgin Mary. Only the Son is God incarnate, born of Mary, yet all three persons work inseparably.[39] Thus, although Augustine may appear to be modalist at points, these charges do not always stand up.

Second, if Augustine is accused of modalism this may say more about the historical circumstances in which Augustine was writing than what Augustine actually thought about the Trinity. Certainly, Augustine was more concerned to defend Nicene orthodoxy over and against those non-Nicene formulations that were prevalent at the time. Because Augustine sees most of his opponents as veering more towards tritheism and subordinationism rather than modalism, he is understandably more concerned to defend against the former as opposed to the latter.[40]

However, despite this, such tensions are detectable within Augustine's appeal to the tradition of the *vestigia trinitatis*. According to Augustine, since we are all born in the image of God it must be possible to detect traces or 'vestiges' of the Trinity in ourselves. He therefore spends Books IX–XV of *De Trinitate* looking for traces of the Trinity in humankind. Although he does not seek to prove the trinitarian nature of God through the *vestigia* and readily maintains that the role of this is limited because of the creature-Creator distinction,[41] he nevertheless identifies a range of 'trinities' he perceives within human existence. He begins with the instance of love. There are always three things in love he says: 'he that loves, and that which is loved, and love'.[42] This leads Augustine to postulate a model of the Trinity as Lover, Beloved and mutual love. Next Augustine turns to the mind. For Augustine, the mind is at the centre of human self-awareness – it knows itself and loves itself. Detecting a similar trinitarian pattern here then he refers to the mind

---

[37] Augustine, *Letters*, 100–155, II/2, trans. Roland Teske, ed. Boniface Ramsey (New York, 2003), 120.17, p. 138.

[38] Augustine, 'Answer to the Arian Sermon', 15, p. 153.

[39] Augustine, *Serm*, 52.8, pp. 53–4.

[40] See Brenner, 'Augustine and Karl Rahner', p. 29.

[41] Augustine follows the Nicene tradition in maintaining a firm qualitative distinction between God and humankind. Humankind is created ex nihilo and is contingent; God, on the other hand, is necessary. When applied to the vestigia, this means that the human mind can only ever reflect so much of the Trinity; it cannot reveal the Trinity in its completeness, hence God always remains 'other' and can never be reduced to humanity.

[42] Augustine, *On the Trinity*, IX.2, p. 221.

itself, the love of the mind and the knowledge of the mind.[43] Most significantly however, Augustine presents the trinitarian formula of memory, understanding and will.[44] Such examples serve to demonstrate Augustine's ultimate concern to safeguard the unity of the divine operations, for although there may be three things in love, there is, in the end, only ever *one* love; although the mind is certain of memory, understanding and will, there is only ever *one* mind; although there may be three persons in God, ultimately God is *one*.[45] But do not such analogies stress the unity of God at the expense of the threeness of God?

At first glance, it may seem as so, given that Augustine posits an understanding of the triune God as essential unity in divine Triplicity.[46] For Augustine, the triune persons do not exist in respect to themselves but in respect to each other. Hence, although the three remain distinct they cannot be separated for whatever they are called in respect to themselves they must also be called together. 'These three are one' he says, 'in that they are one life, one mind, one essence'.[47] And so Father, Son and Holy Spirit are consubstantial with one another, interpenetrating one another, sharing in the same single essence whilst remaining distinct in the way they relate to one another. The Father begets the Son, the Son is begotten of the Father and the Spirit proceeds from the Father and the Son. Importantly, however, Augustine's aim here is to defend the inseparability of the triune operations; a belief which is shared by Greek thinkers also as we will see when we consider Gregory's theology next.[48] Indeed, Augustine's various trinitarian analogies seek to communicate this very point. Certainly, Although Augustine struggles in places to express how the unquestionable doctrine of inseparable operations affirmed at Nicaea and Constantinople might be compatible with the belief that the triune persons are distinct in terms of their relation to one another, this does not prevent him from declaring that God is nevertheless one in such a way that neither person can take the place of the others.[49]

---

[43] Ibid., IX.4, p. 226.

[44] Ibid., X.17–19, pp. 253–6.

[45] There has been much debate on whether Augustine considers the *vestigia* to operate inductively or deductively; whether the mind reveals something about the Trinity or whether the Trinity reveals something about the mind. Whereas authors like Colin Gunton (*The Promise of Trinitarian Theology*) have argued for the former, others such as Matthew Drever ('The Self Before God') have argued for the latter, maintaining that 'the Trinity is the basis for the self' (p. 235). Since Augustine begins with the claim that humankind have been made in the image of the triune God, it does indeed seem more likely that Augustine favours the latter rather than the former.

[46] Prestige, p. 236.

[47] Augustine, *On the Trinity*, X.18, p. 259.

[48] Ayres makes this point well by referring to an example from Gregory of Nyssa. See 'Remember That You Are Catholic', p. 48.

[49] See Augustine, *Serm*, 52.2, p. 51.

According to Augustine then, we can talk about the Trinity in terms of distinctness of 'persons' and inseparableness of 'operation' or 'working'.[50] Although there are three separate distinct divine persons, there is only ever one divine essence; one divine love and one divine will. Although Father, Son and Holy Spirit each have their own memory, love and understanding, they love as one, understand as one, and act as one. What is clear then is that Augustine does not deny the diversity or threeness of God. Indeed, Augustine's main contribution is that he safeguards the divine mystery and incomprehensibility of God by holding the oneness and threeness of God in tension. God is not more one than three: there is real distinction within the Godhead (as signalled by the divine processions) yet all three persons work together as opposed to independently.

Gregory of Nazianzus

The Cappadocian Fathers (Basil of Caesarea [or Basil the Great], Gregory of Nyssa and Gregory of Nazianzus) are commonly cited as three key contributors to Eastern theology in general and Eastern trinitarian thought in particular. If a common assumption in relation to Augustine has been that he (as a 'typical' example of 'Western' trinitarian thought) begins with the oneness of God and then moves to the threeness of God, a common assumption in relation to the Cappadocian Fathers (as typical examples of 'Eastern' trinitarian thought) has been that they begin with the threeness of God (the divine economy of persons or the three *hypostases*) and then move towards the oneness of God, or the oneness of the divine *ousia*.[51] Besides constituting a massive generalization, this is not completely accurate.[52] A brief look at Gregory of Nazianzus will make the point.

Like Basil and Gregory of Nyssa, Gregory of Nazianzus subscribes to the Nicene claim that God is one *ousia* and three *hypostases*. For him, the former connotes the nature of God whereas the latter connotes the properties of the three persons.[53] God is thus a plurality who, at the same time, constitutes equality of nature, union of mind and identity of motion.[54] There is one Godhead but three distinct *hypostases*. Relations between the trinitarian persons are typified by *koinōnia*, by communion and by the mutual indwelling of each person in the Godhead. Each person, according to Gregory, participates equally in the Godhead and therefore

---

50 Ibid., 52.14, p. 56.

51 See for example Prestige, p. 242 and Kevin Giles, *The Trinity and Subordinationism: The Doctrine of God and the Contemporary Gender Debate* (Downers Grove, Illinois, 2002), p. 41.

52 See also Najeeb G. Awad in his article, 'Between Subordination'.

53 Ibid., p. 191.

54 Gregory of Nazianzus, 'Select Orations of Gregory Nazianzen', in Philip Schaff and Henry Wace (eds), *A Select Library of Nicene and Post-Nicene Fathers of the Christian Church*, trans. Gordon Browne and James Edward Swallow (Edinburgh, Grand Rapids, 1989), pp. 203–436, esp. Oration XXIV.II, p. 301.

shares equally in (and comprises equally of) the substance of God. God the Father cannot 'be' without God the Son and God the Holy Spirit; this is true also of the other two *hypostases*. For Gregory then, the three *hypostases* are distinguished by their relations of origin: God the Father is the unoriginate, unbegotten, non-corporeal, timeless, emitter and begetter; God the Son is the begotten Son of the Father; God the Holy Spirit is the emission of the Father, proceeding from the Father.[55] God is therefore *one* because there is only one Godhead which is co-constituted of Father, Son and Holy Spirit.

This, however, is not to say that Gregory presents *relation* as prior to *essence* as some have argued.[56] For Gregory, relation and essence are connected; that God 'is' means that God is in relationship, in communion. God *is* Trinity. Augustine, however, would not have disagreed! This said, difficulties appear when Gregory's understanding of the monarchē of God the Father is scrutinized in more detail. Certainly, Gregory's understanding of the Father as 'cause' appears somewhat ambiguous. On the one hand, Gregory seems to suggest that the Father is not the source or first principle (*aitia*) of the Godhead whilst on the other, he seems to maintain the Father as the eternal source of both Son and Spirit and thus as ontologically greater to them. Such a tension, at points, can appear to compromise the equality of the three *hypostases* and present the Father as ontologically greater within the trinitarian Godhead.

In his *Orations*, there are numerous passages which seem to reflect this tension. In Oration 31:14, for example, he writes:

> When then we look at the Godhead, or the First Cause, or the Monarchia, that which we conceive is One; but when we look at the Persons in Whom the Godhead dwells, and at Those Who timelessly and with equal glory have their Being from the First Cause – there are Three Whom we worship.[57]

The implication here is that the Godhead constitutes the first cause, principle or monarchē as opposed to this resting with God the Father alone. Gregory confirms the co-equality of Father, Son and Spirit, seemingly dismissing any claims that the Father is greater in rank.[58] However, in Oration 25:15, where Gregory speaks

---

55 Ibid.

56 Awad, 'Between Subordination', p. 192.

57 Gregory of Nazianzus, Oration XXXI.XIV, p. 322.

58 Najeeb Awad thus argues that Gregory does not understand the Father as the source or principle (*aitia*) of the Godhead itself but as the originator or cause (*arche*) of the Son and Spirit. When Gregory says that the Father is the cause or origin of Son and Holy Spirit, he is saying something about the *persons* of God as opposed to the essence of God; he is not citing God the Father as the substance, principle or source of the Godhead but saying that God the Father eternally generates the Son and Holy Spirit *without* being superior in being to them. For Awad, the Godhead is characterized by *koinonia* and so reflects a logic of mutuality, sharing and equality. See Awad, 'Between Subordination', pp. 181–204.

directly to Maximus, he warns against making the Father subject to another source and against viewing the Son and Holy Spirit as being without source. In the Third Theological Oration, he argues that the three *hypostases* are distinct on the basis of their eternal origin in God the Father.[59] To be source then seems to be the particular work of the Father. Indeed, Gregory posits the Father as the one 'to Whom the order of Persons runs its course', seemingly insisting that the Son and Holy Spirit are equal to the Father on the basis that they both refer back to the Father as single cause.[60]

This tension in Gregory's work, much like tensions in Augustine's thought, testifies to the struggle of expressing the threeness of God alongside the oneness of God. Certainly, Gregory maintains that the Holy Spirit and the Son are each *homoousios* with God the Father, and so does not seem at any point to suggest that the Father's special property of causation equates to the Son and Holy Spirit's ontological subordination within the eternal life of God. The principle of *koinōnia* is certainly pivotal to Gregory's understanding of the Trinity, with each person participating *equally* in the Godhead. However, the equality and unity of the three, it seems, is only upheld because the Father eternally generates the other two persons.

The difficulty with Gregory's trinitarian thought then is that, at points, it seems to indicate that God's substance logically begins with the person of God the Father and thus that the Father alone is God in the absolute sense.[61] The Father is the ultimate cause and origin of all things, including God the Son and God the Holy Spirit. This implies that God is fundamentally Father and that the Son and Spirit are divine because of their relation to the Father. Given that the Son and Holy Spirit only share in the divine *ousia* because of their personal characteristics and therefore because of their originating in the Father, it is primarily the Father who seems to be equated with the divine essence. To be sure, this does not represent the entirety of Gregory's thought, however, the danger is that such views, where they appear, imply that God the Father is the ultimate monarch, source and principle of the Trinity and that God the Son and God the Holy Spirit are subsequently inferior.[62] His main contribution, however, is that like Augustine, he successfully maintains a tension between the oneness and threeness of God. It is not that God is more three than one but that God is inwardly distinct at the same time as being one due to the inseparability of the divine operations.

---

59 Gregory of Nazianzus, Oration XXIX.III, pp. 301–2.

60 Ibid., Oration XLII.15, p. 390.

61 See Giles, *The Trinity and Subordinationism*, p. 43.

62 Awad ('Between Subordination') argues that this difficulty is resolved by distinguishing between Gregory's use of *arche* (cause/origin) and *aitia* (source/principle). According to Awad, Gregory understands God the Father as the *arche* of God the Son and God the Holy Spirit but not the *aitia* of the Godhead or Trinity itself. The ultimate principle or source is the Godhead, not God the Father (p. 194). Gregory's ambiguous use of these terms however makes it difficult to assert this position with total conviction.

Karl Rahner

Together with Karl Barth, Karl Rahner is often considered to be one of the main thinkers responsible for placing the Trinity back on the theological agenda within the modern period.[63] Critical of what he perceives to be the scholastic abstraction of the Trinity by thinkers such as Aquinas (whose thought he sees as originating from Augustine), he seeks to make clear the relevance of the Trinity for contemporary Christian living. In his text, *The Trinity*, Rahner identifies his dislike of Western trinitarian theology, accusing it of placing too much stress on the oneness of God. Believing himself to be more in keeping with Greek, pre-Augustinian theology, he proposes that discussion on the Trinity begin with the economy of God, that is, with how God is revealed in and to the world, refusing to separate the treatise 'On the One God' from the treatise 'On the trinitarian God'.

As a basic critique of Western Christianity, particularly it would seem of Augustine, he begins *The Trinity* by accusing most Christians of living as if the trinitarian God did not exist.[64] He states that despite the confession of the triune God, most Christians live as 'mere monotheists'. Of course, it is debateable as to how accurate Rahner's critique of Western theology, particularly Augustinian theology, is. However, for Rahner, this perceived deficiency in Western thought compels him to present the famous axiom that 'the "economic Trinity" is the "immanent Trinity" and the "immanent Trinity" is the "economic Trinity"'.[65]

Rahner's point here is that God is not to be perceived as being just inwardly or eternally trinitarian but also trinitarian in relation to how God deals with or organizes the world (that is in relation to the divine 'economy' or 'house of God'). Thus, for Rahner, God is not essentially or ontologically one and relatively three; God is immanently diverse and immanently relational. As such, Rahner is clear that the two treatises 'On the One God' and 'On the Triune God' must be held together at all times with God in relation to humankind being completely identical to God in relation to Godself.[66] In fact, Rahner asserts that 'no adequate distinction can be made between the doctrine of the Trinity and the doctrine of the economy of salvation'.[67] God must be towards humankind in salvation history as God is in Godself otherwise a dualism is created in which we may acceptably postulate the existence of two Trinities, and this, for Rahner, is absurd. Consequently, he claims that God's relation to humankind in a threefold manner reveals God's very being as immanently triune, as God for us.[68] Thus Rahner argues that God should

---

[63] See for example comments by Patricia A. Fox in her book, *God as Communion: John Zizioulas, Elizabeth Johnson and the Retrieval of the Symbol of the Triune God* (Collegeville, Minnesota, 2001), pp. 25–6.

[64] Rahner, p. 10.

[65] Ibid., p. 21.

[66] Ibid.

[67] Ibid., p. 24.

[68] Ibid., p. 35.

never be separated from God's relation to the world, as if God exists differently by Godself, for to do so would mean that God in God's own reality would not be the God we worship;[69] it would connote, as Catherine LaCugna claims, 'a fantasy about a God who does not exist'.[70]

In expressing such a view, Rahner suggests that God communicates in a threefold manner rather than as a divine 'whole'. What this means is that each person is upheld as being peculiar and distinct, that only the *logos* becomes incarnate and that only the Spirit sanctifies.[71] However, Rahner argues that reference to three 'persons' does not mean there are three consciousnesses, 'rather the one consciousness subsists in a threefold way'.[72] In short, the one self-communication of the one God occurs in three different manners so that 'the one God subsists in three distinct manners of subsisting'.[73] Rahner then chooses to refer to the triune relations as 'manners of subsisting' rather than as 'persons' because such language, he contends, implies unity between the three whereas 'person' does this to a lesser extent. According to Rahner, '"manner" at least suggests the possibility that the same God, as distinct in a threefold manner, is concretely "three-personal", or the other way around, that the "three-personal" co-signifies the unity of the same God.'[74] Hence, for Rahner, such language implies that God is not other than triune and that the same trinitarian God is present in all three manners.

Rahner, therefore, favours a trinitarian logic focused on the threeness of God rather than one based on an abstract understanding of divine essence. He, however, specifically cites the oneness of God within the person of God the Father,[75] suggesting that God is unified by the perfect interrelationship of the Son and

---

69 George Newlands, *Trinitarian Perspectives* (Edinburgh, 1994), p. 137. Such an axiom has obvious implications for the incarnation. If the economic Trinity is the immanent Trinity and vice versa then Jesus' humanity cannot be separated from his position within the Godhead as the eternal Word of God. As Rahner (p. 33) puts it, 'what Jesus is and does as man reveals the Logos himself; it is the reality of the Logos as our salvation amidst us … [H]ere the Logos with God and the Logos with us, the immanent and the economic Logos, are strictly the same.'

70 Catherine Mowry LaCugna, *God for Us: The Trinity & Christian Life* (New York, 1991), p. 230.

71 Ted Peters, *God as Trinity: Relationality and Temporality in Divine Life* (Louisville, Kentucky, 1993), p. 99.

72 Rahner, p. 107.

73 Ibid., p. 109.

74 Ibid., pp. 111–12.

75 Ibid., p. 58. Rahner justifies his starting point by stating that if we begin from the divine essence then there is a tendency to imply a Godhead behind the Trinity which subsequently gives rise to the threefold existence (see pp. 58–9). He states that we must always begin with the Father simply because in the Old Testament it is the unoriginate God who is revealed. It is only in the New Testament, through the revelation of the Son, that God is known as 'Father' and therefore as always acting in communion with the Son and the Spirit. In this sense God is logically (not ontologically) Father before God is Son and Holy Spirit.

Holy Spirit with the first person. As such, he claims that all subsist within divinity precisely *because* all relate to one another.

However, there are problems with his argument. First, it is debateable how far Rahner's critique of 'Western' trinitarian theology, especially Augustinian theology, can be maintained. We have already seen that a straightforward reading of Augustine as beginning with the oneness of God and as compromising the threeness of God is not particularly accurate. Rahner however upholds this very firmly. It is also debatable how far 'Eastern' or Greek trinitarian thought begins with the threeness of God since we have already seen that for thinkers like Gregory of Nazianzus at least, it is the oneness of the Godhead which is paramount. In this sense, the base from which Rahner establishes his trinitarian thesis is questionable.

Second, although it is clear that Rahner is trying to safeguard himself against any potential charges of tritheism (demonstrated by his choice of terminology), he consequently runs the risk of falling into modalism[76] and subordinationism. Suggesting that God exists in three distinct manners of subsisting, although safeguarding God's unity, tends to imply that the Son and Holy Spirit subsist within the *one* God, which is the *Father*. As such, the Son is not only presented as economically subordinate to the Father (that is subordinate in terms of his relationship with the Father within the economy of salvation) but also eternally subordinate (therefore subordinate to the Father within the immanent Trinity).

Brenner sees this as resulting mainly from Rahner's famous axiom. He argues that because Rahner posits the economic Trinity as identical to the immanent Trinity and vice versa, he rids himself of any conceptual resources for distinguishing between the status of the Son in the economy of salvation and the status of the Son within the eternal life of the trinitarian God. If God in relation to humankind is the same as God in relation to Godself then whatever we say of the Son in relation to the economy of salvation must be said also of the Son in relation to the immanent life of God. In this case, the missions and processions of God are not presented as distinct.[77]

For some this leads to a range of theological difficulties. If the immanent Trinity is the economic Trinity and vice versa then God struggles to find meaning outside the context of humankind and the world. Brenner thus criticizes Rahner for reducing theology to anthropology; he comments, 'Rahner's blurring of the two leaves one wondering whether Rahner's vision of God can survive Ludwig Feuerbach's critique that God is merely a projection of humanity.'[78] A line of contingency is seemingly constructed between God and the world to the extent that it is difficult to see how and why the Trinity could or should exist at all if humanity was not present.[79] And yet this scenario need not be the necessary result

---

[76] See Bruce Marshall, *Trinity and Truth* (Cambridge, 2000), p. 188.

[77] Brenner, 'Augustine and Karl Rahner', p. 35.

[78] Ibid., p. 37.

[79] David Cunningham, *These Three are One: The Practice of Trinitarian Theology* (Malden, Massachusetts, Oxford, 1998), p. 38. Also see M. Schluter, *Christianity in a*

of enforcing Rahner's axiom. If the economic Trinity is the immanent Trinity then what this means is that God is not other than the God who is revealed in the economy of salvation. There are not two trinities – one in relation to Godself and one in relation to the world. The God who is active in the history of salvation *is* the triune God. This, however, does not reduce God to the world or to a projection of humanity. What is revealed in the economy of salvation is that God is incomprehensible and that God will be who God will be. Thus, by claiming that the economic Trinity is the immanent Trinity (and vice versa), one confesses that the unfathomable God has made Godself known in and through the world and that God cannot be separated from this relationship. It also maintains, however, that God still remains hidden.

John Zizioulas

John Zizioulas is one of the most influential Orthodox theologians of the last century.[80] Influenced by Cappadocian thought, he echoes many of the same concerns as Vladimir Lossky, an equally influential Orthodox theologian.[81] He provides one example of what I wish to call an 'ethical-pastoral' modelling of the Trinity, common within contemporary trinitarian thought. Assuming the accuracy of the distinction between 'East' and 'West' and their respective emphases on the 'threeness' and 'oneness' of God, Zizioulas is one of a number of contemporary theologians who see themselves as more in keeping with an 'Eastern', Greek trinitarian logic, stressing the relationality and community of God as Trinity. Within this setting, the *koinōnia* of the Trinity is considered to provide an ethical model for human relationships and human societies.

Zizioulas is primarily concerned with citing God's being within the community of trinitarian relationships as opposed to within a single abstract essence. Indeed, in his essay, 'The Doctrine of God and the Trinity Today: Suggestions for an Ecumenical Study', Zizioulas expresses his growing concern that the Trinity is often overshadowed by a desire to maintain and stress the unity and oneness of God. As the Trinity forms a major stumbling block for interfaith dialogue, there is a growing need, he argues, to clarify and indeed decipher the exact meaning of such unity. If God is one because there is only one divine essence then the threeness of God follows logically after the oneness of God. Moreover, if God is first and foremost a single divine essence, then this essence stands to determine the person of God and therefore means that God cannot be free. On the other hand, if God's being is about *person* as opposed to *substance*, then God is completely

Changing World: Biblical Insight on Contemporary Issues (London, 2000), pp. 9–10.

[80] This point is affirmed by Aristotle Papanikolaou in *Being with God: Trinity, Apophaticism and Divine-Human Communion* (Notre Dame, Indiana, 2006), p. 1.

[81] For an example of Lossky's thought see *The Mystical Theology of the Eastern Church* (New York, 1997).

free to determine God's own selfhood.[82] This is clearly a departure from the likes of Rahner and Barth who wish to problematise talk of God as 'persons' on the grounds that this serves to endorse rather than undermine modern individualism, and tritheism.[83]

However, like Rahner, Zizioulas contends that the unity of God is found primarily within the person of God as Father, for the Father is the ontological principle of God.[84] Indeed, this, according to Zizioulas, is the profound contribution made by the Cappadocians. It is God the Father who constitutes the *archē* (origin/cause) and *aitia* (source/principle) of the Trinity; God exists as Father, Son and Spirit not because this is determined by God's divine essence but because the Father chooses it to be so eternally. It is the Father who begets the Son and the Father who sends forth the Spirit.[85] It is, therefore, because the Father freely chooses to be in eternal communion with the Son and Spirit that the Trinity exists and it is within this *free* communion that the being of God finds its place.[86] Critical of those trinitarian theologies which locate the unity of God within the divine substance, a tendency which he readily associates with 'Western theology', he identifies the ways in which the theology of the Greek Fathers provides a useful corrective. He writes:

> Among the Greek Fathers, the unity of God, the one God, and the ontological 'principle' or 'cause' of the being and life of God does not consist in the one substance of God but in the *hypostasis*, that is, *the person of the Father*. The one God is not the one substance but the Father, who is the 'cause' both of the generation of the Son and of the procession of the Spirit.[87]

For Zizioulas then, the Father reveals the being (or *ousia*) of God as being-in-communion. He argues, 'God as person – as the hypostasis of the Father – makes the one divine substance be that which it is: the one God.'[88] Such an identification of God's being (*ousia*) with person (*hypostasis*) as opposed to essence, according to Zizioulas, makes a biblical doctrine of God possible and also means that the Father can be referred to as the ground of God's being without this slipping into Monism.[89] This also, according to Zizioulas, reinforces a connection made by the Greek

---

[82] John D. Zizioulas, 'The Doctrine of God and the Trinity Today: Suggestions for an Ecumenical Study', in Alasdair Heron (ed.), *The Forgotten Trinity: A Selection of Papers presented to the BCC Study Commission on Trinitarian Doctrine Today* (London, 1991), pp. 19–32, esp. p. 25.

[83] See Rahner, pp. 114–15 and Karl Barth, *Church Dogmatics*, I/1, 'The Doctrine of the Word of God', trans. and ed. G.T. Thomson (Edinburgh, 1936), pp. 401–3.

[84] Zizioulas, *Being as Communion*, p. 41.

[85] Zizioulas, 'The Doctrine of God', p. 27.

[86] Zizioulas, *Being as Communion*, pp. 41 and 44.

[87] Ibid., pp. 40–41.

[88] Ibid., p. 41.

[89] Ibid., pp. 88–9.

fathers where being is grounded in person rather than abstract essence. Indeed, for Zizioulas, personal relations within the Trinity are not something to be added as an extra to the 'real' being of God; that God *is* means that God *is* Trinity, for God to *be* means for God to be relational.[90] Indeed, Zizioulas argues that the three persons are one God because they are united in 'an unbreakable communion (*koinonia*)'.[91]

However, does the citing of God's being within the person of God the Father mean that the Father is eternally and ontologically greater than the Son and Holy Spirit? Zizioulas argues not: so long as 'person' is complemented by 'substance', God the Son can be viewed as subordinate to the Father without this necessarily meaning that he is less than God or less than human – Jesus is *homoousios* with the Father, sharing in the same substance, but is not the ultimate reason for God's existence. For Zizioulas, the three persons are distinct in terms of their causative relations and these can be said of the Trinity *ad intra*.[92] For Zizioulas, the Father is the eternal cause of the divine existence; the principle, source and *monarchē* of the Godhead.

However there are problems with this argument. First, we have already seen how the trinitarian thought of Gregory of Nazianzus (as one example of Cappadocian thought) does not straightforwardly fit with Zizioulas' caricature of 'Eastern' approaches to the Trinity. Nazianzus certainly does not maintain that person precedes essence (like Zizioulas presumes of Cappadocian thought in general), nor does he always insist on the *monarchē* of God the Father. Often, Gregory seems to insist that it is the Godhead itself which constitutes the being of God rather than locating this exclusively with the person of God the Father.

It is also true that if the relationality and freedom of the Godhead are attributed to the person of the Father alone, as Zizioulas suggests, then the Father *alone* would be God in person[93] and in an absolute sense. The Son and Holy Spirit would not be God in person in this way. Such a view 'deprives the Godhead of its essential trinitarian nature and paves the way for relations of superiority and inferiority or for "degrees of deity" in the Trinity'.[94]

Despite these problems, one of Zizioulas' main contributions to contemporary trinitarian thought is his articulation of *ekstasis*. Such a term, he argues, signifies that God, as love, creates an 'immanent relationship of love "*outside Himself*"'.[95] This, according to Zizioulas, is the heart of the Trinity and as such the heart of

---

90 Ibid., p. 88.

91 John Zizioulas, 'The Doctrine of the Holy Trinity: The Significance of the Cappadocian Contribution', in C. Schwöbel (ed.), *Trinitarian Theology Today* (Edinburgh, 1995), pp. 44–60, esp. p. 48.

92 John Zizioulas, 'On Being a Person: Towards an Ontology of Personhood', in Christoph Schwöbel and Colin E. Gunton (ed.), *Persons, Divine and Humans: King's College essays in Theological Anthropology* (Edinburgh, 1991), pp. 33–46, esp. p. 38.

93 See Awad, 'Between Subordination', p. 188.

94 Ibid.

95 Zizioulas, *Being as Communion*, p. 91.

God's relationship with the world. Because the Father reveals the Father's being as communion, as one who freely chooses to be in communion with the Son and Spirit, this 'being' means that the Father is also free and in the Father's *ekstatic* love does in fact choose to create humanity so as to bring humanity into communion with God.[96] As such, Zizioulas claims that we are drawn into the triune dance and encouraged to take part. Being made in the image of God, we are also free to be in communion ourselves.[97] Hence, according to Zizioulas, human personhood necessarily finds its fulfilment in relationship with God, and with one another.[98]

This is an important contribution to contemporary debate. Although I consider Zizioulas' stress on the monarchē of God the Father to be misplaced, I do nevertheless appreciate his use of *ekstasis* to signify something meaningful about the being of God. However, that God is the kind of God who chooses to be in relationship, both internally and with the world, I contend, is not signalled ontologically by the person of God the Father but by the Godhead itself, more specifically by the *koinōnia* which characterizes the triune life. It is because all three *hypostases* mutually dwell with one another that God cannot help but be in relationship with the world and, thus, cannot help but draw humankind into the eternal dance of the Trinity. This is revealed within the economy of salvation through the incarnation of God in Christ and through the healing and restoring presence of the Spirit.

Jürgen Moltmann

As a contemporary German Protestant theologian, Jürgen Moltmann is one of a number of current theologians who present 'suffering' as integral to an understanding of the Trinity. Related to the ethical pastoral model, the 'suffering model' incorporates the notion of a suffering God, drawing heavily on the significance of the crucifixion and the suffering of Christ. If the Trinity provides a model by which to live, then it also witnesses to God's solidarity with those who suffer and to the eschatological movement of God to restore creation and redeem suffering.

Late twentieth-century and contemporary theology has tended to challenge the classical notion of the impassibility of God prominent in the patristic and medieval periods, instead drawing attention to the suffering God and the significance of Jesus' suffering on the cross. Such a shift has taken place due to a number of factors, including the numerous atrocities witnessed in the twentieth century (particularly the two world wars and the Holocaust), the rise of Protest Atheism (specifically

---

96 Ibid., p. 58.

97 Ibid.

98 Peters, p. 36. Also see Costa Carras, 'The Holy Trinity, the Church and Politics in a Secular World', in Andrew Walker and Costa Carras (eds), *Living Orthodoxy in the Modern World: Orthodox Christianity and Society* (New York, 1996), pp. 189–216. Such a social emphasis has been taken up more fully by Leonardo Boff in his book, *Trinity and Society*.

the work of Alfred North Whitehead, Charles Hartshorne, John Cobb and David Griffin), and a resurgence of interest in Luther's 'theology of the cross'.[99]

Jürgen Moltmann writes within the context of this general shift presenting his understanding of God, suffering and the Trinity within two central texts, *The Crucified God*[100] *and The Trinity and the Kingdom of God.*[101] Moltmann's theology is Christological and even Christocentric, hinging on the fact that Jesus has revealed God per se as a suffering God.[102] Because Jesus suffers and the humanity and divinity of the Son cannot be divided, Moltmann argues that suffering must be taken up into the very being of God.[103] However, he goes on to state that since the cross takes place within trinitarian history, it cannot result in the death *of* God but must instead point toward death *in* God.[104] Such a distinction is fundamental to Moltmann's theology. Here, death represents the *potential* of God; it signifies that God is not immune or unaffected but that God has the capacity to suffer and even die.

Placing the cross within a trinitarian framework, Moltmann insists that God cannot be reduced to Jesus' death for the cross involves more than Jesus' crucifixion. Hence it is too simplistic to say God dies. Indeed, Moltmann states that the Father suffers as well as the Son, but in a different way.[105] The Father forsakes the Son and delivers him to death and therefore suffers the grief of the Son's death, whereas the Son suffers the abandonment of his Father and also the physical pain of death itself.[106] Both are united in the same will, for the Son wills to surrender and the Father willingly delivers him, and yet both are at the same time separated through the Father's abandonment.[107] It is, therefore, the Spirit who, according to Moltmann, unites the two,[108] bridging the gap between the godforsakenness of sinners and the righteousness of God.[109] For Moltmann, the suffering of Jesus has significance for the entirety of the triune life. Since each person depends on the

---

99 Martin Luther's 'theology of the cross' emerged during 1518 and 1519. See Martin Luther, 'Disputations held at Heidelberg, 1518', in J. Atkinson (trans. and ed.), *Luther: Early Theological Works, Library of Christian Classics*, XVI (London, 1962), pp. 274–307.

100 Jürgen Moltmann, *The Crucified God: The Cross of Christ as the Foundation and Criticism of Christian Theology*, trans. R.A. Wilson and John Bowden (London, 1974).

101 Jürgen Moltmann, *The Trinity and the Kingdom of God: The Doctrine of God* (Munich, 1981).

102 Ibid., p. 21. See also Moltmann, *The Crucified God*, pp. 205–6.

103 Newlands, *God in Christian Perspective*, p. 111.

104 Moltmann, *The Crucified God*, p. 207.

105 Ibid., p. 203.

106 Peter Toon and James D. Spiceland, *One God in Trinity* (London, 1980), p. 119.

107 Ibid.

108 Peters, p. 103.

109 Toon and Spiceland, p. 119.

others,[110] the suffering of Christ cannot be separated from God per se. All suffer, but all do not die; 'death is something that happens in the midst of the relationships that make up God's triune life'.[111]

Moltmann therefore claims that it is on the cross that God reveals Godself as love.[112] As Migliore comments: 'In Moltmann's formulation, the love of God, manifest supremely in the event of the cross, is the central content of the doctrine of the Trinity; and the doctrine of the Trinity is the form or comprehensive framework for understanding the event of the cross.'[113] Indeed, for Moltmann, the history of the trinitarian God is a history of self-giving love, revealed prominently in the cross of Christ,[114] yet love cannot be love without suffering. Hence in the second chapter of his book, *The Trinity and the Kingdom of God*, Moltmann discusses the passion of God arguing that traditional views which interpret God's divinity in terms of impassibility are somewhat flawed.[115] If God is incapable of suffering then this, he maintains, renders Christ's passion a simple human tragedy and denies the particularity of Jesus.[116] Such a view, he argues, presents humankind as having an ability which God fails to possess, exposing God as less than God. Consequently he criticizes the patristics for making a false assumption that God either had to have an essential incapacity for suffering or had to be fatally subjected to it.[117] For Moltmann, God actively suffers and this means God chooses to suffer out of love for humankind.

'Active suffering' refers to 'the voluntary laying oneself open to another and allowing oneself to be intimately affected by him; that is to say, the suffering of passionate love'.[118] As such, Moltmann suggests that God is not compelled to suffer out of necessity but actually chooses to do so out of love. God's active suffering then constitutes God's free choice to be affected by the world. Indeed, he argues that to love another is to voluntarily leave oneself open to the suffering the other brings, hence within this context divine suffering does not amount to a deficiency

---

110 This point is important to Moltmann's trinitarian perspective. He claims that each person is dependent on the other two in order to secure their own identity. The self-giving of the Son on the cross therefore affirms the identity and deity of the Father and confirms the Sonship of Jesus. As deity is connected to God's Lordship (rule) then the self-giving of each person to the others constantly confirms the Lordship of each. Moltmann therefore argues that the triune God comes to be characterized by a mutual sense of submission.

111 Fiddes, p. 238.

112 Moltmann, *The Trinity and the Kingdom of God*, p. 23.

113 Daniel L. Migliore, 'The Trinity and the Theology of Religions', in Miroslav Volf and Michael Walker (eds), *God's Life in Trinity* (Minneapolis, 2006), pp. 101–17, esp. p. 108.

114 Jürgen Moltmann, *The Church in the Life of the Spirit* (New York, 1977), p. 161.

115 Moltmann, *The Trinity and the Kingdom of God*, p. 22.

116 Ibid.

117 Ibid., p. 23.

118 Ibid.

in God but actually means that God has the *power* to suffer.[119] Moltmann thus maintains that the salvation history attested to in the Bible is a history of Father, Son and Holy Spirit and moreover, a history in which the divine persons affect the world and are affected by the world.[120]

Such a view conflicts with the trinitarian perspectives of the likes of Augustine and Aquinas, defining God's perfection in relation to suffering and vulnerability rather than in terms of God's immunity from such characteristics. However, despite such an emphasis, Moltmann does not consider suffering to be the final word, either in relation to God or in relation to the world. Indeed, although Moltmann is firm in saying that God *does* suffer, he is also firm in saying that such suffering prepares the way for redemption, for unless God suffers, he says, suffering cannot be taken into God and therefore cannot be redeemed.[121] Moltmann is, therefore, clear that suffering must be placed within an eschatological context and within the context of hope: God suffers with us in order that we might be redeemed and finally taken into communion with the trinitarian God. As such, Moltmann argues that the Christ event anticipates the new creation, when suffering will be redeemed and what was true for Jesus will be true for us also.

The role of the Spirit is fundamental in this process. For Moltmann, the Spirit is the universal giver of life and the consummator of the redemptive work of Christ. The Spirit makes all things new, enables life to flourish, brings hope in the midst of hopelessness, and establishes peace and justice. The Spirit draws creatures into community with God and thus invites humankind to participate in the eternal life of the Trinity.[122] As Migliore puts it, 'The Spirit opens the eternal life of the triune God to the world. That the Trinity is an *open Trinity* means that the divine life has a surplus or overflow of love that gives life to creatures and enables them to become active participants in the triune life of love and the mission of God in the world.'[123] For Moltmann then, the Spirit of God is present in suffering and in hope for transformation; revealing God's solidarity with those who suffer as well as the eschatological *telos* of transformation towards which all creation is orientated.

In light of this, Moltmann argues that it is only at the eschaton that the immanence of God will be fully glimpsed and God finally revealed as 'all in all'.[124] Of course, this images God as in a state of becoming and implies that God somehow remains incomplete without the final redemption of the world. Indeed, Moltmann argues that the trinitarian life will only be fully realized when creation is redeemed. The

119 Jürgen Moltmann, 'The Motherly Father: Is Trinitarian Patripassionism Replacing Theological Patriarchalism?', in Johannes-Baptist Metz and Edward Schillebeeckx (eds), *God as Father?* (Edinburgh, New York, 1981), pp. 51–6, esp. p. 55.

120 See Giles, *Trinity and Subordinationism*, p. 95.

121 Moltmann, *The Trinity and the Kingdom of God*, p. 34.

122 Jürgen Moltmann, *Experiences of Theology* (Minneapolis, 2000), p. 326.

123 Migliore, 'The Trinity and the Theology of Religions', in Miroslav Volf and Michael Walker (eds), *God's Life in Trinity* (Minneapolis, 2006), pp. 101–17, esp. p. 112.

124 Toon and Spiceland, p. 113.

benefit with this understanding of the immanent Trinity, however, is that God in Godself cannot be disassociated from the world since the openness of the triune life posits the world as integral to the self-identity of God. However, there are problems with Moltmann's view.

O'Collins, for example, argues that because Moltmann places so much emphasis on Christ and his relation to the Father, he may run the risk of underestimating the role of the Spirit within the triune Godhead.[125] Yet it seems that Moltmann challenges such trends in his work. He criticizes 'Western' theology for subordinating the person and work of the Spirit and rejects any claims that the Son can be seen as 'prior' to the Spirit. This is indeed the grounds on which he rejects the *filioque* clause formed and utilized by the West. Son and Spirit enjoy a mutual relationship of exchange and reciprocity. The Spirit precedes and empowers the mission of Christ but is at the same time sent by Christ.

There also appear to be a number of difficulties with Moltmann's account of the suffering God. If God really participates in the event of the cross and all three persons share in perichoretic relations of mutual exchange and reciprocity, then must we not say that God is just as much involved in the dying of the Son as the bereavement of God the Father?[126] If the triune God is typified by *koinōnia*, then must we not speak of the death *of* God rather than just death *in* God? According to Paul Fiddes, Moltmann's distinction between the death *of* and death *in* God is problematic for this reason. He consequently prefers to speak of God as experiencing a 'threshold situation' where there is a complex experience of transition from life to death.[127] Speaking of death *in* God, however, need not be so problematic. Although the perichoretic relations shared by the three persons must mean that all are affected by death, we must be careful that we do not slip into Patripassionism, assuming that the Father suffers as the Son. Such a view fails to do justice to difference within the triune community. Indeed, it is the placing of 'death' within a trinitarian framework which is Moltmann's real achievement. For him, it is too simplistic and actually rather inaccurate to say God dies because only the Son dies. This is not to say, however, that the Father and Holy Spirit are unaffected by the death of the Son. All suffer and all experience death, but the Son's suffering and experience of death is not the *same* as the Father's.

It is, however, the case that by identifying the necessary place of suffering within love, Moltmann seems to suggest that humans are made one with God through taking up their own crosses and thus by their own suffering. As has already been noted in Chapter 1, this sort of idea runs a dangerous ideological course, justifying and even sacralizing suffering and must be questioned in a feminist setting. It is true that the placing of suffering within an eschatological framework

---

125 G. O'Collins, 'The Holy Trinity: The State of the Question', in Stephen Davis, Daniel Kendall, Gerald O'Collins (eds), *The Trinity: An Interdisciplinary Symposium on the Trinity* (Oxford, 1999), pp. 1–25, esp. p. 7.

126 This is a question posed by Fiddes, pp. 238–9.

127 Ibid., pp. 239–41.

which looks forward to a time when pain will be redeemed may not inspire a drive and incentive for change in the here and now. However, such identification with suffering need not propose a view of God as one who endorses suffering. To be sure, 'God's love is not a beautiful solidarity in suffering but an identification which is utterly intolerant of the evil which is the opposite of love.'[128] To identify God with suffering is not to say that suffering is intrinsically good but that God is with those who suffer and also, importantly, that God opposes the injustice and evil linked with such suffering.

It is also the case that for Moltmann, the future is not just *futurum*, 'further steps in an already unfolding process', but also *adventus*, 'a coming event "on the way towards the present."'[129] In the case of the latter, the future is not simply about something which is still to come but also about something which meets us and affects us in the present; it is both present and anticipated. Viewed through this lens, Moltmann's eschatological reading of suffering need not simply amount to a passive resolution which consequently serves to justify and even glorify pain. Although communicating God's identification with those who suffer and are weak, it may also testify to God's rejection of suffering and to God's present action to restore and redeem it. As a social doctrine, the Trinity may inspire human efforts to reject and oppose suffering and injustice revealing Moltmann's theology as a theology of hope, *par excellence*.

A Trinitarian Thesis

Thinking the Trinity

What then can we say about what it means to think the Trinity in light of this discussion? From what has already been said, it should be clear that there are certain aspects of the arguments presented which I wish to take forward and others which are unhelpful and that I wish to leave behind. What this section aims to do then is to clarify what these aspects are and what the main features of a trinitarian understanding of God might comprise.

God is not-one: The significance of community and relationship First, to think God as Trinity means to understand God as not-one. Although it has been argued that it is too presumptuous to assume that Western trinitarian theology places more emphasis on the unity of God and Eastern trinitarian theology more emphasis on the threeness of God, it is nevertheless the case that the talk of essence as the unifying principle of God implies that the *absolute* reality of God is characterized

---

[128] Newlands, *God in Christian Perspective*, p. 113.

[129] John Polkinghorne, 'Jürgen Moltmann's Engagement with the Natural Sciences', in Miroslav Volf and Michael Walker (eds), *God's Life in Trinity* (Minneapolis, 2006), pp. 61–70, esp. p. 62.

by oneness as opposed to threeness. Hence whilst such associations are refuted by Augustine, the language he uses still carries these kinds of overtones. His attempts to safeguard against subordinationism sometimes lead him into what looks likes like modalist territory.

We must also be mindful of comparable difficulties within seemingly alternative views which cite God's being within the person of God the Father. The likes of Rahner and Zizioulas who follow this trajectory risk subordinating the Son and Spirit because they wish to maintain the Father *alone* as the *archē* (origin/cause) and *aitia* (source/principle) of divinity. Such approaches threaten to reinforce a patriarchal notion of God, depicting God the Father as self-sufficient and without an equal, thereby repeating problems already addressed in the first chapter.[130]

In order to avoid these kinds of problems then, it is helpful to turn again to the trinitarian thought of Gregory of Nazianzus and thus locate the oneness of God within the Godhead itself and thus within the *koinōnia* shared by all three *hypostases*. If the Godhead constitutes the unoriginate principle, substance and *monarchē* of God then divine essence is neither grounded in the person of God the Father (as with the likes of Rahner and Zizioulas) or seemingly separated form the triune relations. According to this understanding, God the Father is not ontologically superior or different in 'rank' to the Son or Holy Spirit since all are equal and all co-exist eternally with one another. All are, therefore, God equally.

Of course, if the *monarchē* of God is rooted in the Godhead then what it means for God to *be* is not something separate from what it means for God to *be* three. To confess God as Trinity means to confess God as relational and as divine community. It means to cite God's being in mutual relationship and *perichoresis*, and so in the mutual indwelling of the three *hypostases* within one another. Each person freely and equally participates in the life of the others; 'a life of mutual relationship grounded in the understanding of God as a relational community'.[131] Within this context, there is no underlying oneness beneath or outside of the threefold personhood of God. God is ontologically and eternally diverse because God is ontologically and eternally Trinity. This, however, is not to propose three gods, for such a view defeats Christian monotheism. Instead it is to suggest, in agreement with Leonardo Boff that God is 'one' precisely because God is three; because the three *hypostases* overlap and never act in isolation of one another. As Boff argues, 'Father, Son and Holy Spirit do not emerge as separate or juxtaposed, but [are] always mutually implied and related. Where is the unity of the Three found? In the communion between the three divine Persons.'[132] To understand God as Trinity then is to locate God's oneness in community and mutuality and in the inseparable operations of Father, Son and Spirit. This is not to collapse the

---

130 Gavin D'Costa, *Sexing the Trinity: Gender, Culture and the Divine* (London, 2000), p. 17.

131 Karen Baker-Fletcher, *Dancing with God: The Trinity from a Womanist Perspective* (St Louis, Missouri, 2006), p. 57.

132 Boff, p. 4.

divine operations into sameness but to say that although distinct, all three operate in communion with one another and so in unity with one another. Because there is mutual indwelling, all three *hypostases* act together as one.

Within this context God's unity does not equate to a disintegration of difference. Rather, to confess faith in God as Trinity means to confess faith in a God who is by nature diverse and communal and to understand God as 'not-one'. Communion is the expression of mutual love and life and of a liveliness which is overflowing and dynamic.[133] This, however, is not to retreat from Christian monotheism. It simply means that God cannot be reduced to the 'abstract monotheism' Moltmann warns against where the living and dynamic relations of the triune persons are dissolved into sameness.

To confess God as Trinity then is to say that God is inwardly as well as outwardly diverse and relational and to cite difference within the very being of God. Trinitarian faith does not separate the existence of God from the existence of God as loving and relational. As Cynthia Rigby puts it, 'God's loving and relating are not only something God *does* but also something God really *is*.'[134] Trinitarian faith asserts that as diversity-in-communion, the triune God meets humankind as a dynamic presence of love in relationship. It confesses that as Trinity, there is no hierarchy in God because all three *hypostases* share equally in the eternal Godhead. Relations within this community are equal, mutual and reciprocal with each 'person' seeking the glory of the others and freely giving to them. The Father is not *more* God than the Son, nor is the Son *more* God than the Holy Spirit. Because all three together constitute the divine Godhead, all three together are equally God. As Augustine puts it, 'The Father is God, and the Son is God, and the Holy Spirit is God.'[135]

The dance of difference: the triune relations as distinct The unity of God then can be said to be established on the grounds of God's community and inter-relationality. However, if difference lies at the heart of divine being, what can we say about how the three persons are distinct?

Traditionally, the peculiarities of Father, Son and Holy Spirit have been determined in relation to causation. Nicene orthodoxy provides a clear example of this depicting God the Father as the unbegotten cause of all things, the Son as begotten of the Father and the Holy Spirit as proceeding from the Father (and from the Son according to the West). However, given that associations with generation imply that God is somehow sexed, that the Father produces the Son and so on, such an emphasis repeats the difficulties previously outlined in relation to the feminist critique in Chapter 1 and should, therefore, be avoided. Certainly, if God

---

133 Boff, p. 5.

134 Cynthia L. Rigby, 'Scandalous Presence: Incarnation and Trinity', in Amy Plantinga Pauw and Serene Jones (eds), *Feminist and Womanist Essays in Reformed Dogmatics* (Louisville, London, 2006), pp. 58–74, esp. p. 63.

135 Augustine, 'Answer to the Arian Sermon', 15, p. 153.

is *not* generative (because God *qua God* has no body or sex) then distinguishing the triune relations in this way is misleading, implying that the Father in some way precedes the Son and Holy Spirit so as to bring them into existence. This risks bringing hierarchy into the Trinity and as such, risks compromising the mutuality and co-equality of the three. Depicting the triune relations in terms of origin risks either a fall into subordinationism or a fall into Sabellianism.[136]

Given my desire to stress the co-equality of the three, I propose a different understanding, distinguishing the three *hypostases* in terms of their individual operations. Of course, this may seem strange given that I have already supported the inseparable operations of the triune persons, however, to say the three are inseparable is not to deny their distinctiveness. In agreement with Sallie McFague, I suggest we distinguish the Father as Creator, the Son as Redeemer, and the Holy Spirit as Restorer. It is not that *only* the Father creates or that *only* the Son redeems. It is not that *only* the Spirit sanctifies, for the divine *hypostases* act together and their operations are indeed inseparable. All three *hypostases* are responsible for creating and redeeming the world,[137] hence Augustine is right to say that although only the Son, and not the Father, was born of the Virgin Mary, his birth was the work of both Father *and* Son.[138] Distinguishing the divine *hypostases* in terms of operations means that each 'person' is identified *primarily* in relation to different works. For example, redemption is wrought by the life, death and resurrection of the Son, and yet it is through the Father and by the power and life of the Spirit that redemption takes place. In the same way, although God the Father is Creator, the Father creates through the Son and by the Spirit hence all three *hypostases* are involved in the work of creation. Although only the *logos* becomes incarnate, incarnation is an event within the eternal life of God – a point made particularly well by Rahner.

As such, God is understood here as a relationship of three divine *hypostases* in dynamic movement and activity. The Trinity encapsulates an eternal dance of difference wherein each person operates in union with the other divine *hypostases*, in accordance with one will and in the fulfilment of one act. Such oneness results from the perfect communion which is shared between the *hypostases*. Thus, although there is one act, God communicates in a threefold manner because God *is* God in three distinct ways. What this essentially establishes then is that God is three not only in relation to the economy of salvation but also in relation to Godself. There can be no meaningful distinction between the economic and immanent Trinity.

The immanent and economic Trinity If the triune relations are distinct *ad intra trinitatis* as well as *ad extra trinitatis* and the way God operates towards the world says something about God's eternal being, then there can be no clear or meaningful

136 D'Costa, p. 89.

137 Marshall, *Trinity and Truth*, p. 43.

138 Augustine, *Serm*, 52.8, pp. 534.

distinction between God in Godself (the immanent Trinity) and God in relation to the economy of salvation (the economic Trinity). God cannot be something different in Godself to what God is in relation to the world as this would signify a Trinity behind the Trinity – a God behind God. If God communicates with the world through the incarnate Son and through the redeeming power of the Spirit, as testified in the Bible, then God must be this kind of God in Godself. As such, the God-world relationship must be integral to God's own eternal self-identity making it nonsensical to speak of God as though God were separated from the world.

This, however, is not to suggest that revelation makes God available for our knowing. Certainly, we only know the immanent Trinity on the basis of what happens in the economy of salvation.[139] This reinforces that speculation about this God's being outside of this God's act is fruitless and indeed inappropriate. If the Trinity exposes God as the kind of God who is *with* as opposed to *without* humankind, then such speculation is unfounded. This, however, is not to say that the Christian God is ultimately knowable and fathomable because God decides to act in the world. What is revealed in revelation is the unfathomableness of God. Although God reveals Godself rather than a copy or analogy of the inner life of the Trinity, God still remains absolute mystery. Hence Rahner usefully defines the self-communication of God as a self-communication 'in which that which is given remains sovereign, incomprehensible, continuing, even as received, to dwell in its uncontrollable incomprehensible originality'.[140] Revelation then makes visible the invisible God and so continues to communicate that 'God is known by God and by God alone.'[141] God's relation with the world does not take away from God's otherness. God continues to remain hidden and incomprehensible because, as Barth puts it: 'His nature is not one which … lies in the sphere of our power. God is inapprehensible.'[142]

To argue that there is no meaningful distinction between the immanent and economic Trinity then is to say that in God's hiddenness, God cannot be reduced to the world. The world does not exhaust God. As Trinity God includes but also reaches *beyond* the world. This is a panentheistic depiction of the God-world relationship rather than a pantheistic one. According to this view, the world is taken into the triune being through the historical reality of Jesus and the consuming, redeeming power of the Holy Spirit, without suggesting that the world constitutes the entirety of God. The world *participates in* God rather than *is* God. God then is not other than God is in revelation. God is Trinity in relation to the world and

---

139 See also Bruce Marshall, 'Trinity', in Gareth Jones (ed.), *The Blackwell Companion to Modern Theology* (Malden, MA, Oxford, UK, Victoria, Australia: Blackwell, 2004) pp. 183–203, esp. p. 188.

140 Rahner, p. 37.

141 Karl Barth, *Church Dogmatics*, II/1, The Doctrine of God, ed. G.W. Bromiley and T.F. Torrance, trans. T.H.L. Parker, W.B. Johnston, Harold Knight and J.L.M. Haire (Edinburgh, 1957), p. 179.

142 Ibid., p. 187.

internally. In the economic Trinity we have an accurate revelation of the immanent Trinity[143] but God still remains hidden and unknowable in God's revealedness. As Sallie McFague puts it, 'There is, as it were, a limit on our side, not on God's.'[144]

To confess faith in the Trinity then is to assert boldly that God is a God who chooses to be *with* as opposed to *without* the world. That God, through God's *ekstatic* love is the kind of God who freely decides to create an immanent relationship of love outside of Godself. Communion within the Trinity then overflows to incorporate the world so that relationship with the world is integral to what it means for God to be as Trinity.

Temporality, change and suffering If the immanent Trinity is the economic Trinity, then it follows that suffering, change and temporality cannot be located outside of the eternal being of God. If God's relation to the world in and through the person of Jesus Christ is not something separate from God's being, then the suffering, temporality and tangibility of Jesus must find some place within the triune God. This means that God's perfection cannot be straightforwardly outlined in terms of immutability and impassibility as in the case of traditional philosophical theology, for this is to either deny the reality of the cross or the divinity of Christ. If Jesus, as fully God, suffers and dies then God must also in some way suffer and die. However, given that Jesus finds his place within a wider trinitarian framework as one of three divine *hypostases*, the death and suffering he experiences should not be transferred straight forwardly onto the entirety of the Godhead. It is only the Son who is crucified and only the Son who dies.

The three *hypostases* then, although operating in relation to one another, always remain distinct. Moltmann is right when he says that even though the Father, Son and Holy Spirit all suffer, they suffer in different ways. In other words, to argue that because Jesus is temporal, suffers and dies, God must also be temporal, suffer and die is too simplistic. This reduces the Trinity to the person of God the Son and the person of God the Son to the historical person of Jesus of Nazareth, dissolving difference within the triune community. It is helpful to suggest that Jesus' suffering and death point towards death *in* God as opposed to the death *of* God. Just as the triune community cannot be reduced to the person of the Son but includes the person of God the Son, so the triune God cannot be reduced to the suffering the Son endures but must nevertheless include it.

To think God as Trinity then means to think God as involved in suffering, temporality and change but not in such a way as to reduce God to this. That God *is* Trinity means that there is sufficient space in God for suffering, temporality and change to exist without this exhausting God. Karl Barth's understanding of the humanity of God is helpful here since this depicts God's deity as constitutive of God's involvement with the world. For Barth, God's deity is not compromised

---

[143] Giles, *The Trinity and Subordinationism*, p. 28.

[144] Sallie McFague, *Models of God: Theology for an Ecological, Nuclear Age* (Philadelphia, 1987), p. 72.

by God's participation in time and space but on the contrary reveals that God is the kind of God who chooses to be affected by the world. God meets humanity in the person and humanity of Jesus. Indeed, for Barth, Christ represents God's movement towards humanity and humanity's movement towards God.[145] Christ reveals God both in a state of humiliation – as true God becoming true 'man', taking on human suffering and the sin of the world, and in a state of exaltation – as true 'man' raised up as true God.[146] This, however, does not mean that God needs humanity in order to be complete, but that God chooses humanity in total freedom, and through love decides to be its partner.[147] Understood through this lens, God's involvement in temporality, suffering and change do not undermine God's deity but are actually seen as constitutive of it. This neither compromises the freedom of God nor reduces God to these qualities.

Hope, eschatology and redemption This brings me to my final point. If suffering, temporality and change participate in God but do not exhaust God, then there is also room for hope, healing and redemption. Indeed, we can say with Karl Rahner and Leonardo Boff that God takes suffering and temporality into God's being so as to restore and redeem it. Understood this way, suffering can never have the final word. We can maintain that the world is liberation bound, that in the end, all will be well because God directs all things towards the fulfilment of God's creation. Such a vision is traditionally signalled through the resurrection of Christ. However, this is not to say that such restoration and healing is purely futuristic or that humanity's role within redemption is purely passive. To lay hold of such a vision is to make manifest the coming reign of God in the present through *orthopraxis*; through acts of justice, love and equity. It is not a glamorization of suffering (which is deeply unhelpful when seeking to develop a *feminist* theology) but a recognition that suffering is not the end: '*because God is God, it means that suffering is not all that God does*'.[148] God suffers but because God is triune, this means that suffering *participates* in God and, as a result, does not exhaust God. Instead, suffering is included in God and is redeemed by God through this process of participation. God then identifies with those who suffer and with those who seek justice and the end of suffering.

Such an understanding testifies to the non-reducible nature of the Trinity, affirming that there is enough space in the Godhead for suffering and redemption to co-exist. It also testifies to the healing work of the Spirit, 'renewing, comforting, instructing, guiding, and encouraging the people of God; not only healing them, but also *empowering* them with gifts to go out and heal others'.[149] It proclaims that 'resurrection' is not just an event in the past but also an event which is both present

145 Karl Barth, *The Humanity of God* (London, 1961), p. 47.

146 Ibid., p. 46.

147 Ibid., p. 50.

148 Mary Grey, *Introducing Feminist Images of God* (Sheffield, 2001), p. 60.

149 Baker-Fletcher, p. 163, emphasis mine.

and still to come. Because Jesus died and rose again, evil, suffering and death cannot and will not overcome the world. The resurrection establishes the world as being liberation bound and provides a promise of deliverance from tyranny. Suffering, although integral to the eternal life of God, can never be the last word about God.

Conclusion: Thinking God as Trinity

Thinking God as Trinity then means to think God in ways that do not dilute God to *either* this *or* that. As Trinity, it is not enough to define God as one and it is not enough to define God as three. God is *both* one *and* three ultimately revealing the logic of the Trinity as one of inclusion. If the triune *hypostases* are distinct in terms of their operations then the Father cannot be reduced to the Son nor the Son to the Holy Spirit and so on. Each person occupies their own space in the trinitarian Godhead.

Understanding God as Trinity then asserts that there is irreducible difference within God. Death, suffering, temporality and change all find their place within the trinitarian being of God through God's eternal decision to become embodied in the particular person of Jesus of Nazareth. However, because the Trinity does not connote the one God in a threefold repetition, because we do not fall into the modalist trap of presenting the Son as identical to the Father and the Holy Spirit, it enables us to also say that God cannot be reduced to suffering, temporality or change. The incarnation reveals God's identification with the world and with suffering but it does not limit God to this. The incarnate Christ is also the eternal *logos* and although there can be no *logos* without the flesh (on the basis that incarnation has always been integral to the eternal identity of the Son), the *logos* is, nevertheless, not contained by the flesh. What it means for Jesus to be the Christ is not limited to the historical incarnation of God in time but finds its significance *also* in relation to the eternal life of God. In this sense the body and the world, rather than placing boundaries around God are taken up into the eternal impenetrable identity of God through the incarnate *logos*.

Aside from this we must also remember that the three divine *hypostases* operate together. Creation is not simply and exclusively the work of God the Father nor is redemption simply and exclusively the work of the Son or restoration and sanctification solely the work of the Holy Spirit. Although there is irreducible difference within the trinitarian community there is also uninterrupted communion and relationship which enables the triune God to act as one. All three *hypostases* are present at every moment and this again enables us to say with confidence that although God identifies with suffering, God can never be reduced to this.

What we have in a trinitarian understanding of God then is not so much a technical equation which seeks to square the circle of three-in-oneness but a doctrine which reveals that the immanence and transcendence of God belong together. A doctrine which announces that there is space in God – space for movement, space for community, space for difference, space for participation and space for love. The question we now face then is to what extent thinking God in this way is useful for feminist theology. How then are we to determine this? On what basis are we to articulate this usefulness? The next part of this book seeks to establish this through a consideration of theological methodology. By outlining firmly what it means to do theology from a feminist point of view we are able to turn again to this doctrine and consider the ways in which it might affirm and be affirmed by the central values which underpin this particular theological approach. The next chapter begins this process by stressing the importance of orthodoxy and contextualization in the doing of theology; Chapters 4 and 5 then move this methodology in a more distinctly *feminist* direction through an emphasis on women's experience.

PART TWO
Feminist Theological Methodology

Chapter 3

Working Towards an Orthodox-Contextual Theological Methodology:

A Dialogue with Karl Barth and Friedrich Schleiermacher

At the heart of our discussion here lies the crucial question, how do we go about doing theology? This chapter answers this question by drawing attention to two main features which I consider to be important to theological method: a grounding of theology in context and a grounding of theology in orthodoxy. Here, a concern for orthodoxy signals the importance of upholding the ontological priority and objective reality of God's self-revelation, as well as a firm confession that Jesus Christ is God incarnate. Humankind can only know God because God has decided to make Godself known in human history, thus, theology depends on the free decision of God to reveal Godself as Godself in the first place. In keeping with Nicene and Chalcedonian orthodoxy, this asserts that God exists objectively as Trinity and that God has made Godself known in the economy of salvation through the person of Christ.

Rooting theology in 'context' however signals the role of experience in the doing of theology. Theology always begins with context rather than with a trans-cultural received tradition or a pre-determined deposit of faith.[1] In keeping with contemporary moves away from more classical deductive approaches to theology, this establishes experience as the practical and necessary starting point of theological reflection. Although it is only possible to know God because God has eternally decided to reveal Godself as Godself in and through the world, theological reflection always begins with experience because there is nowhere outside of this to which we might escape. Both emphases are important since contextualization prevents theology from slipping into abstraction, fantasizing about God outside of context, whereas orthodoxy prevents theology from collapsing into anthropology and from reducing God to nothing more than the sum of human experience.

In order to develop these two emphases I dialogue in some detail with the methodological perspectives of Friedrich Schleiermacher and Karl Barth. Schleiermacher (1768–1834) is useful because he places much of his focus on 'feeling' and experience within religion. As the so-called 'father' of modern theology, he is frequently accused of presenting the Trinity as an appendix to his theology

---

[1] See my short extract on 'Contextual Theologies' in M. Davie, T. Grass, S. Holmes, J. McDowel and T. Noble (eds), *New Dictionary of Theology* (InterVarsity Press, forthcoming).

and for reducing theology to anthropology and these are important concerns which must be confronted if context is to be established as the logical starting point of theology. Barth (1886–1968) is useful here because he articulates the self-revelation of God (as Trinity) as the starting point of all theology. This roots theology in the priority of God in revelation rather than in the human self-consciousness as with Schleiermacher. Barth thus provides a degree of correction to the problems foreseen with Schleiermacher's method. Where Schleiermacher's method seems to be overly anthropocentric, reducing the objective and ontological reality of God (and thus of the Trinity) to consciousness of the self, Barth establishes the objective reality of God as triune as the very ground of his theological method. Barth then succeeds in securing the ontological freedom of God whereas Schleiermacher struggles to maintain this. However, it is also the case that where problems arise with Barth's method, Schleiermacher provides a suitable corrective. Where Barth seems to underestimate the active role played by human beings in interpreting revelation and, thus, in knowing God, Schleiermacher insists that theology must begin with what is directly apprehended by the human self-consciousness. Schleiermacher is, therefore, used to help establish context and experience as the logical and necessary starting point of theological method whereas Barth is used to help establish the priority of God's revelation and the incarnate Christ as the ontological starting point of theological method. This distinction is important and will be revisited as we take a closer look at both thinkers.

The Role of Context in the Doing of Theology

What then does it mean to emphasize the role of context in the doing of theology? At a basic level it means to recognize that *all* theology is contextual. We only know God through context and through experience hence theology can never claim to have access to a God outside of this. Traditional sources of theology such as the Bible and tradition do not provide direct access to the being of God, they are themselves rooted in experience. The Bible, for example, is written in context about context and read in context. It speaks of different human experiences of God's activity in the world rather than making this activity directly available to us. It cannot be separated from the past context in which it was written or from the present context in which it is read. Rosemary Radford Ruether famously presents this as part of her critique of malestream theology asserting that there are no objective, absolute theological principles, ideas or symbols, just ideas, principles and symbols which filter from human context. *All* theology is contextual. 'What have been called the objective sources of theology; Scripture and tradition', she says, 'are themselves codified collective human experience.'[2] Thus, although the Bible and tradition are important as sources of theology, experience necessarily underpins each.

2 Rosemary Radford Ruether, *Sexism and God-talk: Toward a Feminist Theology* (Boston, 1983), p. 12.

One of the implications of this approach is that the search for 'original' meaning in revelation – for example, in the corpus of the Bible – is fruitless. One cannot get *behind* experience to a de-contextualized core because experience plays a formative role in the doing of theology. Experience does not connote a 'skin' we can peel away to reveal a kernel of unmediated truth. As Rebecca Chopp notes, the Word is not an unmediated Word which is simply *channelled* through human words. Such a view, she argues, is 'philosophically suspect' in contemporary theology.[3] Instead, human language and experience play a part in shaping knowledge about God. To root theology in context then is to understand that context not only constitutes the *vehicle* through which God communicates but that context also *informs* what is communicated. This, however, does not mean that the Bible and tradition are redundant as sources of theology. It is not that the text is 'empty' (as some post-moderns would want to suggest) since this would deny that revelation took place.[4] It is simply that one cannot take the 'text' out of 'con-text'.

In order to outline further what it means to do theology from the starting point of experience, I turn now to Friedrich Schleiermacher. Schleiermacher is helpful because he responds to Enlightenment concerns which tended to highlight the importance of reasonable faith by presenting a more open and personal approach to theology. For Schleiermacher it is inward feeling and experience rather than intellectual knowledge or religious dogma which are of primary importance. Religion, for him, is not about what we can know concerning God's being or nature but about what we can *experience*. Schleiermacher, then, is useful because he depicts the 'essence' of religion (and of Christianity in particular) as 'feeling', making this fundamental to his theology.

Friedrich Schleiermacher

Schleiermacher's theology develops and matures from his early thinking to the crystallization of his theology in *The Christian Faith*. This is of particular importance when we consider his definition of religion. In his seminal work, *On Religion*, Schleiermacher dedicates the first speech to identifying the root of religion. Here he states that religion is grounded in the feeling to apprehend God rather than within human reason. One should not look to dogma or doctrine as the heart of religion but to what gives rise to such things. In short, Schleiermacher states that religion is first and foremost concerned with inward emotions and dispositions. He goes on to discuss this in more detail in the second speech by distinguishing 'feeling' from physics and morality. Religion is not primarily a way

---

3 Rebecca Chopp, *The Power to Speak: Feminism, Language, God* (New York, 1989), p. 6.

4 For an interesting discussion on the role of scripture and tradition in theological method in light of the challenge of postmodernism, see Najeeb George Awad's article, 'Should We Dispense with *Sola Scripture*? Scripture, Tradition and Postmodern Theology', *Dialog: A Journal of Theology*, 47/1 (2008): 64–79.

of thinking or a way of acting, he says,[5] for '... it resigns, at once, all claims on anything that belongs either to science or morality'.[6] According to Schleiermacher, religion constitutes '... the immediate consciousness of the universal existence of all finite things, in and through the Infinite, and of all temporal things in and through the Eternal'.[7] In other words, religion is the feeling that everything finite is part of an eternal whole; that all things are united in and through God.[8] This has two implications: first that infinity and finiteness are not antithetical, and second that God is not separate from the world.

Schleiermacher's understanding of religious 'feeling', however, becomes more specific in *The Christian Faith.* In Chapter 1 he relates feeling to immediate self-consciousness,[9] however, he is quick to assert that this does not simply constitute self-contemplation but refers specifically to *pious* feeling which he defines as 'the consciousness of being absolutely dependent'.[10] Self-consciousness then is the pious feeling or awareness that one is dependent on something else for one's existence and that the whole of the finite world is naturally suited for an encounter with Infinity.

Schleiermacher understands the self-consciousness at two levels, on the one hand as a feeling of freedom (the spontaneity of the self), whilst on the other as a feeling of dependence (receptivity). The first expresses the existence of the subject for itself, constituting the feeling of spontaneous movement and action and the sense that one is free and can in fact affect the world. The second expresses one's co-existence with all others, the feeling that one's activity is, like the rest of the finite world, limited through a dependence on something else.[11] Both exist alongside one another. Thus, one can never be absolutely free because there are limits as to how far one can actually affect the world. One can, however, be absolutely dependent given that all spontaneous movement is actually dependent in the first place on something outside of itself.[12] Absolute dependence then, according to Schleiermacher, constitutes an awareness of God. Because everyone shares this sense of dependence, we also consequently share in a consciousness of the divine. Thus, for Schleiermacher, religious feeling actually constitutes consciousness of

---

5 Friedrich Schleiermacher, *On Religion: Speeches to its Cultural Despisers*, trans. John Oman (New York, 1958), p. 27.

6 Ibid., p. 35.

7 Ibid., p. 36.

8 Ibid., pp. 49–50.

9 Ibid., p. 6.

10 Ibid., p. 12.

11 Friedrich Schleiermacher, *The Christian Faith*, trans. and ed. H.R. Mackintosh and J.S. Stewart, second edn (Edinburgh, 1999), 4, pp. 12–18, and Robert R. Williams, *Schleiermacher the Theologian: The Constructions of the Doctrine of God* (Philadelphia, 1978), p. 32.

12 Schleiermacher, *The Christian Faith*, 4.3, pp. 15–16.

God as the 'whence' of all things: to be aware of one's absolute dependence is in fact to be conscious of being in relation with God.[13]

However, Schleiermacher is clear that it is not a case of either being conscious of God or not since all possess the feeling of absolute dependence. The question is then to what degree one is conscious of the divine. Schleiermacher refers to two extremes: the evil condition of Godlessness or God-forgetfulness and the redeemed condition of Blessedness and perfect communion with God.[14] According to Schleiermacher, God-consciousness does not necessarily mean fellowship with God. Where the God-consciousness does not dominate the moment there is God-forgetfulness,[15] hence, the feeling of absolute dependence is not adequately recognized nor is it the ground of one's life. In this instance, there is no fellowship with God and the individual is guilty of sin. Within this context, redemption signifies the passing from less God-consciousness to more, from turning-away-from-God to turning-towards-God.[16] As a result of this, Schleiermacher argues that Jesus is unique because unlike other human beings, he 'has an absolutely potent God-consciousness'.[17] Jesus is the *only* human to have manifested perfect God-consciousness and communion with God. Unlike other human beings, Jesus is not in need of redemption. He is instead, 'the One in whom the human creation is perfected'.[18] He has, therefore, been criticized quite strongly for providing a heterodox Christology which undermines the claims of Chalcedon, presenting Jesus as a mere 'ideal type' of human being.

We will look at Schleiermacher's Christology in a little more detail later on, what is significant for now, however, is to note the way in which Schleiermacher rejects knowledge of God outside the religious self-consciousness. Theology is rooted in the religious self-consciousness and so it cannot speak deductively about God. This carries important implications for his understanding of the Trinity and for the place of this doctrine within his theological method.

The Place of Dogmatics and the Doctrine of God and the Trinity

In *The Christian Faith*, Schleiermacher goes about identifying the relation of Dogmatics to Christian piety. He begins this section by asserting that 'Christian doctrines are accounts of the Christian religious affections set forth in speech'.[19] Doctrine then is the inner religious experience formalized and externalized in language. It constitutes the move from inward feeling, which may not be specific, ordered or synthesized, to definite speech. As such, dogmatic propositions constitute

---

13 Ibid., 4.4, p. 17.

14 Ibid., 2.2, p. 54.

15 Ibid., 2.2, p. 55.

16 Williams, p. 102.

17 Schleiermacher, *The Christian Faith*, 89.2, p. 367.

18 Ibid.

19 Ibid., 15, p. 76.

what Schleiermacher calls 'diadactic' speech in that they aim at the highest degree of definiteness.[20] Doctrine as diadactic speech is an immediate reflection on the self-consciousness,[21] that is, an immediate reflection on one's direct experience of God. In this sense, religious feeling is primary and religious dogma secondary and derivative. This means that doctrine cannot be seen as something separate to religious feeling but must instead be seen as rooted in it. As Schleiermacher puts it, 'doctrines in all their forms have their ultimate ground so exclusively in the emotions of the religious self-consciousness, that where these do not exist the doctrines cannot arise'.[22]

Given that Schleiermacher argues that doctrine proceeds from religious self-consciousness and all we can know about God is what we apprehend in immediate religious experience, then direct knowledge of the being of God or the nature of God is, according to Schleiermacher, impossible. Indeed, he argues that it is impossible to know God as eternal, omnipotent, omniscient and omnipresent directly and primarily within the religious self-consciousness since such knowledge concerning the innate attributes of God can only be *derived* from the primary God-consciousness.[23] To this extent, such knowledge follows secondarily rather than being apprehended directly or immediately.[24] It is within this general framework that the doctrine of the Trinity is placed.

God and the Trinity As a doctrine, Schleiermacher maintains that the Trinity is derived from the God-consciousness and as such cannot say anything directly about the being of God per se. It simply reflects on the God-consciousness and in the light of this constructs a picture of God that is consistent. As such, Schleiermacher understands the Trinity as following logically after experience of God, hence it does not occupy a central place within his methodology.

It is still common to assume that Schleiermacher subordinates the Trinity within his methodology presenting it as merely speculative. Barth certainly makes this assumption arguing that we are quite within our right to assume that for Schleiermacher, 'no constitutive meaning attaches to it'.[25] However, such an emphasis seems to somewhat misinterpret Schleiermacher's perspective. Of course, that Schleiermacher includes the Trinity at the very end of his volume does seem to imply that the doctrine is somehow insignificant or trivial. However, it may be that Schleiermacher's thinking here is not so straightforward; not so much that the Trinity *should not* be primary but that it *could not*.

---

[20] Ibid., 16, p. 78.

[21] Keith W. Clements, *Friedrich Schleiermacher: Pioneer of Modern Theology* (London, 1987), p. 137.

[22] Schleiermacher, *The Christian Faith*, 15.2, p. 78.

[23] Stephen Sykes, *Friedrich Schleiermacher* (Working, 1971), p. 30.

[24] Schleiermacher, *The Christian Faith*, 50.4, p. 200.

[25] Karl Barth, *Church Dogmatics*, I/1, 'The Doctrine of the Word of God', trans. and ed. G.T. Thomson (Edinburgh: T & T Clark, 1936), p. 348.

Given Schleiermacher's views on religious feeling, it would be methodologically impossible for him to consider the Trinity in advance of his comments on the God-consciousness. Since he has, by this stage, already set in place the secondary nature of religious doctrine, he simply uses this final section in order to plant the Trinity within this context. Hence, it is not that the Trinity is auxiliary but that it is only known indirectly through reflection on the God-consciousness. Thus, he says:

> All that is essential in this second Aspect of the Second Part of our exposition is also posited in what is essential in the doctrine of the Trinity; but this doctrine, as ecclesiastically framed, is not an immediate utterance concerning the Christian self-consciousness, but only a combination of several such utterances.[26]

For Schleiermacher, the main concern of the doctrine of the Trinity is to unite the divine essence with the human essence; to say that the same divine being is in Christ as is in the Church.[27] As such, the doctrine filters from that which is directly apprehended by the religious self consciousness. According to Schleiermacher, we experience Christ and redemption directly through the preaching of the Word within the Christian community. We experience Christ as being in and as working through the Church and thus experience his influence on our own consciousness of God. This is an immediate experience of redemption which tells us something indirectly about what God is like. There is, therefore, for Schleiermacher, a relationship between what is known immediately through the God-consciousness and the being of God. Although we always begin with the immediacy of the religious self consciousness, we can go on to speak about the being of God. This, however, is not mere speculation as some suggest, but a matter of abstracting information from the God-consciousness and, thus, a matter of *interpretation*.

Related to this, Christ's relation to the world through the incarnation and redemption are not considered by Schleiermacher to be separate from the divine essence.[28] If God in Godself is not separate to God for us, then the divine essence cannot be separated from redemption. Schleiermacher thus argues that however God reveals Godself in and through the world must be true of God *ad intra*. One should not speculate concerning the being of God outside the world or the incarnation since God has revealed Godself as Godself through the world and through the life of Christ.

This leads Schleiermacher to formulate a view of the Trinity as both hidden and revealed.[29] God is not one thing in Godself and another in relation to the world,

---

26 Schleiermacher, *The Christian Faith*, 170, p. 738.

27 Ibid., 170.1, p. 739.

28 Ibid.

29 For Schleiermacher, unity is God concealed and Trinity is God revealed (See Schleiermacher, 'On the Discrepancy Between the Sabellian and Athanasian Methods of Representing the Doctrine of the Trinity', trans. with notes and illustration by M. Stuart, *The Biblical Repository and Quarterly Observer*, XVIII (April 1936): 316–17.

there is a correspondence between the two as revealed through Jesus Christ. God is neither wholly other, transcendent and distant from the world, nor completely identical to the world (the pantheistic critique). God cannot be reduced to either but must instead involve both. Given this, he argues that divine monarchy should not be separated from the economy of salvation, for it is only through the historical incarnation that the ontological monarchy of God is known in the first place.

Schleiermacher, then, should not be criticized for presenting a merely economic Trinity. Indeed, for Schleiermacher God is a bipolar God,[30] on the one hand failing to be totally identified with the world, whilst on the other, failing to be totally transcendent of and unrelated to it.[31] Whereas the former constitutes what Schleiermacher calls the 'absolute inwardness'[32] of God, the latter constitutes what he calls the 'absolute vitality' of God.[33] As absolutely inward, God is qualitatively different from the world.[34] God is free and is not tied to the world through necessity. Conversely, the absolute vitality of God signals that God is fully expressed in and through the world; that the world is the means by which God manifests Godself and thus points towards an essential relationship between the two.[35] Thus, for Schleiermacher, there is distinction in God – God is wholly revealed and wholly hidden at the same time, in the same way that God is both eternal and historical, co-eternal and co-equal. There is distinction in God without there being any essential difference between God and God's revelation.

Assessing the Contribution of 'Context' in Theological Method

Schleiermacher's contribution to discussion surrounding theological method then is noteworthy. He outlines an understanding of the Trinity which carries resonance with that proposed previously in Chapter 1 presenting God as the coincidence of opposites, as both hidden and revealed and maintains that God is neither wholly other nor totally identical to the world. As absolute inwardness and absolute vitality, God is immanent in the world and yet still remains free. What Schleiermacher, however, does insist upon is that knowledge of the absolute inwardness of God can only be induced and derived from reflection on the God-consciousness. In

30 Williams, p. 87.

31 Ibid., p. 84.

32 Schleiermacher, *The Christian Faith*, 51.2, p. 203.

33 Hence Williams argues that, for Schleiermacher, God constitutes the 'coincidence of opposites' (p. 149).

34 The divine attributes Schleiermacher associates with this are eternity and omnipresence. These are negative attributes in that they are inactive and merely formal. See *The Christian Faith*, 51.2, p. 202.

35 The divine attributes Schleiermacher associates with this are omnipotence and omniscience. These are positive attributes in that they are active, expressing God's active presence within the world. See *The Christian Faith*, 50.3, pp. 51, 198 and 200–203.

other words, experience provides the gateway into knowledge of God. Indeed, Schleiermacher does not begin his theological method with a view of infallible revelation or received tradition. Instead, his methodology begins with what he considers to be immediate religious experience, denying any dichotomy between revealed and natural theology.[36] Whatever is experienced immediately within the religious self-consciousness constitutes revelation of God. Thus, one cannot talk about revelation outside human experience because it is through this context that God is made known in the first place. Such a methodological perspective then rightly insists that it is impossible to know the being of God directly and that this is always mediated through experience and articulated through reflection on experience. What Schleiermacher helps to demonstrate is that theology must always begin with concrete experience and with the historical person of Jesus Christ because this is how revelation meets us. Revelation meets us through context.

There are however a number of difficulties with Schleiermacher's method and these help identify more general problems with a contextual approach to theology.

Theology as anthropology First, Schleiermacher's method may be in danger of being overly anthropocentric, relativistic and non-objective. There seems to be an over emphasis on the human to the extent that God is almost entirely collapsed into the human self-consciousness. Schleiermacher argues that to be aware of one's absolute dependence is to be aware of God and so appears to be in danger of collapsing God into 'feeling' and the objectivity of God into the human self-consciousness. This threatens to reduce God to human experience. The first potential problem with a contextual theological method then is that knowledge of God may be presented as synonymous with knowledge of the self and God therefore as a projection of human experience.

At the same time, however, Schleiermacher seems to resist this difficulty. He refers to God as the source of the God-consciousness and as, therefore, prior to it. Jesus' perfect God-consciousness is given by God and it is because God makes consciousness of God possible in the knitting together of creation that humankind can be conscious of God and redeemed by the perfect God-consciousness of Jesus Christ. In other words, the objective reality of God is preserved by Schleiermacher, at least in theory. The problem is that Schleiermacher, in placing so much emphasis on the human self-consciousness, fails to pay sufficient attention to the being of God. He certainly struggles to make a compelling case for the objective reality of the *Trinity* as the source of the God-consciousness, and this is a weakness. For Schleiermacher, because the Trinity follows logically *after* the God-consciousness he fails to establish the Trinity as the ontological root of the God-consciousness.

Experience as immediate Schleiermacher also seems to present experience itself as something which is self-evident, basic, intuitive and immediate. The feeling of absolute dependence is presumably experienced directly by every human being

[36] Avery Dulles, *Models of Revelation* (Dublin, 1983), p. 70.

in the same way just as the experience of redemption (which Schleiermacher also holds to be primary) is presumably generic amongst Christians. In this sense, Schleiermacher, although allowing more space for interpretation than Barth, still seems to hold to a kind of theological foundationalism. This causes problems because it fails to recognize the role of culture in constructing interpretations of experience, and fails to recognize difference between different religions.

In the first instance we must admit that culture affects the way we interpret experience. In this sense, any appeal to a generic or universal notion of human experience is questionable because experience is always an act of interpretation which takes place with the context of cultural history.[37] It is because of this that George Lindbeck argues that language and symbol make it possible to feel and experience. For him, it is in relation to these reference points that feeling and experience can in fact be mapped.[38] The point we have to recognize then is that to say experience is *primary* in theological method is, at the same time, to admit that experience is always an interpreted reality rather than something which is immediate or self-evident. It is always enmeshed in a complex array of cultural conceptual tools, symbols and discourses.

In addition to this, Schleiermacher's notion of a universal, generic, 'core' religious experience seems to overlook differences between religions and as such, difference between religious experiences. Again, Lindbeck comments: 'Adherents of different religions do not diversely thematize the same experience; rather they have different experiences.'[39] Thus, we must admit that although experience is primary, it is not an uninterpreted reality; experience is mediated and diverse and a contextual method must recognize this complexity.

Jesus as paradigmatic of human being Schleiermacher's method is also problematic because it seems to compromise the uniqueness of incarnation. Like most liberal protestants, Schleiermacher was more concerned with cultural relevance and human experience than with religious orthodoxy. Thus, tradition was only upheld if supported by experience and those things that were deemed irrelevant to the contemporary human situation were rejected. Hence, it is within this context that Schleiermacher frames his Christological perspective. Admittedly, Schleiermacher does not deny the significance of Christ but his significance is somewhat unconventional. Christ is the archetypal human, the perfectly enlightened man who achieved the fullness of humanity through his perfect God-consciousness. Redemption then does not so much refer to the specific historical event of the cross but is, instead, more symbolic. It constitutes the passing from God-forgetfulness to blessedness and thus connotes an internal, subjective transformation.

---

[37] See Francis Schüssler Fiorenza, *Foundational Theology: Jesus and the Church* (New York, 1984), p. 299.

[38] George Lindbeck, *The Nature of Doctrine: Religion and Theology in a Postliberal Age* (Louisville, Kentucky, 1984).

[39] Ibid., p. 40.

According to Schleiermacher Jesus is the *only* one who can redeem humanity's Godlessness because he is the *only* human in which consciousness of God dominates consciousness of the self. He is 'the only other in which there is an existence of God in the proper sense'.[40] Jesus' perfect apprehension of God, however, cannot be explained through reference to human history or as a product of natural human development because everyone within this context is tainted by sin.[41] Christ then is a 'miraculous fact' which speaks of a new implanting of God-consciousness of supernatural origin.[42] However, this is not to say that Christ establishes anything new in creation. Instead, Schleiermacher argues that Christ shows what has always been possible without sin and thus reveals the God-consciousness as created by God at the outset of creation. It is through sharing in Jesus' perfect God-consciousness (which is how Schleiermacher models redemption) that human nature has the ability to be free from sin. Thus, Schleiermacher insists that the domination of our God-consciousness by our self-consciousness and by sin is something that has been overcome by redemption, and so something that no longer presents an insurmountable problem.[43] He thus argues that the essence of redemption is that 'the God-consciousness already present in human nature, though feeble and repressed, becomes stimulated and made dominant by the entrance of the living influence of Christ'.[44] As a result, the individual 'attains a religious personality not his before'.[45]

Of course, this implies a *quantitative* as opposed to *qualitative* distinction between Jesus and other human beings and as such, is rightly criticized for presenting an overly low Christology.[46] Given that Christ is interpreted in an historical sense, as one perfectly conscious of God and only in this sense as God manifest in the world, Schleiermacher can only hope to present a partial (and therefore inadequate) trinitarian theology. Indeed, such a view of the Trinity fails to meet the criterion previously outlined in Chapter 2 since it fails to communicate the uniqueness and divinity of Christ sufficiently and risks compromising his status as a co-equal member of the Godhead. As Barth rightly argues, 'one cannot speak of God by speaking of man in a loud voice'.[47] If Christ is simply presented as being *more* divine than us then this relativizes his uniqueness. What we need then is to understand Christ beyond the historical context of the world and to understand God beyond the God-consciousness. Although Schleiermacher is right in stressing

---

40 Ibid., 94.2, p. 388.

41 Ibid., 89.4, p. 365.

42 Ibid., 93.3, p. 381.

43 See the point made by Edwin Chr. Van Driel on p. 261 of his article, 'Schleiermacher's Supralapsarian Christology', *Scottish Journal of Theology*, 60/3 (2007): 251–70.

44 Schleiermacher, *The Christian Faith*, 106.1, p. 476.

45 Ibid.

46 This point is made by Kevin W. Hector on p. 308 of his article, 'Actualism and Incarnation: The High Christology of Friedrich Schleiermacher', *International Journal of Scottish Theology*, 8/3 (2006): 307–22.

47 Karl Barth, *The Word of God and the Word of Man* (New York, 1957), p. 196.

access to God through the God-consciousness and experience, the objective reality of God should still be maintained.

Of course, there are those who disagree with this critique. Mary Strufert,[48] for example, argues that Schleiermacher does not present an exemplary model of redemption but insists on the divinity of Jesus. According to her interpretation of Schleiermacher, Christ is divine because the effect of Christ is available to us in the present through the preached word. Christ does not remain external as a teacher or example but becomes internal and made known to us through the preaching of the word. Kevin Hector[49] is also clear that for Schleiermacher, Christ is distinct from humanity because in his life, he apprehends God's pure activity and perfectly reproduces it. This, he insists, is key since for Schleiermacher, God is pure act whereas humanity is made up of activity and passivity. Because Christ perfectly reproduces the activity of God in every moment, Schleiermacher, according to Hector, maintains that Jesus is God incarnate and distinct from humankind.

This certainly seems to be consistent with Schleiermacher's thought. In section 94.2 Schleiermacher asserts that Jesus is the only one in whom there is an existence of God in the truest sense. Here he argues that Jesus is the only one who portrays God purely and in whom the God-consciousness asserts itself as pure activity. Whereas the human God-consciousness is dominated by self-consciousness, Jesus' God-consciousness perfectly apprehends God's activity.[50] Despite this, however, it does seem to me that only a quantitative distinction can ever be upheld between Jesus Christ and the rest of humanity. As we have already noted, for Schleiermacher, Christ introduces a new element into the corporate life of human sinfulness through his perfect God-consciousness; a consciousness which is itself given by God. Christ enables humankind to share in his God-consciousness and thus enables humankind to continue the divine activity which was begun in him.[51] The problem here is that there is no clear ontological distinction between the being of Christ and that of other human beings. Human beings are able to be fully and perfectly conscious of God just like Jesus was. Although Jesus Christ may constitute the ground of incarnation being different from other human beings because he enables humankind to be conscious of God in the first place, it seems that humankind can now achieve the same degree of God-consciousness as him and thus become divine in this way. Because of this, his depiction of the divinity and uniqueness of Christ is not strong enough. Again, this may be symptomatic of a method which focuses too much on experience, for in this context, it is not

---

48 Mary J. Streufert, 'Reclaiming Schleiermacher for Twenty-first Century Atonement Theory: The Human and the Divine in Feminist Christology', *Feminist Theology*, 15/1 (2006): 98–120.

49 Kevin W. Hector, 'Actualism and Incarnation: The High Christology of Friedrich Schleiermacher', *International Journal of Scottish Theology*, 8/3 (2006): 307–22.

50 Schleiermacher, *The Christian Faith*, 94.1, pp. 387–8.

51 Van Driel, 'Schleiermacher's Supralapsarian Christology', p. 261.

surprising that Schleiermacher's understanding of Christ is in danger of reducing Christ to the historical Jesus and is rather ambiguous.

In response to these difficulties then, I propose we supplement such a contextual starting point with a reaffirmation of the objective reality of God and a reaffirmation of the uniqueness of Jesus as the Word made flesh. Insofar as these measures align with Christian orthodoxy as it has been outlined at Nicaea and Chalcedon, they form part of what I call an 'orthodox' theological method. If up until now we have argued for the contextual nature of all theology, what this next section seeks to do is to argue for the priority of God in revelation. Although we only know God through experience and through context, this does ultimately demand that God reveal Godself as Godself in the world in the first place. Hence, whilst we might refer to experience as the logical starting point of theological method, it is the priority of God as Trinity which constitutes the ontological starting point.

Towards an 'Orthodox' Theological Method

A concern for orthodoxy here does not feature as a naive adoption of the claims of Nicaea and Chalcedon. It is certainly not that such yardsticks provide direct access to the nature of God as this would contradict what we have just argued previously. This section does, however, begin from the conviction that the affirmations of faith articulated through the Apostles' Creed, the Nicene-Constantinopolitan Creed and in the Chalcedonian definition do say *something* meaningful about what God is like. Although based on experience and interpretation, the theology provided here which is derived from a reflection on the presence and activity of God in the world as testified to in the Bible and as witnessed to through the life of faith, does say something, although indirect and partial, about God. Thus, I affirm in keeping with the Nicene-Chalcedonian formulation that Jesus Christ is fully God and with Nicaea that Father, Son and Holy Spirit are *all* equally God and that God exists in Godself as Trinity. What this *really* means is, however, unobtainable due to the incomprehensibility of God and the limitations experience places on epistemology.

This, then, is a 'generous orthodoxy'[52] because it remains open to the voice of the other and so does not claim to know God fully, directly or universally. It has a modest view of theological knowledge whilst respecting the claims of Nicaea and Chalcedon. Indeed, it recognizes that orthodoxy did not develop in a vacuum nor as the result of a disembodied process. Orthodoxy was framed by men in a patriarchal setting and so there is a need to approach its claims with a hermeneutics of suspicion. A generous orthodoxy, however, does acknowledge

[52] Taken from Hans Frei, *Theology and Narrative*, ed. George Hunsinger and William Packer (New York, 1993), p. 208. For a different account of how feminist theology might relate to 'orthodoxy' and a 'generous orthodoxy' in particular see Kathryn Greene-McCreight, 'Feminist Theology and a Generous Orthodoxy', *Scottish Journal of Theology*, 57/1 (2004): 95–108.

that Nicaea and Chalcedon say *something* meaningful about God despite these limitations – that God is Trinity, that God is creator, saviour and sanctifier, that Jesus is fully God and fully human and the Holy Spirit is co-equal to Father and Son. Indeed, such claims are presented here as important features of the Christian confession of faith.

Informing a contextual theological method with these broad brush strokes of Christian orthodoxy means that God cannot be easily confined to experience as is the danger with Schleiermacher. God objectively exists and is not reducible to what is mediated through experience. Although context and experience cannot be escaped and necessarily limit what we can know of God, this does not mean that God is something different to what God reveals in the world. The immanent Trinity is the economic Trinity and there is no God behind the God revealed in salvation history, however what is revealed in the world does not allow us direct, immediate access into the being of God because it is a revelation which is always *interpreted.* The self-communication of God does not take place in a bubble nor does it meet us in the abstract. Who God is in the world is itself mediated through experience, so we always approach revelation from this starting point.

In order to further develop what it means to insist on the priority of God in revelation, I turn now to a brief discussion of Karl Barth. Barth is useful because he proposes a stress on God, rather than experience, as the starting point for theology. Indeed, Barth proposes that a central difficulty with Schleiermacher's theology concerns his anthropocentric starting point, a problem we have already discussed. According to Barth, this simply amounts to a sort of 'theological arrogance' in which the believer views themselves fit to apprehend God autonomously.[53] As such, Barth provides an important corrective to Schleiermacher's overly anthropocentric theological method.

Karl Barth

Whereas Schleiermacher places religious feeling at the very centre of his methodology, Barth insists that knowledge of God is unobtainable outside divine intervention. Barth is critical of the modernist, liberal agenda because he sees in it the attempt to build up a prolegomena on general anthropological grounds as opposed to on Christological ones. He argues that God reveals Godself through the Word and as such cannot be known outside of this. What we know of God we only know because of God's decision to reveal Godself through Christ. Hence for Barth, 'Revelation takes place vertically from heaven.'[54] Faith does not constitute human religious experience but is determined by God.[55] As sinful human beings, we are completely unable to speak the Word of God ourselves.[56]

---

[53] Stephen Sykes, *The Identity of Christianity: Theologians and the Essence of Christianity from Schleiermacher to Barth* (London, 1984), p. 181.

[54] Barth, *Church Dogmatics*, I/1, pp. 378–9.

[55] Ibid., p. 281.

[56] Ibid., p. 160.

To speak about the Word of God is, for Barth, to speak about an event, an act of God which rests on God's free decision to reveal Godself as Godself. As such, it constitutes the language of God to humanity and the means by which God communicates Godself to the world.[57] For Barth, God's Word is never available in a straightforward way. It is not a deposit of truth or a set of statements which can be consulted; it is as an event which connotes that God has spoken, speaks and will speak.[58]

For Barth, God's Word takes on a three-fold form, as Church proclamation, Holy Scripture and revelation itself,[59] or put another way, as the preached Word, the written Word and the revealed Word.[60] The preached Word refers to the proclamation of the Church. As realities of revelation, Barth states that proclamation and the Church have come into existence and have only done so through the Word of God (that is Christ), for if God did not reveal Christ in the world then there would be nothing to proclaim.[61] He therefore argues that if the proclamation of the church is a true reality of revelation then the Word of God, that is Christ, will be its commission,[62] object,[63] judgement,[64] and will constitute the event itself.[65] As such, he claims that the preaching of the Word of God communicates the actual grace of God, for it is only through God's free decision to reveal Godself through human language that the words of people (human speech-acts) *become* the Word of God (the divine speech-act).[66]

The proclaimed Word of God, however, is a realized proclamation 'on the basis that God's word has already been spoken, that revelation has already taken place'.[67] What this means is that proclamation points back to the biblical proclamation. The church has not the confidence to appeal to herself as the divine Word.[68] Scripture tells us what God's past revelation actually is and therefore constitutes the concrete form of proclamation.[69] It gives the church 'her marching orders'[70] and is thus the means by which she can claim authority. For Barth then, scripture may be described

---

57 Ibid., p. 150.

58 John Webster, *Karl Barth*, second edn (London, New York, 2004), p. 55.

59 Barth, *Church Dogmatics*, I/1, pp. 149–50.

60 For a full detailed account of what Barth means by each of these see Barth, *Church Dogmatics*, I/1, pp. 98–135.

61 Ibid., pp. 98–9.

62 Ibid., pp. 99–101.

63 Ibid., pp. 101–3.

64 Ibid., pp. 103–4

65 See Ibid., pp. 104–11.

66 Ibid., p. 106. Also see Thomas F. Torrance, *Karl Barth: Biblical and Evangelical Theologian* (Edinburgh, 1990), p. 89.

67 Barth, *Church Dogmatics*, I/1, p. 111.

68 Ibid., p. 112.

69 Ibid., pp. 113–14.

70 Ibid., p. 114.

as the beginning of the revelatory event whereas church proclamation, on the other hand, constitutes the continuation of it in the world. Both stand alongside one another with scripture always occupying the upper hand.[71]

The revealed Word of God, however, stands out from the previous two forms. Whereas proclamation and the Bible are the Word of God derivatively and indirectly, revelation itself is the Word of God originally and directly.[72] The revealed Word of God (revelation itself) refers to the freedom of God's grace; to God's free decision to reveal Godself as Godself. This freedom, however, does not connote an abstract principle but an act or event; it refers to 'the event in which God, being free, allows his free grace scope to operate'.[73] As such, it cannot be separated from Christ as the Word-made-flesh. Indeed, Barth argues that 'To say revelation is to say "the Word became flesh."'[74] Jesus is the divine act itself and thus constitutes the limit and ground of what can be said of the Bible and proclamation.[75] As such, revelation is defined as the unveiling of the veiled God in the person of Jesus Christ.[76]

One of Barth's main strengths here is that he potentially allows for a contextual reading of revelation. Through his insistence that the Word of God is not communicated directly and straightforwardly and that both the Bible and Proclamation point beyond themselves to an 'other' which is the Word of God directly, he undermines any attempt to identify either the written Word or the preached Word with the being of God directly. This reinforces Barth's view that God cannot be known in God's primary objectivity – in Godself. Instead, God is known in God's secondary objectivity, as God is revealed to the human knower. This said, however, it is still the case that for Barth, revelation depends on the Lordship of God, on God choosing to reveal Godself as Godself and, thus, demands the priority of God's free decision and a response of passive acceptance, obedience and faith on the part of humanity. The extent to which this allows for a genuinely contextual theological method then is debateable and is something we will consider in more detail later.

Barth also, however, establishes a rather attractive Christological centre within his methodology. This grounds theology in particularity and identifies that the God revealed in Christ (the incarnate Word) is not something separate from God in Godself, echoing the view of the economic and immanent Trinity proposed in Chapter 2. Again, this potentially allows for a contextual starting point in theological method and is, therefore, to be commended. Such a strength is seen particularly in Barth's understanding of the Creator-creature relationship.

---

71 Ibid., pp. 114–15.

72 Ibid., p. 131.

73 Ibid., p. 132.

74 Ibid., p. 134.

75 Ibid., p. 132.

76 Ibid., pp. 133–4.

The Creator-Creature Relationship and the Particularity of Christ

The relationship between God and humanity is considered at some length by Barth in his *Church Dogmatics* and in *The Humanity of God.* After developing his view somewhat, Barth contends that Christ, as revelation itself, reveals God's free decision to turn towards humanity, thus revealing a God who chooses relationship with the world.[77] This, however, does not mean that God can be, or should be, reduced to the world or to God's relationship with humanity. In fact, he clearly rejects the anthropocentric starting point of Schleiermacher stating that God must transcend the Christian religious self-consciousness.[78] Thus, in his earlier work, he strongly argues that the deity of God primarily means that God is wholly other. He refers to what he calls an 'infinite qualitative distinction' between God and humanity,[79] that is a distinction in *kind* rather than simply degree, positing God as perfect and humanity as totally sinful. Consequently, Barth argues that it is only through God's choice to turn towards humanity in the person of Jesus Christ that relationship with God is possible in the first place. God alone initiates the relationship and so remains sovereign because of this.[80]

However, we must not misunderstand Barth here. He is not saying that humanity and God are totally opposed but that humanity is able to be open to God precisely because God is first open to humanity.[81] Indeed, Barth argues that it is integral to human 'being' (ontology) to be open to God; because Jesus, the Word of God is both creature and God then the 'essence of all the minimal requirements for a view and concept of real man is that man cannot be seen or understood apart from God';[82] the nature of the human is communal being.[83] This openness towards God is, thus, according to Barth, first established by God in Christ and then practiced freely by humankind through a life of gratitude and faith.[84]

For Barth then, God's deity includes his decision to be for and not against humanity, with as opposed to without humanity: God's deity includes God's humanity because God remains God despite God's bending down to meet

[77] Ibid., pp. 158–9.

[78] Karl Barth, *The Humanity of God* (London, 1961), p. 40.

[79] Ibid., p. 42.

[80] Ibid., p. 45.

[81] For more on this see Kenneth Oakes' article, 'The Question of Nature and Grace in Karl Barth: Humanity as Creature and as Covenant Partner', *Modern Theology*, 23/4 (2007): 595–616.

[82] Karl Barth, *Church Dogmatics*, III/2, The Doctrine of Creation, ed. G.W. Bromiley and T.F. Torrance, trans. H. Knight, G.W. Bromiley, J.K.S. Reid. R.H. Fuller (Edinburgh, 1960), p. 72.

[83] See p. 33 of John Yocum's article, 'What's Interesting about Karl Barth? Barth as Polemical and Descriptive Theologian', *International Journal of Systematic Theology*, 4/1 (2002): 29–44.

[84] See Oakes, 'The Question of Nature and Grace', p. 606.

humankind in the person of Jesus Christ.[85] Barth argues that Christ reveals God both in a state of humiliation – as true God becoming true man, taking on human suffering and the sin of the world, and in a state of exaltation – as true man raised up as true God.[86] In other words, Christ reveals that this is the kind of God God decides to be; if Jesus as God is for humankind then openness towards humankind must be integral to the being of God.

According to Barth then, Jesus is both humanity's partner and God's. God elects to be God known in and as Jesus Christ and also elects humanity through the incarnation of the Word. Jesus is, thus, the electing God and the elect human. That God chooses to become known through the particular man of Jesus not only signals God's self-election but also an eternal and unbreakable covenant between God and humanity.[87] It proclaims that the doctrine of God must have humanity as part of its content because God has elected to be 'God for us' through the particularity of Christ.[88]

Such an emphasis on Christ as the particular focal point of revelation means, again, that Barth's methodology has quite an attractive Christological centre. Indeed, his emphasis on the particularity of Christ is one of Barth's most important and commendable contributions to debate surrounding theological method. He affirms that 'theology can think and speak only as it looks at Jesus Christ and from the vantage point of what He is'[89] and thus rejects any attempts to speak about God from a position of abstraction or speculation (something he considers philosophical enquiry to be guilty of). Revelation cannot be separate from particularity.[90] This clearly aligns with my own concern to uphold the particularity of the historical reality of Jesus as *the* Word-made-flesh and the place of humanity in the doctrine of God.

The difficulty with Barth's view of revelation, however, is that such a perspective may run the risk of depicting revelation as flowing in a one-way direction from God to humanity, and as such undermines the possibility of natural theology.[91] Indeed, Barth is clear that knowledge of God is only obtained through Christ's

---

85 Barth, *The Humanity of God*, p. 46.

86 Ibid.

87 See Yocum, 'What's Interesting about Karl Barth?', p. 33.

88 Karl Barth, *Church Dogmatics*, II/2, The Doctrine of God, ed. G.W. Bromiley and T.F. Torrance, trans. T.H.L. Parker, W.B. Johnston, Harold Knight and J.L.M. Haire (Edinburgh, 1957), p. 509.

89 Barth, The Humanity of God, p. 55.

90 Also see Webster, p. 76.

91 According to Barth as presented in the Gifford Lectures of 1938, humankind does not have the capacity to know God by itself. Human reason is incapacitated by sin to the extent that humankind only knows God because of divine grace. Also see Roger Gustavsson's discussion of Barth and natural theology in his article, 'Hauerwas's W*ith The Grain of the Universe* and The Barthian Outlook', *Journal of Religious Ethics*, 35/1 (2007): 25–86 and Trevor Hart's comments in his essay 'Revelation' in John Webster (ed.), *The Cambridge Companion to Karl Barth* (Cambridge, 2000), pp. 37–56.

mediation (that is through the Word), not through a generic human consciousness of God as in the case of Schleiermacher. Revelation starts and ends with Christ, not with human activity. What then of the role of humanity as *active* agents in the process of revelation?

We will deal with this criticism in more detail later however there are two points to note at this stage. First, that humanity are not *de facto* passive. Barth clearly argues that humankind are capable of spontaneous movement towards God (of what Barth calls 'readiness'),[92] however he is also clear that this rests on God's prior openness towards humankind (therefore on the readiness of God).[93] Humanity's readiness comprises their capacity for obedience and gratitude in response to the gift of Christ given in God's self-revelation; God's readiness comprises God's free giving of Godself as the source of revelation. Barth's point then is not that humanity are not free but that humanity's activity depends on their receptivity of God's self-revelation; that humanity's capacity begins not with human self-consciousness but with the 'act' of God in Christ.[94]

As a result, and this is the second point I wish to make, it is fair to say that Barth tends to underplay the *active* role of humanity in receiving and interpreting revelation and the effects of human context on determining the meaning of revelation. For Barth 'Christian faith and speech are essentially *response* and not essentially *source*.'[95] The implication is that revelation is *addressed* to humankind (even if this takes place within the context of particularity) rather than being a process in which humankind actively play a part as constructors of meaning.

Revelation as Trinity

What then of the place of the Trinity within Barth's theological method? To answer this, let us first consider Barth's understanding of the Trinity in more detail. For Barth, the answer to the question 'what does God do in revelation?' is threefold: God reveals Godself as Godself in the person of Jesus Christ and continues to do so through the impartation of the Holy Spirit. That God freely chooses to reveal Godself as God *really* is, according to Barth, points towards the Lordship of God.[96] Hence he argues that Father, Son and Holy Spirit are all equally Lord. Yet Barth is clear that this does not signal three Lords. There is only one Lordship, and this takes on a threefold form as Revealer, Revelation and Revealedness.

The oneness of God then is of the utmost importance in Barth's trinitarianism. Reference to God's revelation as a single act which takes on a threefold form

---

92 Barth, *Church Dogmatics*, II/1, The Doctrine of God, ed. G.W. Bromiley and T.F. Torrance, trans. T.H.L. Parker, W.B. Johnston, Harold Knight and J.L.M. Haire (Edinburgh, 1957), p. 65.

93 Ibid.

94 See Webster, p. 80.

95 See Hart, 'Revelation', p. 41, emphasis mine.

96 Barth, *Church Dogmatics*, I/1, p. 353.

demonstrates Barth's concern to remain faithful to the orthodox statement that God is one. There cannot be three objects of faith otherwise there would be three gods.[97] The peculiarities of the three are distinguished in terms of their relations of origin: the Father is Begetter, the Son the Begotten and the Spirit the one who brings forth. The Father is the veiled, hidden Revealer God, the Son the Revelation and the manifestation of what was previously hidden and the Spirit the Impartation and meaning of the revelation itself.[98] This leads Barth to assert that, 'The name of Father, Son and Spirit means that God is the one God in a threefold repetition.'[99] God is one in 'three "modes of being"'.[100]

Barth has, however, been charged with having modalist tendencies here, upholding the oneness of God at the expense of God's threeness. To be sure, Barth is keen to avoid tritheism and his insistence on the language of 'mode of being' rather than 'person' reflects this desire. To say that God constitutes three 'modes of being', he maintains, affirms that there is only one divine 'I'[101] and that this 'I' appears in three distinct modes. The charge is that such a view underplays the three-personal nature of God and fails to take sufficient account of difference within the being of God. Such a criticism, however, is on one level, questionable. Barth presents the language of 'mode of being', not as a corrective to the orthodox, traditional meaning of 'person' but because he is worried about the meaning this word carries within a modern context. He is clear that there are not three autonomous and separate subjects within God, hence he presents the notion of 'mode of being' in the hope that this will better communicate the meaning of the original language.[102] He is not trying to say that God is more one than three as this would undermine the original meaning of the language of person.

On the other hand, however, there is no denying that speaking of the three *hypostases* as three 'modes of being' does, nevertheless, imply a modalist understanding of the Trinity. Even if Barth's theology denies this claim, his choice of language has the unfortunate implication of suggesting it. Just as the traditional language of 'person' may be interpreted in a tritheist way which was unintended by those who formulated the Nicene Creed, so the language of 'mode of being' may be interpreted in modalist ways unintended by Barth.

What then can we say about the place Barth ascribes to the Trinity within his theological method? Whereas Schleiermacher places the Trinity at the end of his methodology, Barth places it at the start within the prolegomena of his *Church Dogmatics*. Such a privileged position is secured through Barth's two-tiered understanding of revelation. On the one hand he agrees with Schleiermacher,

---

97 Ibid., p. 401.

98 Ibid., p. 417.

99 Ibid., p. 402.

100 Ibid., p. 407.

101 Ibid., p. 403.

102 For more on this see Iain Taylor's article, 'In Defence of Karl Barth's Doctrine of the Trinity', *International Journal of Systematic Theology*, 5/1 (2003): 33–46.

suggesting that the doctrine of the Trinity is constituted as a doctrine of the church and is therefore reflection on revelation as opposed to being revelation itself; however, on the other he forcefully argues that to speak of revelation is to speak of Father, Son and Holy Spirit and, thus, to speak about the being of God.

Trinity as reflection on revelation and as revelation itself In his discussion of the Trinity in the *Church Dogmatics*, Barth says that 'the Trinity of God cannot claim to be directly identical with the statement about revelation, or with revelation itself'.[103] The statement about revelation refers to the claim that God reveals Godself as Lord, indicating that God freely chooses to reveal Godself as Godself. What Barth is saying here then is that the doctrine of the Trinity is not directly identical to the being of God. To say Trinity is not exactly the same as to say revelation. Hence Barth maintains that:

> The doctrine of the Trinity is an analysis of this statement, i.e. of what it designates. The doctrine of the Trinity is a work of the Church, a document of how she regards that statement, or its object, a document of how she knows God …, only indirectly, a document of revelation itself.[104]

According to Barth then the doctrine of the Trinity constitutes *reflection* on revelation and as such, follows logically after it. Biblical material, he maintains, requires that we firstly ask *who* the God is who reveals Godself as Godself through the Word.[105] For Barth it is only through reflection on this question that the doctrine of the Trinity comes about,[106] for to say that God reveals Godself as Lord is to say that God freely chooses to reveal Godself through the person of Jesus Christ and to affect the world through the Holy Spirit. Hence he classifies the Trinity primarily as 'theologoumenon'; as dogma, and to this extent as a formulation of the church.[107]

However, Barth does not stop here. Concerned to stress the centrality and priority of the Trinity within theological method he states that this doctrine nevertheless constitutes the starting point of all dogmatics. This is so, Barth claims, because reflection on revelation actually leads to the realization that the God who reveals Godself as Godself is in fact the trinitarian God. Thus, revelation and the Trinity are indirectly identical; God *is* Trinity and this *is* what revelation reveals.

At the beginning of his section on the triune God, Barth boldly asserts, 'God reveals Himself as the Lord and that according to Scripture signifies for the concept of revelation that God Himself in unimpaired unity yet also in unimpaired

103 Barth, *Church Dogmatics*, I/1, p. 353.

104 Ibid., p. 354.

105 Ibid., p. 341.

106 Ibid., pp. 353–7.

107 Ibid., p. 431.

difference is Revealer, Revelation, and Revealedness.'[108] Thus, at the very outset of his discussion in the *Church Dogmatics*, Barth claims that to say God reveals Godself as Lord is to say that God in Godself is triune.[109] This however is not to contradict his previous view that the doctrine of the Trinity is derivative, for the doctrine is secondary in the sense that it is only realized through reflection on revelation. However, Barth furthers this by saying that revelation necessarily reveals God as ontologically both the Revealer, event and effect of revelation,[110] and thus as a trinitarian God. Because God's revelation cannot be separated from the form it takes and the content disclosed, revelation cannot be separated from the Trinity. For Barth, God is what God reveals and how God affects the world. The biblically directed question of *who* is revealed by this self-revealing God contains its own answer: Godself. The two related questions of 'what is revealed' and 'what does this effect'[111] are also answered in the same way: what is revealed is Godself and it is Godself who affects the world. Thus, according to Barth, Godself cannot be separated from God's self-revelation in Jesus or from what God creates, affects and achieves in humanity through the power of the Holy Spirit.[112] To say God, is to say Trinity.

Assessing the Contribution of Orthodoxy in Theological Method

Barth then is notably different to Schleiermacher in the sense that he insists on the Trinity as the ontological grounds of all dogmatics. Although Schleiermacher does suggest that God is the source of the God-consciousness, at least in theory affirming the objective reality of God apart from the God-consciousness, Barth makes a much stronger case for the objective reality of God and certainly for the ontological priority of the Trinity in his theological method. Indeed, he states that to relegate the Trinity to a later stage in theological method means that it runs the danger of lapsing into speculation.[113] For Barth, because revelation begs us to ask *who* is revealed and this necessarily demands a trinitarian answer, the Trinity must come ontologically first. Although for Schleiermacher the Trinity amounts to more than just speculation, it is true that he fails to establish the Trinity as the source of the God-consciousness. For him, the Trinity always remains second order and this is where Barth's methodology is stronger and, therefore, preferable.

To be sure, Barth succeeds in establishing both the centrality of Christ as the revealed Word and the centrality of the Trinity in theological method. Christ is not only quantitatively different (therefore different in degree) from humankind

[108] Ibid., p. 339.

[109] Ibid., p. 251.

[110] Ibid., p. 343.

[111] Ibid., p. 341.

[112] Ibid., p. 343.

[113] Ibid., p. 346.

– a charge previously levelled at Schleiermacher, but also qualitatively different (therefore different in kind). Based on his understanding of analogy, Barth argues that the move from Christology to anthropology must be an indirect one. Jesus, although like humankind, is also unlike humankind: 'between the man Jesus and ourselves as men there stands not only the mystery of our sin, but primarily and decisively the mystery of His identity with God'.[114] Christ's relationship to God is ontologically different from our own and this always remains the case. To this extent his methodology upholds an orthodox understanding of the person of Christ and also retains an orthodox understanding of God as ontologically triune (outcomes Schleiermacher struggles to achieve). These are commendable features reflecting the trinitarian thesis presented in the previous chapter in which God is seen to be Trinity *ad intra* as well as *ad extra*. Yet there are problems with Barth's theological methodology and these are symptomatic of an 'orthodox' theological method which seeks to establish the priority of God as its ontological starting point.

The role of interpretation Although Barth insists that God's threefold self-communication as Revealer, Revealed and Revealedness in the economy of salvation exposes God in Godself as Trinity, thus affirming no meaningful distinction between the economic and immanent Trinity, he does seem to simultaneously overlook the role of interpretation and mediation in the process of revelation. Whilst I have argued in Chapter 2 that God's trinitarian communication in the economy of salvation (God *ad extra*) cannot be separated form the trinitarian God in Godself (God *ad intra*), this is not to say that revelation in the economy of salvation is immediate or that we can claim direct access to the being of God. Certainly we can maintain that it *is* the triune God who is made known in the world but *we* only know this God through our own interpretation of what has been revealed – in other words, we cannot bypass our own context as receivers of revelation. Revelation thus connotes a blending together of context and God's self communication in the world to the extent that the latter is never known by the recipient outside the setting of the former. The theological enterprise always involves a limitation on our part because we cannot 'see' God except through the lens of our own interpretation and experience.

This, however, does not mean that we say with the likes of Sallie McFague that we cannot speculate about a really existing God. Instead we must recognize that God has made Godself known and therefore that some degree of knowledge is possible. That knowledge is, however, tentative, partial and mediated because it is derivative and inductive. Context does provide a gateway into knowledge of God and this knowledge does correspond to a God who is *real* but we only know in part. What *we* interpret on the basis of what God has revealed is not identical to who God is in Godself, but this does not in anyway deny that God is who God is in revelation. We can still say that God *is* Trinity because we maintain a

[114] Barth, *Church Dogmatics*, III/2, p. 71.

correspondence between what God communicates and what we know, however, such knowledge is based on interpretation. Postulating the triune God then as the ontological ground of all theological knowledge is more than mere speculation because God has revealed Godself in the world. It is, however, still a claim which is based on interpretation.

Revelation then is best understood as a process since it always assumes a recipient and so always involves interpretation. Barth's theological method falls down because revelation is assumed to connote the direct and uncomplicated transfer of communication from the mind of God directly to the mind of human beings.[115] Humanity receives what God reveals but that God is known through the world does not affect what is being revealed. As such, Barth misses the significant role played by humanity in hearing, receiving and understanding revelation. David Cunningham, for example, understandably retorts that Barth reduces humankind to a passive audience 'who can only "watch" as the mystery of God is unveiled'.[116] For him, revelation is always revealed to someone and so requires active reception on the part of the recipient. 'Revelation', he says, 'cannot bypass the human will as though it were medicine injected with a syringe.'[117]

The logos asarkos and the Logos ensarkos A further difficulty with Barth's theological method is his understanding of the notion of election. If Jesus as the Subject and Object of election shows that God is the kind of God who is for human beings then what are we to say about the relationship between divine 'act' and 'being'? Does God's free act of self-revelation in Christ determine the being of God or does the being of God give rise to the act of God in Christ? The problem is that if the latter is true, then this implies a pre-established essence which is simply demonstrated by the incarnation. If the former is true then this may collapse the being of God into salvation history and the *Logos asarkos* (the Logos 'without the flesh') into the *Logos ensarkos* (the Logos 'within the flesh').

This has been a scenario much debated within recent discussion. Bruce McCormack, for example, strongly maintains that Barth's mature understanding of Christ as the Subject (rather than just Object) of election means that his former insistence that the internal life of the Trinity (God *ad intra*) precedes the act of God in Christ (God *ad extra*) can no longer be maintained. For McCormack, Barth's Christology, specifically his understanding of election, means that God's 'being' must be constituted by God's 'act'. Hence, it is not that God's triune being determines God's act as then the incarnation becomes a mere function or role that God performs and something which simply affirms God's pre-determined being.

---

[115] Paul D. Janz makes this point on p. 323 of his article, 'Divine Causality and the Nature of Theological Questioning', *Modern Theology* 23/3 (July 2007): 317–48.

[116] David Cunningham, *These Three are One: The Practice of Trinitarian Theology* (Malden, Massachusetts and Oxford, 1998), p. 100.

[117] Ibid., p. 101.

Instead, it is election and incarnation that determine God's being.[118] Because of this, McCormack maintains that there can be no straightforward distinction between the immanent and economic Trinity or between the *Logos asarkos* and the *Logos ensarkos*. If the starting point for understanding the being of God is not speculation but is the particular act of God in Christ, then we must say, according to McCormack, that God's taking on flesh informs the being of God.[119]

Others such as Paul Molnar, George Hunsinger and Edwin Chr. Van Driel have opposed this reading of Barth.[120] For van Driel, for example, positioning divine election as constitutive of divine being presents creation as also essential to divine being and compromises divine freedom. He therefore disagrees with McCormack, insisting that 'for Barth, the incarnation does not constitute the divine being, but the divine being constitutes the incarnation. Incarnation is possible because of the kind of being God is'.[121] George Hunsinger reflects this position arguing that for Barth, the Trinity is ontologically prior to the act of election. 'Election', he says, 'is an act of the Holy Trinity in which God determines himself *ad intra* for the sake of his saving work *ad extra.*'[122] Hunsinger provides a compelling reading of Barth engaging with key passages which endorse this view and critiquing the interpretation of others which have been used to suggest that Barth changes his mind about the ontological priority of the Trinity.

Determining what Barth *really* thought, however, is difficult. On the one hand he seems to suggest that the act of incarnation carries ontological significance for who God is in Godself and this seems to be evidenced by Barth's understanding of the humanity of God and the essence of human being, both of which I have discussed already. It also seems that for Barth, God's being *for* the world is manifested in Christ as both the subject and object of election. However, Barth is also very clear that the Trinity is primary and this is hard to ignore. In CD IV/2 for example, Barth clearly argues that election presupposes Trinity:

> The triune life of God, which is free life in the fact that it is Spirit, is the basis of His whole will and action even *ad extra*, as the living act which He directs to

---

118 See Bruce McCormack's pivotal 'Grace and Being: The Role of God's Gracious Elements in Karl Barth's Theological Ontology', in John Webster (ed.), *The Cambridge Companion to Karl Barth* (Cambridge, 2000), pp. 92–110. Also see his more recent article 'Seek God Where He May be Found: A Response to Edwin Chr. Van Driel', *Scottish Journal of Theology*, 60/1 (2007): 62– 79.

119 McCormack, 'Grace and Being', pp. 93–5.

120 See Paul Molnar's *Divine Freedom and the Doctrine of the Immanent Trinity: A Dialogue with Karl Barth and Cotemporary Theology* (London, New York, 2002), George Hunsinger's, 'Election and the Trinity: Twenty-five theses on the Theology of Karl Barth', *Modern Theology,* 24/2 (2008): 179–98, and Edwin Chr. Van Driel's article 'Karl Barth on the Eternal Existence of Jesus Christ', *Scottish Journal of Theology*, 60/1 (2007): 45–61.

121 Van Driel, 'Karl Barth', p. 52.

122 Hunsinger, 'Election and the Trinity', p. 181.

> us. It is the basis of His *decretum et opus ad extra*, of the relationship which He has determined and established with a reality which is distinct from Himself and endowed by Him with its own very different and creaturely being. It is the basis of the election of man to covenant with Himself, of the determination of the Son to become man, and therefore to fulfil the covenant.[123]

When Barth says this, however, he is not insisting that God in Godself is something separate from God in relation to the world since maintaining a connection between the immanent and economic Trinity seems paramount to Barth. Barth, in my opinion, is not changing his mind about the priority of God's triune being when he insists on the priority of humanity's election in and through the person of Jesus Christ. For Barth, it is more a case of 'being' and 'act' existing *alongside* one another, *simultaneously*. As Alan Torrance notes, 'it is fundamentally incompatible with Barth's trinitarian/ecclesial approach to consider God's being in isolation from God's *being with* humanity as the incarnate Son/Word and the Holy Spirit.'[124] In other words, in one very important sense, Barth does not see this as a 'chicken-or-egg' scenario. It is not that being predates act – that God is Trinity *and then* decides to be incarnate – since God's decision to elect humanity through Christ is an *eternal* decision. Barth does, however, insist that in order for God to be free, God must be God whether or not God decides to be incarnate in the world, hence he says, '… nothing would be lacking in His inward being as God in glory, as the Father, Son and Holy Spirit, as the One who loves in freedom, if He did not show Himself to the world.'[125] It seems then that what is paramount for Barth here is upholding the freedom of God. God did not *need* to elect humanity; however, God freely chooses to be the electing God and to be with as opposed to without humankind.

However, this is problematic if we assume, as a result, that talk of God in Godself without the incarnate Christ and without relation to the world can take place and is in fact meaningful. If God has freely and eternally chosen to be *this* kind of God (that is an electing God), then it makes no sense to refer to the being of God without referring to the act of God in Christ. Thus, the self-revelation of God in the world reveals that humanity is taken into the being of God and that relation with the world is something God has chosen not to be without. Hence, although God could have been otherwise, it is not so, and because it is not so, it will never be so and never has been so. To speak about the eternal Trinity, then, in separation from election and thus, in separation from the *Logos ensarkos*, as though the triune God had not eternally decided to become God with us, is nonsensical. Election takes place within the eternal life of God.

---

[123] Karl Barth, *Church Dogmatics*, IV/2, The Doctrine of Reconciliation, ed. G.W. Bromiley and T.F. Torrance, trans. G.W. Bromiley (Edinburgh, 1958), p. 345.

[124] Alan Torrance's essay, 'Trinity', in John Webster (ed.), *The Cambridge Companion to Karl Barth* (Cambridge, 2000), pp. 72–91, esp. p. 74.

[125] Karl Barth, *Church Dogmatics*, IV/1, 'The Doctrine of Reconciliation', ed. G.W. Bromiley and T.F. Torrance, trans. G.W. Bromiley (Edinburgh, 1956), p. 213.

Indeed, such a reading is helpful for my own methodology since it coheres well with the understanding of incarnation and Trinity previously articulated in the opening two chapters. It suggests that we see the *Logos ensarkos* as internal to the trinitarian being of God. God *is* the *Logos ensarkos*, hence there can be no God behind the God of salvation history. However, the incarnate Christ does not reveal a God who is reducible to or fathomable by the world but a God who always remains incomprehensible and ineffable. In other words, that God *is* the *Logos ensarkos* means that the world cannot be separated from God, but God still remains ineffable since it is the ineffable God who is revealed through the incarnate Christ.

Towards an Orthodox-Contextual Theological Method

What then does it mean to propose an orthodox-contextual approach to the doing of theology? To begin with, such an approach can be defined as one which takes context and experience seriously and identifies this as the logical starting point of theological enquiry. We start with human interpretation rather than with direct knowledge of the being of God. Although the priority of God as triune can and must be upheld as the *ontological* starting point of theology (that is to say theology rests on the ontological grounds that God in God's freedom has decided to reveal Godself as Godself in human history), at a logical and practical level, theology always begins with experience; from who *we* are rather than from who *God* is. This is a key point. Although the latter ontologically precedes the former (because the fulfilment of our human 'being' is found in communion with the triune God who *chooses* to be our partner), we only know the latter through the former (because we can never know God outside of human experience or outside of context). Thus, theology begins with experience, not because God can or should be reduced to this, but because there is no where else to begin. To insist on the Bible as the starting point of theological method, for example, is not to say something different. This also means to start with experience since we start with the experiences of those recorded in the text and with the ways in which these have been interpreted in the past and are interpreted from our own contexts today.

Such an understanding of theological method allies with the postmodern acknowledgement that reality in itself (what Kant refers to as the 'noumenal' world) can never be known or accessed directly. Lyotard, for example, maintains (in keeping with Wittgenstein) that meaning is located within the context of different 'language games' and is, thus, without a unifying discourse.[126] He is clear that postmodernism signals the end of grand narratives; a disbelief and scepticism of totalising, unifying theories which claim to see the world as it *really* is. There is no unifying view of knowledge or of reality. Seen in these terms, revelation is no

[126] Jean-François Lyotard, *The Postmodern Condition: A Report on Knowledge* (Manchester, 1984), pp. xxiv and 10.

longer seen as unitary; it does not connote direct access to the being of God but God as experienced in the world. Revelation is always an interpreted, mediated reality.

Revelation as Mediation

An orthodox-contextual theological method, then, understands revelation as mediation. This means that context plays an *active* role in determining the nature of revelation. We do not simply receive revelation 'from above', we affect it 'from below'. Our reading of the Bible is affected by context and the Bible itself arises from context. In this sense, the word of God should not be viewed as an abstract or decontexualized word that simply 'addresses' or 'confronts' context; it is not simply a vertical word which filters from heaven, it is an *incarnate* word and as such, a word that cannot be separated from experience. In this sense, Pannenberg's criticism is timely:

> Theology has to learn that after Feuerbach it can no longer mouth the word 'God' without offering any explanation; that it can no longer speak as if the meaning of this word were self-evident; that it cannot pursue theology 'from above,' as Barth says, if it does not want to fall into the hopeless and, what is more, self-inflicted isolation of a higher glossolalia, and lead the whole church into this blind alley ....[127]

The meaning of revelation is not self-evident, yet, nor is it totally relative. As a mediated reality, we acknowledge that the 'content' of revelation cannot be separated from the vehicle (or 'form') through which knowledge is communicated. Mediation does not constitute a third entity which operates between God and human experience; the message is not something separate from the messenger. The task of theology then is not to *de*contextualize scripture by discovering what God has *really* said and then to *re*contextualize this so that it makes sense in the contemporary world.[128] Context *informs* theology rather than simply functioning as the vehicle through which particular truths are communicated.

However, context is not a fixed, objective, stable or self-evident reality in itself. To assert this is to be guilty of problems inherent within Schleiermacher's notion of religious 'feeling'. Context and experience always constitute complex, shifting, interpreted realities and are always, in the end, themselves mediated through language. Understanding revelation as mediation then means that it is impossible to access a fixed or stable (foundational) reality underneath context – to take leave of experience – but also that context itself cannot be seen as a self-evident, static reality. The vehicle of revelation becomes integral to revelation

---

127 Wolfhart Pannenberg, *Basic Questions in Theology: Collected Essays* (Philadelphia, 1970), pp. 189–90.

128 David F. Wells, 'The Nature and Function of Theology', in R.K. Johnston (ed.), *The Use of the Bible in Theology: Evangelical Options* (Atlanta, 1985), pp. 175–99.

itself, necessarily citing revelation as indivisible from its socio-linguistic context and echoing postmodern sensibilities that meaning cannot be separated from the 'text'. It is only God as experienced who is available for knowing directly and this is a complex and mediated experience rather than a self-evident one.

However, this is not a non-foundationalist, fideist rendering of theological knowledge. It is not that theology has no foundation since this has clearly been rejected through adopting the Barthian stance that theology relies on the ultimate priority of God's grace and, as such, the free decision of God to make Godself known in and through Christ and the church. In this sense, an orthodox-contextual method adopts a critical realist stance on the nature of knowledge and reality. There *is* an objective reality 'out there', there is such a thing as God in Godself and it is God in Godself who meets us in revelation, however this is a *critical* realism because the data we receive about this reality is always mediated, and is, therefore, always interpreted and never, therefore, direct. Knowledge of God as a mediated reality is complex and fallible; it is a contextual, embodied knowledge but a knowledge which, nevertheless, rests on the ontological priority of God's givenness in revelation and which is always in correspondence to this reality.[129] The Spirit of God makes God knowable enabling us to say something meaningful about God on the basis of what is mediated through context and through interpretation.

Contextualization as Grounded in the Particularity of Jesus Christ

If we are to contend that the hidden God has become known in and through the particular man Jesus, a point made in this chapter as well as in the previous two chapters, then we have to admit that revelation is inherently contextual and embodied; that God chooses to communicate through context and that this is fitting for God. As Nancy Eiesland comments: 'Christology is the natural domain of contextualization since the Incarnation is the ultimate contextual revelation ... Christology is fundamentally about human experience and human bodies as partially constitutive of God.'[130] Jesus establishes that it is through the particular that the Living God is made known.[131] If God reveals Godself as Godself in the economy of salvation then context and bodies are not 'other' than God but integral to revelation itself. According to this view, creaturely existence can be seen as a continuation of divine reality (rather than in opposition to it). Humanity is not in opposition to God because God has made a covenant with them through the incarnate Word. Because the *hypostasis* of humanity is contained within the being of Jesus Christ, there can be no human

---

[129] Kevin Diller presents a similar view in his article, 'Does Contemporary Theology Require a Postfoundational Way of Knowing?', *Scottish Journal of Theology*, 60/3 (2007): 271–93.

[130] Nancy L. Eiesland, *The Disabled God: Towards a Liberatory Theology of Disability* (Nashville, 1994), p. 99.

[131] See Stephen B. Bevans, *Models of Contextual Theology*, revised and expanded edn (Maryknoll, New York, 2002), p. 12.

existence independent of him. Thus, rather than seeing Christ as paradigmatic of some form of ideal human 'being' (as in Schleiermacher), I argue, with Barth, that human 'being' is instead located and contained within the incarnate Christ. In saying this, we assert that human 'being' must say something meaningful about God, hereby reinforcing the understanding of Christ as the ontological foundation of the principles of incarnation and sacrament previously proposed in Chapter 1.

This said, however, although God is known through context and this is what the incarnation reveals, context does not constitute a mirror reflecting the reality of God back at the world in perfect focus. What is revealed in the world can never be identical with God in Godself because we only know the former through what *we* receive and interpret. It is not that the God revealed in the world is different form God in Godself but that there is a limitation on our side. Although there is a correspondence between what *we know* and interpret of God in the world and *God* as God reveals Godself in the world, between the interpretations of experience of God recorded in the Bible, for example, and how God is in Godself, God is never immediately or directly known because what we know through context is always partial. This, however, is the nature of revelation – it can be no other way. Bodies and context *do* say something meaningful about God because Christ reveals this to be the case through the incarnation. Although what they say is limited, revelation within these terms is cast as *present* as well as past and future event. Revelation does not simply connote the particular self-revelation of God in Christ and the specific future of the eschaton. Because Christ reveals incarnation and sacrament as cosmic principles, that is, as principles inherent within the cosmos, we must say that God is known today, even if only partially.

Experience as 'Source' and 'Norm'

Understanding revelation in this way means that experience is not simply upheld as the vehicle through which the traditional sources of scripture and tradition are given and received, it is to say something stronger. If the 'form' of revelation cannot be separated from the 'content' (although not being reducible to this), then experience as 'form' must also affect and influence the substance of what is revealed. As was argued earlier, it is impossible to peel away the skin of experience in order to reveal a kernel of truth unaffected by this. Revelation is rooted in experience. As well as being informed and shaped by experience, however, theology is also judged according to experience. To say that theology begins logically and practically with experience then is to say that all theology is contextual but also, that experience (as source) constitutes the *criterion* (or norm) against which theological claims are measured and assessed. If there is no access to revelation outside of experience, then experience must serve as judge. Theological assertions then are validated by experience so that truth claims are considered 'true' on the basis that they have been experienced as such within (and by) the Christian community.

It is the role of *present* experience which is of particular import here. An orthodox-contextual theological method takes into account the faith experiences which have been recorded in the past through scripture and preserved by tradition (since engagement with such sources is important for any 'Christian' theology), however, it also takes account of experience in the present. Specifically, it maintains that experiences recorded in the past are *only* authentic when they animate what is experienced in the present; when the words of the Bible and tradition are heard as 'good news' in the here and now.[132] This will be particularly apparent when we consider women's experience in the next chapter, as the past has not always been conducive to affirming women's voices and female personhood. Experience recorded in the past must pass through what Stephen Bevans calls, 'the sieve of our own individual and contemporary collective experience.'[133] Thus, rather than the Bible confronting and addressing present experience as a body of truths which is directly given and only channelled through context, present experience is placed in critical dialogue with the Bible. We critically reflect on the Bible and tradition in light of present experience so that such experience can illuminate and challenge experiences recorded in the Bible and tradition, and so that experiences contained within the Bible and tradition can illuminate and challenge present experience. If the Bible is be read as 'good news' in the present, we must, as Jacquelyn Grant argues, 'read and hear the Bible and engage it within the context of our own experience. This is the only way that it can make sense to people who are oppressed.'[134]

Conclusion

An orthodox-contextual method then recognizes the priority of God in revelation whilst also insisting on experience as the necessary and logical starting point of all theology. Although it affirms that God *has* made Godself known in the economy of salvation, this cannot be known outside of experience and outside of interpretation; hence, God in Godself as revealed in the history of salvation can never be known immediately. Barth is criticised because he fails to understand the extent to which experience plays a part in God's self-communication. Although Barth is right in stating that revelation is not directly equated to the Bible or tradition since it is an event of which the Bible and tradition speak, we only know God through these contexts and thus through these various avenues of experience. Insofar as this is the case, the event of revelation (and thus the ontological priority of God's free decision to reveal Godself as Godself [as Trinity] in the person of Christ) which takes ontological priority in theological method cannot be separated from what is known of this through the witness of the apostles in the New Testament, and as a

[132] For a similar view within feminist circles, see Letty Russell's *The Future of Partnership* (Philadelphia, 1979), p. 22.

[133] Bevans, p. 5.

[134] Jacquelyn Grant, *White Women's Christ and Black Women's Jesus* (Atlanta, Georgia, 1989), p. 212.

result of what is interpreted through context. Hence there can be no direct access to God in Godself. The practical starting point of theological enquiry is always experience. As James Cone thoughtfully comments:

> Christian theology is human speech about God, it is always related to historical situations, and thus all of its assertions are culturally limited. Although God, the subject of theology, is eternal, theology itself is like those who articulate it limited by history and time. It is not universal language; it is interested language, always reflecting the values and aspirations of a particular people in a particular time and place.[135]

Of course, if experience is the logical and practical starting point of theology, and it is *present* experience which takes priority, then we have to ask *whose* experience theology is to begin with. If the past experiences recorded in the Bible, for example, must be tested by present experience then where are we to start and what justification can be given for this? The following chapter takes these questions forward and moves discussion surrounding theological method towards a distinctly *feminist* focus.

---

[135] James H. Cone, 'The Story Context of Black Theology', *Theology Today*, 32/2 (July 1975): 144–50, esp. p. 144. Also see his monograph, *God of the Oppressed* (Maryknoll, 1975), p. 36.

Chapter 4

From 'Experience' to '*Women's* Experience':

Towards a Feminist Theological Methodology

Identifying experience as source and norm in theological method does indeed raise important questions. Whose experience is to be privileged as normative and on what basis? In pushing discussion in a more distinctly *feminist* direction, this chapter proposes the use of *women's* experience in the doing of theology. The underpinning justification for this is that theology has in the past overlooked its contextual nature (as evidenced in part by Barth), specifically its grounding in *male* experience, and assumed its claims to be universal and objective. As such, it has assumed the experiences of men from which it emerges to speak for all and has therefore marginalized the voices and experiences of women. Jacquelyn Grant thus defines the feminist critique of theology as one which exposes the assumed grounding of theology in so-called objective sources of truth as a grounding of theology in the experiences of the dominant culture. In this respect, feminist theology, she argues, shakes the very foundations of theology.[1]

Of course, such a starting point is not without its problems. The proliferation of different feminist, womanist, lesbian, Mujerista, African and Asian women's theologies over recent years has exposed any sense of a shared, generic, 'naturalized' female experience to be illusory, even dangerous. Women experience differently and have different experiences depending on a variety of factors, including geographical location, economic position, class, race, age, sexuality, physical ability and so on. As such, it is now generally seen as problematic to claim women's experience as an innocent foundation for Christian feminist claims.[2] Despite such problems, however, this chapter seeks to make a case for the use of women's experience. It argues that women's experience continues to constitute a meaningful and important starting point for feminist theology so long as such an appeal is established on non-foundational grounds, is justified on ethical and pragmatic grounds, and draws on the experiences of women which are shared and critiqued within Christian *feminist* communities of resistance.

---

1 Jacquelyn Grant, *White Women's Christ and Black Women's Jesus* (Atlanta, Georgia, 1989), p. 10.

2 See Marian Ronan, 'Reclaiming Women's Experience: A Reading of Selected Christian Feminist Theologies', *Cross Currents* (1998): 218–29.

A New Starting Point: Women's Experience as 'Source' and 'Norm'

Valerie Saiving is perhaps the first thinker to highlight the challenge women's experience posed to traditional theology. In her landmark essay, 'The Human Situation: A Feminine View' published in 1960, Saiving argues that the human condition has theologically been defined in accordance to male experience alone. Specifically, 'sin' has been explained as pride and self assertion, and 'love' as selflessness.[3] For Saiving, this is problematic because the meaning of these theological categories is assumed to be universal when in fact it only reflects *male* experience. She forcefully argues that whilst men may experience sin as self-assertion, women who mother, experience sin in terms of self-negation, as the 'underdevelopment or negation of the self.'[4] It is not that women who mother pay too much attention to themselves, it is that they do not pay enough. As such, Saiving argues that women do not experience the human condition in the same way as men and thus exposes the grounding of theological ideas on exclusively *male* experience.

In many respects, Saiving marks the beginning of a conversation in feminist theology surrounding the use of women's experience. Other voices have, however, been significant in directing the focus of feminist debate. Rosemary Radford Ruether, for example, famously notes the challenge of women's experience to so-called 'malestream' theology and insists that this starting point will not only change the form and content of theology but also the very way in which theology is done. Doing theology from the basis of *women's* experience, she argues, will lead to a paradigm shift in theological reflection.

According to Ruether, *all* theology is contextual. Feminist theology then, she maintains, is not doing anything new by beginning with experience. Beginning with *women's* experience, however, is revolutionary since such experience has previously been marginalized or excluded from theology.[5] Indeed, in a more recent essay, she argues that feminist theology begins from the central claim that Christian theology has been produced from male elite experience.[6] The use of *women's* experience in feminist theology, she thus contends, 'explodes as a critical force', exposing classical theology as grounded on explicitly *male* experience.[7] Whatever

---

[3] Valerie Saiving, 'The Human Situation: A Feminine View', in Judith Plaskow and Carol P. Christ (eds), *Womanspirit Rising: A Feminist Reader in Religion* (New York, 1992), pp. 25–42, esp. p. 26.

[4] Ibid., p. 37.

[5] Rosemary Radford Ruether, *Sexism and God-talk: Toward a Feminist Theology* (Boston, 1983), p. 13.

[6] Rosemary Radford Ruether, 'Methodology in Women's Studies and Feminist Theology', in Arvind Sharma (ed.), *Methodology of Religious Studies: The Interface with Women's Studies* (Albany, 2002), pp. 179–206, esp. p. 179.

[7] Ruether, *Sexism*, p. 13.

undermines the full-humanity of women must be rejected as non-redemptive[8] and this includes theological symbols: 'if a symbol does not speak authentically to experience, it becomes dead or must be altered to provide new meaning'.[9] Women's experience then, which for Ruether includes women's experience of the divine, oneself, the community and the world,[10] must be used to determine what counts as being theologically appropriate and must operate as both source and norm in the doing of theology.

Although much has happened in the feminist arena since Ruether's writing of this work in the early 1980s, views like hers and Saiving's have been formative in mapping the direction of feminist discussion in this area. Part of this discussion has involved a reflection on the place and role of the Bible in theology. Ruether, for example, argues that the Bible and tradition are to be interpreted in relation to women's experience. For her, Christian preaching and teaching are never simply about finding out what the Bible says and then applying unchanging truths to our present day context. The Bible only operates as the 'Word of God' when we tell our *own* liberating stories through dialogue with the text.[11]

Such views have been echoed in part by Elisabeth Schüssler Fiorenza, a feminist biblical scholar. Drawing attention to the way in which the Bible has served to marginalize and silence women, she proposes that the Bible does not tell the full story about women's role in the ministry of Jesus or in the early church.[12] It does not provide an historical account of what actually happened. The gospels are 'paradigmatic remembrances'[13] of events rather than complete accounts of the historical Jesus. They are expressions of communities and individuals who attempted to say what the significance of Jesus was for their own situations.[14] According to Fiorenza, this is a particular telling of biblical history and it is a telling which overlooks the experiences and voices of women. Women are invisible in the text, however, Fiorenza argues that the way forward here is not to abandon Christianity as being irredeemably sexist (as is the Post-Christian response) but to uncover and recover the history of women in the early Christian churches. Fiorenza thus argues that there are indications within the New Testament that women were far more active, both in the Jesus movement and the early Christian movement, than has previously been assumed.

Central to Fiorenza's method is a hermeneutics of suspicion towards biblical material. She is clear that the Bible serves a patriarchal agenda and operates in

---

8 This is what Ruether refers to as the 'critical principle' of feminist theology. Ibid., p. 18.

9 Ibid., pp. 13–14.

10 Ibid., p. 12.

11 Ruether, 'Methodology in Women's Studies', p. 199.

12 Elisabeth Schüssler Fiorenza, *In Memory of Her: A Feminist Reconstruction of Christian Origins* (London, 1995), p. 68.

13 Ibid., p. 102.

14 Ibid.

the interests of those (men) who authored its accounts. 'Without question', she says, 'the Bible is a male book.'[15] Because it excludes women's experience and further perpetuates the denial of their identities it *cannot* be normative in Christian theologizing. She thus proposes that the Bible operate as 'prototype' as opposed to 'archetype' in theological method[16] – as 'source' and as continuous with present revelation as opposed to as a 'norm' which is fixed, stable and directly identifiable with revelation. What counts as the 'Word of God' for Fiorenza is only those passages which are interpreted as liberating by the feminist-Christian community, the *ekklesia gynaikon*. Christian theology, she argues, begins with the experiences of those who are struggling for liberation against patriarchy and other forms of oppression; it does not begin with what is seemingly received through scripture or tradition.

The contribution of feminist theology to discussion surrounding theological method is, therefore, extremely significant. At the heart of early feminist critique was the recognition that theology was perspectival and ideological, filtering from *male* experience in particular and representing the interests of an elite group. In time, however, it became apparent that such a starting point was not so straight forward and needed to be accompanied by far more critical insight. A central problem was detected surrounding the nature of difference. If women's experience was to be both source and norm, did this not assume that all women were the same, sharing a particular way of seeing the world which was distinct from men? Did it not serve conveniently to silence certain women's experiences, repeating the 'sins' identified previously with 'malestream' theology? In short, feminist theologians had to grapple with the question of *whose* experience was to be privileged and on what basis?

Problems with Articulating Women's Experience as Source and Norm

Assuming Difference between Women and Men

In her book, *Feminist Theology/Christian Theology: In Search of Method*,[17] Pamela Dickey Young sets about constructing a theological method which she considers to be both true to her identity as a Protestant Christian as well as true to her identity as a feminist. In so doing, she establishes women's experience as source and norm alongside the apostolic witness of Christ in the Synoptic gospels. She, like those feminist theologians mentioned above, is concerned to make clear the vast difference brought about by grounding theological reflection in women's,

[15] See Elisabeth Schüssler Fiorenza's essay, 'The Will to Choose or to Reject', in Letty M. Russell (ed.), *Feminist Interpretation of the Bible* (Louisville, London, Leiden, 1985), pp. 125–36, esp. 130.

[16] Fiorenza, *In Memory of Her*, p. 33.

[17] Pamela Dickey Young, *Feminist Theology/Christian Theology: In Search of Method* (Eugene, Oregon, 1990).

as opposed to men's, experiences. Listening to women's 'bodily', 'socialized', 'feminist', 'historical' and 'individual' experience, she argues, will make a significant difference to the theology which is done.[18] The problem here, however, as with other early accounts of what it means to begin theological enquiry from this starting point, is that the desire to expose women's experience as absent from theology leads to the implication that such experience exists as a self-contained, foundational entity which is shared by all women and which can be simply added alongside male experience. Young, for example, assumes that there is such a thing as *women's* 'bodily', 'socialised', 'feminist', 'historical' and 'individual' experience; that there is some kind of shared 'raw material' upon which feminist theology can draw which is distinct from the 'raw material' upon which 'male' theology has drawn.[19]

Of course, there have been those feminists who have seen great value in asserting such an essentialist reading of 'woman'. Some have sought to celebrate 'woman-nature' or the 'eternal feminine' in order to valorize what patriarchy has tended to belittle and subordinate. Mary Daly, for example, in her book, *Pure Lust*, draws sharp distinctions between men and women suggesting that men have defined women and dragged them away from their own 'country' and race.[20] She urges women to take stock and return to their 'wild', 'original' selves, what she identifies as 'elemental female lust'. This is the heart of the female essence. Such an ontological cosmic commonality, she contends, is shared by all women, and as such is something that cuts across diversities and transcends differences.[21]

In light of the strong influence of social constructionist theories, postmodern and poststructuralist accounts of identity, however, many feminists today tend to criticize such appeals to a female *essence*. To suggest that women are 'naturally' more predisposed to certain urges, character traits or behaviour patterns overlooks the complexity of the human situation, fails to acknowledge the socially constructed nature of the 'natural', and reinforces patriarchal notions of femininity. It implies that women are *naturally* more suited to 'x', often the 'private' domain of nurturing 'mothering' and housework – a point made by Rousseau in the eighteenth century[22] and famously criticized by Betty Friedan in the early 1960s[23] and Nancy

---

[18] Ibid., pp. 53–6.

[19] This is reflected, for example, in her claim that 'most women experience pregnancy and childbirth' (Young, p. 53). Even if many women have the same 'bodily' experiences (such as periods for example), such experiences are never simply 'natural' because they are always mediated through 'lenses of cultural interpretation'. See Ruether, 'Methodology in Women's Studies and Feminist Theology', p. 195.

[20] Mary Daly, *Pure Lust: Elemental Feminist Philosophy* (London, 1984), p. 6.

[21] Ibid., pp. 25–7.

[22] See Jacques Rousseau, *Discourse on the Origin of Inequality. Discourse on the Origin and Foundation of Inequality Among Men*, trans. Donald A. Crex (Indianapolis, Cambridge, 1992).

[23] Betty Friedan, *The Feminine Mystique* (London, 1963).

Chodorow[24] in the late 1970s, and men, *naturally* more suited to 'y', often the rational and intellectual pursuits of the 'public' world of work, business and education. It says that women are *naturally* more caring, emotional and relational and men *naturally* more rational, strong and self-sufficient. However, feminist theology has been quick to challenge such appeals to a generic female essence on the grounds that this overlooks difference – not all women share a maternal urge, not all women are 'naturally' caring and peace loving.

Postmodern and poststructuralist accounts of gender identity and sexual difference have sought to respond to these difficulties by presenting the body as a construct, not simply of culture but more specifically of discourse.[25] According to post-structuralism, subjectivity is produced through discourse. Discourse connotes a particular historical form of language and a type of social action which is always invested with power and which always serves particular agendas.[26] Language then is never vacuous or neutral. It does not *communicate* meaning, it *constructs* meaning; it does not *represent* our experiences, it *produces* them. Seen in these terms, subjectivity is an effect of discourse. There can be no stable subject (or 'self') because the socio-cultural and economic discourses that produce subjectivity are constantly changing.

Judith Butler, for example, offers a poststructuralist critique of the sex/gender dichotomy arguing that bodies are produced (that is brought into being) through 'performativity'.[27] Bodies are not naturalized entities over which gender is worn (much like a mask). Instead, gender is performed through the unconscious repetition of 'acts' which serve to construct and reinforce particular discourses about what constitutes 'male' and 'female' identity.[28] Sex 'materializes' through the embodiment of such norms to the extent that sexual difference is then perceived as 'natural.'[29] It is because such acts are so convincing that they give the impression of a naturalized male or female body, when in fact such realities are illusory.

When considered in relation to the use of women's experience in theological method, this critique raises a series of opportunities and threats. One key advantage is that it undermines the myth of biological determinism – of a straightforward

[24] Nancy Chodorow, *The Reproduction of Mothering: Psychoanalysis and the Sociology of Gender* (Berkeley, Los Angeles and London, 1978).

[25] See Donna Teevan's discussion of poststructuralist feminism in her article, 'Challenges to the Role of Theological Anthropology in Feminist Theologies', *Theological Studies*, 64 (2003): 582–97.

[26] Ibid., p. 587.

[27] See for example Judith Butler, *Bodies that Matter: On the Discursive Limits of 'Sex'* (New York and London, 1993), p. 1. Also see *Gender Trouble: Feminism and the Subversion of Identity* (New York and London, 1990) and *Excitable Speech: A Politics of the Performative* (New York and London, 1997).

[28] Butler, *Gender Trouble*, p. xv.

[29] Judith Butler, 'Critically Queer' in Paul du Gay, Jessica Evans and Peter Redman (eds), *Identity: A Reader* (London and New Delhi, 2000), pp. 108–10.

biological distinction between men and women – understanding 'sex' as a fluid construct. Our bodies 'are not ... the naked *a priori* of pure unmediated experience'.[30] Indeed, according to Butler's critique, there can be no such 'body' as the female (or male) body because this is constructed through acts of performativity and through discourses of power. Straightforward distinctions between assumed naturalized binaries such as sex/gender, male/female, heterosexual/homosexual are problematized. Such a perspective also affirms, in keeping with the previous chapter, that access to reality-in-itself is impossible on account of our individual locatedness within socio-cultural and historical contexts.

One key problem, however, is that such a view makes it all too easy to deny the existence of the material body.[31] If the body is entirely produced through discourse, it has no fixed or stable reality of its own and, hence, we may assume, no materiality of its own. This becomes problematic when wanting to begin theological method with women's experience as the concreteness of women's diverse experiences of oppression is called into question along with the relations of domination and subjugation to which they testify.

Susan Bordo sees this as a tendency with postmodern accounts of the body in general and criticizes such perspectives for replacing the Cartesian dream of transcendence with the postmodern dream of disembodiment.[32] For Bordo, postmodernism is too quick to reduce the body to pure 'text' and to discourse, insisting that there is nothing but a proliferation of difference. She argues that this replaces the fictitious 'Archimedean point' – the modernist, patriarchal fantasy that there is such a thing as 'a view from nowhere' – with an equally fictitious postmodern 'dream of everywhere'.[33] According to the postmodern dream, the body is not tied to one particular location or to the limitations of bodily existence. An individual can take up an endless array of different vantage points. This, for Bordo is nothing short of fantasy.[34] 'What sort of body is it', she asks, 'that is free to change its shape and location at will, that can become anyone and travel anywhere?'; 'no body at all' she replies.[35]

[30] Jane Barter Moulaison, '"Our Bodies, Our Selves?" The Body as Source in Feminist Theology', *Scottish Journal of Theology*, 60/3 (2007): 341–59, esp. p. 345.

[31] Nancy Fraser highlights the advantages of such an argument suggesting that if sex-gender is produced by power, constituting an ideological discourse as opposed to a biological 'given', then this opens up scope for alternative ways of constructing the body. See 'Pragmatism, Feminism, and the Linguistic Turn' in Seyla Benhabib, Judith Butler, Drucilla Cornell, Nancy Fraser (eds), *Feminist Contentions: A Philosophical Exchange* (London, New York, 1995), pp. 157–72.

[32] Susan Bordo, *Unbearable Weight: Feminism, Western Culture, and the Body* (Berkeley, Los Angeles, London, 1999), p. 227.

[33] Ibid., pp. 218–19.

[34] Ibid., pp. 225–9.

[35] Ibid., p. 229.

Another key problem with poststructuralist accounts of subjectivity is that it becomes very difficult to establish women's experience as starting point in feminist theology. Because language *constructs* experience, appeals to 'women's experience', it is argued, assume a pre-linguistic realm of experience which can serve as source and norm.[36] It is not simply that the category assumes a binary opposition between men and women that poses a problem, but that it assumes that there is such a thing as unmediated experience. If this is so, then appeals to women's experience are in fact appeals to constantly shifting linguistic constructs. Women's experience certainly cannot operate as an innocent or stable foundation.

Whilst there are appealing features to this critique, most apparently its destabilization of women's experience as a uniform category, it allows no room for women's agency due to the entirely constructed nature of subjectivity. This is problematic for any feminist theologian committed to liberative praxis and transformation. The subject is wiped out completely and 'woman' reduced to an endless array of subject positions. Indeed, the complete relativization of difference which is represented by theorists such as Butler threatens to erase the historical body altogether and as such, to erase the historical status of women's diverse experiences. Although I do not wish to endorse the opposite extreme of essentialism, it seems that if we are to ascribe to such experiences a transformative value which moves beyond mere conscious-raising, the collapsing of 'women' and 'experience' into discourse is unhelpful and even dangerous.

This said, however, we cannot ignore the critique. Language cannot be separated from subjectivity or from women's lived experiences, hence neither can it be legitimately seen as self-evident. We do not understand or experience the world outside of language, for if this were so then, as Jane Flax rightly notes, the world would have to be 'apprehended by an empty (ahistoric) mind and perfectly transcribed by/into a transparent language'.[37] Yet this need not be an assumption inherent within all feminist appeals to women's experience. Such appeals can be justified, not on the basis of this constituting an innocent, stable, pre-linguistic, ontological and foundational base from which to begin, but on a more methodological and pragmatic basis; on account of the values such experiences inspire.[38] This point will be developed further in the second half of this chapter, however it does seem to me that we can learn from feminist post-structuralism without whole heartedly sanctioning its approach. Whilst there are no bodies or experiences outside of discourse, there are still bodies and there are still experiences and these sometimes shape and construct discourse as well as being constructed by it. The use of women's experience in theological method then, I suggest, demands an understanding of female subjectivity which takes the

---

36 Teevan, 'Challenges to the Role of Theological Anthropology', p. 590.

37 Jane Flax, 'Postmodernism and Gender Relations in Feminist Theory', *Signs*, 12/4 (1987): 621–43, esp. p. 633.

38 See Linda Hogan, *From Women's Experience to Feminist Theology* (Sheffield, 1995), p. 171.

body's position within discourse seriously without loosing sight of the body's materiality and the limitations which accompany this. The challenge is, as Mary McClintock Fulkerson argues, 'not to lose the subject "woman," but to *change the subject* in the sense that the complex production of multiple identities becomes basic to our thinking'.[39]

Assuming Sameness Between Women

Turning then to the second major criticism which has been levelled at the notion of 'women's experience', it has been suggested that such a term not only over generalizes about difference between women and men but also compromises difference between women. Of course the two are related. Sheila Greeve Davaney, for example, criticizes white feminist theologians' appeal to women's experience on the grounds that these have tended to imply a universal and common essence that defined women as 'women' and which provided the content for feminist reflection.[40]

Indeed, this has been the critique levelled by a range of different theologies, including womanist, African, Asian, Hispanic/Mujerista and Latin American women's theologies. In *White Women's Christ and Black Women's Jesus*, Jacquelyn Grant (a contemporary womanist theologian) argues that although feminist theology has provided a significant critique of the sexist nature of European and North American theology, it is shown to be severely limited when evaluated in the light of black women's experience. 'Feminist theology' she argues, 'is inadequate for two reasons: it is *White* and *racist*.'[41] Feminist theology's appeal to women's experience, she claims, has been an appeal to *white* women's experience in particular. This is deeply problematic because white women's experiences are not the same as black women's experiences.[42] Feminist theology is racist, she argues, because it makes a universal claim about women's experience implying that sexism and patriarchy are experienced the same by all women. Of course, at the heart of this universalizing process has been the construction of a dichotomy between women as 'oppressed' and men as 'oppressors'. Bell Hooks and Angela Davis, for example, in the early 1980s drew attention to the fundamental racism inherent within this view, arguing that it failed to recognize that white women

---

39 Mary McClintock Fulkerson, *Changing the Subject: Women's Discourses and Feminist Theology* (Minneapolis, 1994), p. 7.

40 Sheila Greeve Davaney, 'Continuing the Story but Departing the Text: A Historicist Interpretation of Feminist Norms in Theology', in Rebecca S. Chopp and Sheila Greeve Davaney (eds), *Horizons in Feminist Theology: Identity Tradition and Norms* (Minneapolis, 1997), pp. 198–214, esp. p. 200.

41 Jacquelyn Grant, *White Women's Christ*, p. 195.

42 Ibid.

can be (and have been) equally as complicit in oppressing black women as white men.[43] Being a woman may mean different things to white and black women.

Womanist theology has, therefore, exposed the limitations of white-Western feminist theology, liberation theology and black theology by drawing on themes and issues which filter from the particular lived realities of black African-American women. Delores Williams, for example, reflecting on the biblical story of Hagar, highlights key issues she considers to be prominent within black African-American women's experience, including women's experience of motherhood, survival, surrogacy and poverty. She reads the figure of Hagar from the point of view of African-American women's struggles for survival.[44] Other significant voices involved in this global critique have been African feminist women theologians such as Mercy Amba Oduyoye,[45] Asian women theologians such as Kwok Pui-lan[46] and Chung Hyun Kyung,[47] Hispanic/Latino women theologians such as Ada María Isasi-Diaz,[48] María Pilar Aquino[49] and Ivone Gebara,[50] and Latin American women theologians such as Elsa Tamez.[51] Such voices testify to the global and intercultural nature of feminist theology today and to the fact that there is no such thing as 'women's experience' in the abstract. It is always particular experiences from particular women which are being appealed to and this seems to be at the forefront of present day feminist sensibilities. Indeed, Kwok Pui-lan, although noting that feminist theology is no longer defined by the interests of European,

---

43 Angela Davis, *Women, Race and Class* (New York, 1981), and Bell Hooks, *Ain't I a Woman? Black Women and Feminism* (Boston, 1981).

44 Delores Williams, *Sisters in the Wilderness: The Challenge of Womanist God-talk* (Maryknoll, New York, 1993), pp. 15–33.

45 Mercy Amba Oduyoye, *Introducing African Women's Theology* (Sheffield, 2001), and *Beads and Strands: Reflections of an African Woman on Christianity in Africa* (Maryknoll, New York, 2004).

46 Kwok Pui-lan, *Introducing Asian Feminist Theology* (Sheffield, 2000).

47 Chung Hyun Kyung, *Struggle to Be the Sun Again: Introducing Asian Women's Theology* (Maryknoll, New York, 1990).

48 Ada María Isasi-Diaz, *La Lucha Continues: Mujerista Theology* (Maryknoll, New York, 2004) and *Mujerista Theology: A Theology for the Twenty-First Century* (Maryknoll, New York, 1996).

49 María Pilar Aquino, *Our Cry for Life: Feminist Theology from Latin America* (Maryknoll, New York, 1993). Also see 'Theological Method in U.S. Latino/a Theology: Toward an Intercultural Theology for the Third Millennium', in Orlando O. Espín and Miguel H. Díaz (eds), *From the Heart of Our People: Latino/a Explorations in Catholic Systematic Theology* (Maryknoll, New York, 1999), pp. 6–48.

50 See for example Ivone Gebara, 'Women Doing Theology in Latin America', in Elsa Tamez (ed.), *Through Her Eyes: Women's Theology from Latin America* (Maryknoll, New York, 1989), pp. 37–48.

51 Elsa Tamez, 'Cultural Violence Against Women in Latin America', in Mary John Manazan, Mercy Amba Oduyoye and Elsa Tamez (eds), *Women Resisting Violence: Spirituality for Life* (Maryknoll, New York, 1996), pp. 11–19.

American women (as charged by Grant in 1979),[52] argues that it must still be careful to pay attention to how women from diverse cultural and social contexts articulate their difference, without assuming that women's experience is the same everywhere.[53] 'Feminist theologians', she writes, 'must articulate an alternative vision of cultural resistance, contestation and difference, as well as solidarity among women.'[54]

How then are we to respond to this challenge? Are we to uphold difference to the point of rendering any mention of 'women' meaningless or is there some commonality between women which makes the term useable at some level? Is an appeal to some degree of consensus necessary? These are important questions. It seems to me that insisting on difference between women to the point of denying *any* shared characteristics among them is to make a universal claim equally as erroneous and presumptuous as that which denies *any* difference between women. It undermines, silences and erases experiences which women may claim to share with other women. Whilst shared conditions amongst women should not be *assumed*, they may be *discovered* by women through shared conversation at a range of levels, whether locally or globally. I will return to this point later. Asserting women's experience as source and norm in theological method then, in my opinion, must embrace the multiplicity of women's experiences and must destabilize any essentialist, foundational understandings of 'women', however, it must, at the same time, retain a sense of meaning in relation to the category. If this is lost altogether then talk of women's lived experiences simply collapses into theoretical abstraction. Of course, this is a difficult balance to negotiate, however, before we set about providing constructive suggestions as to how we might go about establishing this, I turn briefly to a discussion of one further assumption which has been criticized in feminist reflection on women's experience: the assumption of a privileged feminist or women's epistemological standpoint.

Assuming a Privileged Epistemological Standpoint

This criticism relates to the previous two problems discussed already. If an appeal to 'women's experience' presumes sameness between women and difference between women and men, then it also alludes to a particular *female* way of knowing and as such, seems to suppose that this way of knowing provides a better and more reliable standpoint from which to do theology.

In her book, *The Future of Differences*, Susan Hekman states that a shift towards a politics of difference took place in the late 1980s and early 1990s. This signalled a move from the universal to the particular; from Truth to truths and

52 Jacquelyn Grant, 'Black Theology and the Black Woman', in Gayraud S. Wilmore and James H. Cone (eds), *Black Theology: A Documentary History 1966–1979* (Maryknoll, New York, 1979), pp. 418–33, esp. p. 419.

53 Kwok Pui-Lan, 'Feminist Theology as Intercultural Discourse', pp. 23–4.

54 Ibid, p. 24.

constituted a direct challenge to the standpoint theory articulated by women such as Nancy Hartsock in the 1970s where all women were considered to occupy the same position as the oppressed.[55] To be sure, Hartsock[56] was heavily criticized for her standpoint epistemology. Her claim that the correct vision of reality could only be glimpsed from the standpoint of the oppressed and specifically from the standpoint of oppressed women implied that all women were oppressed and that all men were oppressors. It also assumed (in keeping with Marx) that the oppressed were in a better position to view the world correctly on account of their oppressed position.[57]

In response to difficulties such as this, feminist thinkers began to place more emphasis on difference between women. Sandra Harding, for example, in her search for a feminist epistemology drew attention to the multiplicity of women's standpoints and realities[58] and to the untenable nature of monolithic understandings of 'woman'. For her, women do not see the world from the same perspective. They are divided by the historical realities of class, race, sexuality and so on and so cannot be forced into a single space.[59] She maintains, with Hartsock, that some social locations are better than others as starting points for knowledge and suggests, as a result, that we begin from the position of the marginalized because this illuminates questions that dominant positions cannot see.[60] However, Harding is quick to point out that there is no *essential* female experience from which feminism should or could begin. Feminist theory must issue from the multiple, complex and contradictory lives of women.[61]

In light of this, Harding argues for a view of objectivity which takes women's diverse experiences into account. Suggesting that knowledge in the past has been biased and androcentric and wrongly placed under the banner of 'objectivity', she maintains that female contributions will help to restore a more accurate perspective so that the world is viewed more realistically. In short, she argues that beginning from women's experience makes objectivity more possible. This objectivity she specifically calls 'strong objectivity' because it is not objectivity as

---

55 Susan Hekman, *The Future of Differences: Truth and Method in Feminist Theory* (Cambridge, 1999), pp. 38 and 23.

56 See Nancy C.M. Hartsock, *Money, Sex and Power: Toward a Feminist Historical Materialism* (New York, London, 1983).

57 Nancy C.M. Hartsock, 'The Feminist Standpoint: Developing the Ground for a Specifically Feminist Historical Materialism', in Sandra Harding (ed.), *The Feminist Standpoint Theory Reader: Intellectual and Political Controversies* (London and New York, 2004), pp. 35–54. In the introduction to this text, Harding notes the influence of Marxist thought on early feminist standpoint accounts.

58 See Sandra Harding, *The Science Question in Feminism* (Milton Keynes, 1986).

59 Sandra Harding, 'Rethinking Standpoint Epistemology: What is Strong Objectivity?', in Sandra Harding (ed.), *The Feminist Standpoint-Theory Reader: Intellectual and Political Controversies* (London and New York, 2004), pp. 127–40, esp. pp. 134–5.

60 Harding, 'Rethinking Standpoint Epistemology', pp. 129 and 131.

61 Ibid., p. 134.

understood in the traditional sense of a 'value-free' single truth. Strong objectivity states that by incorporating women's diverse *particular* standpoints, that truth is *more* obtainable.

One reading of this may suggest that Harding implies that patriarchy can be made better by simply 'adding women' into the epistemological equation. It may also be questioned as to why women's contributions would necessarily *improve* the problem: if men have distorted reality, why should women's perspectives necessarily make for a clearer and more accurate view?[62] However, the picture of reality which emerges as a result of listening to women's diverse experiences is only more realistic because it exposes *difference*, not because it produces a uniform vision of reality.

This said, Harding (like Hartsock and other feminist standpoint epistemologies) seems to assume that *women's* experience is the same as *feminist* women's experience.[63] We start from the experiences of those who are marginalized because such experiences illuminate questions those in positions of privilege cannot see. But does this not assume that all women hold feminist values (and indeed that these values are uniform)? What if certain women experience oppression but do not consider resistance to this appropriate or necessary?[64] There is an assumption within this version of feminist standpoint epistemology, which echoes assumptions in Marxist theory, that women can claim 'self-consciousness' (which resembles Marx's vision of 'class consciousness') by realizing their own structural position (and therefore experiences) of oppression within patriarchy.

Of course, appeals to a feminist standpoint also assume that there *is* a correct way to see the world and that the world can be known objectively. Liz Stanley and Sue Wise, in their two texts, *Breaking Out: Feminist Consciousness and Feminist Research*, and *Breaking Out Again*, criticize feminist standpoint epistemology for attributing an epistemological privilege to women's experience[65] and consequently reject the possibility of objective knowledge. In discussing the role of the feminist researcher they argue that 'the kind of person that we are, and how we experience the research, all have a crucial impact on what we see, what we do, and how we interpret and construct what is going on'.[66] Reality is not the same for everyone.[67] For Stanley and Wise then, the idea that some people have a better insight to the truth, that some have a false consciousness and others a more enlightened consciousness,

---

[62] For an interesting and more detailed critique of feminist standpoint epistemology see Mary Hawkesworth, 'Knowers, Knowing, Known: Feminist Theory and Claims of Truth', *Signs*, 14/3 (1989): 533–7.

[63] A point made by Rita Felski in her *Doing Time: Feminist Theory and Postmodern Culture* (New York and London, 2000), p. 197.

[64] Ibid., p.198.

[65] Liz Stanley and Sue Wise, *Breaking Out: Feminist Consciousness and Feminist Research* (London, Boston, Melbourne & Henley, 1983), pp. 119–20.

[66] Ibid., p. 119.

[67] Ibid.

is patronising and denies the views of those who perceive their experiences as 'real' and valid.[68] It also implies that there is a true reality 'out there' which we can either interpret rightly or wrongly and this is, according to them, erroneous. Indeed, they write: 'Different states of consciousness aren't just different ways of *interpreting* the world. We don't accept that there is something 'really' there for there to be interpretations of.'[69] According to this view, there is nothing beyond social life and experience; all we have are 'multiple realities'.[70] In short, reality is socially constructed. So if women's experience has no epistemological privilege, then on what grounds do Stanley and Wise assert this priority?

It is at this point that they refer to what they call the 'personal' essence of feminism; that is, feminism based on the everyday concrete lived experiences of women.[71] This includes women's material realities and everyday experiences of oppression as articulated from the specific positions of the oppressed.[72] Because these positions are multiple, Stanley and Wise claim that knowledge is also multiple. They therefore argue that such a starting point should lead us to do three things: a) reject positivism, b) take other people's truths seriously, and c) learn how people 'do' the truth and enact it in their daily lives.[73] To reject positivism is to deny that research can be objective and therefore means that feminism cannot claim to know the 'truth.'[74] To take other people's truths seriously is not just to tolerate difference but to welcome it,[75] and to learn how people 'do' the truth is to learn how people construct their own reality through routine and mundane habits.[76]

Of course, such measures must be applauded for Stanley and Wise avoid essentialism and embrace difference and particularity with open arms. However, such a totalizing focus on subjective, day-to-day experience starves the feminist agenda of political force. It is necessary and indeed advisable to deal with the specifics of oppression but surely feminism should not be content with ending here; surely some sort of consensus is necessary if transformation is to take place? If we reject positivism and simultaneously deny that there is any objective reality out there or any objective truth regarding the way the world should be, then does this mean that there is no reason for undertaking the struggle for women's liberation or indeed for taking note of it? If we are open to others' views to the extent of

---

68 Ibid., p. 119.

69 Ibid., pp. 130–31.

70 Liz Stanley and Sue Wise, *Breaking Out Again. Feminist Ontology and Epistemology*, second edn (London and New York, 1993), p. 102.

71 Stanley and Wise, *Breaking Out*, p. 135.

72 Liz Stanley, 'Method, Methodology and Epistemology', in Liz Stanley (ed.), *Feminist Praxis: Research Theory and Epistemology in Feminist Sociology* (London and New York, 1990), p. 25.

73 Stanley and Wise, *Breaking Out*, p. 109.

74 Ibid., pp. 109 and 113.

75 Ibid., p. 109.

76 Ibid., p. 112.

respecting them equally with our own does this also run the risk of preventing us from claiming one view to be more valid than another? Indeed, Stanley and Wise state that 'to swamp arguments about "I'm right and you're wrong" is silly and patronising',[77] but surely there is a need to claim the validity of certain perspectives over and above others? Surely feminist theology wants to assert its claims as more adequate than the patriarchal claims it seeks to criticize?

This critique, therefore, highlights the need for a more complex understanding of feminist knowledge, away from the dichotomous model of positivism versus relativity. It calls for a middle ground between the two extremes that recognizes the significance of 'truth' without compromising the diverse standpoints from which women experience the world. This demands that women's experience find some form of justification without claiming either an ontological privilege or without slipping into relativism, since 'In a world of radical inequality, relativist resignation reinforces the status quo'.[78]

Moving Forward: Engaging the Problems and Constructing a Proposal

There are, then, key conditions which must be met if women's experience is to be established as source and norm in the doing of theology. First, any appeal to women's experience must be established on non-foundational grounds. It must move away from essentialist assumptions concerning a female essence or nature, affirming the material reality of the female body but also its construction in and through language, culture and discourse. In so doing, and also in responding to the reality of difference brought to bear by non-white, non-Western, non-heterosexual theologies, a new framing of subjectivity and selfhood is called for; one which takes account of postmodern readings of the self as fluid, multiple and diverse without erasing the subject altogether or collapsing them into discourse.

Second, feminist appeals to women's experience must also be clear about *whose* experience is operating as source and norm. If an appeal to particular experience as normative operates ideologically to silence 'other' voices, then feminist appeals to women's experience must be fully conscious of this in their own theologizing. If women cannot claim an epistemological privilege on account of their gender, and if women's experience cannot be separated from language and discourse, then we must go in search of a non-foundational justification for prioritizing women's experience. If the relativity and subjectivity of Stanley and Wise is to be avoided then we must also frame some vision of consensus between women which does not undermine the reality of difference.

---

77 Ibid.

78 Hawkesworth, 'Knowers, Knowing, Known', p. 557.

Women and Subjectivity

The first condition then calls for a non-foundational understanding of subjectivity which allows space for solidarity between women whilst avoiding the pit falls of essentialism. Whilst the female body must not be viewed as determining a female essence, the material body must, nevertheless, be recognized along with its limitations. In order to map the way forward here, I dialogue with Simone de Beauvoir and Luce Irigaray. De Beauvoir is useful because she presents an understanding of the body as 'situation'; Irigaray is useful because she locates the female body within phallocentric discourse. Both emphases are outlined below and are used to inform my proposed understanding of subjectivity as 'positionality' at the end of this section.

Simone de Beauvoir and the body as 'situation' In her pivotal text, *The Second Sex*, Simone de Beauvoir proposes an understanding of 'women' which filters from her articulation of the body as 'situation'. For de Beauvoir, that the body is a situation means that it is not simply a 'thing' but is actually positioned and contextualized. She states that the body exists as a body in the world and cannot be interpreted in abstract ways. It is 'the instrument of our grasp upon the world'[79] comprising a lived reality which undermines the separation of biological facts from social context. De Beauvoir therefore argues that women are not determined but are in a state of becoming;[80] that we define ourselves through the actions that we take and the way that we live.[81] This is not all however. Although de Beauvoir maintains that both sexes are equally human, she forcefully argues that in respect to reproduction, men are able to retain their individuality whilst women are not.[82] It is women, she says, who have children and are 'enslaved'[83] to them, women who become possessed by what she calls 'foreign forces',[84] making it impossible for them to fulfil their potential as humans. The body as 'situation' then is not simply the instrument of our grasp upon the world, it is 'a limiting factor' for women's projects.[85]

De Beauvoir, however, is clear that it is men (rather than biology) who are responsible for holding women back on account of their bodies.[86] Men, she argues, have prescribed women roles in order to serve their own patriarchal agendas and

---

79 Simone de Beauvoir, *The Second Sex*, trans. and ed. H.M. Parshley (London, Australia, New Zealand, South Africa, 1949), p. 66.

80 Ibid., p. 65.

81 Ibid., p. 69.

82 Ibid., p. 54.

83 Ibid.

84 Ibid., p. 57.

85 Ibid., p. 66.

86 A point echoed by Nancy Bauer. See *Simone Beauvoir: Philosophy, and Feminism* (New York, 2001), p. 200.

to limit women's potential. Men have forced women into the trap of reproduction, childcare and into the kitchen in such a way that women have developed certain character traits. For de Beauvoir then, it is because women resign themselves to their assigned patriarchal situations that they are unable to fulfil their potential as human beings. She therefore argues that women must reject such limitations and go in search of the future; they must begin to make conscious decisions of their own and escape the 'bad faith'[87] in which patriarchy has placed them. In short, every woman must 'shed her old skin and cut her own new clothes'.[88]

De Beauvoir's suggestions are helpful here because she proposes a view of women's subjectivity which is not essentialist but which, nevertheless, recognizes the reality and materiality of the female body. Female physiology is part of every woman's 'situation'.[89] Here, the body is not reduced to 'text' (as is the danger with many postmodern and poststructuralist accounts) nor to a trans-cultural, predetermined essence (as is the danger with more 'foundationalist' accounts). Biology does not determine who women are or will be. Instead, 'The body of woman is one of the essential elements in her situation in the world' but is not enough to define her as 'woman'.[90] To be a 'woman' is to be a body but it is always more than this; it is to *live* the female body in the world. Such an understanding then allows for the recognition that female bodies are enculturated bodies which take on meaning within an array of cultural, geographical, historical and social settings. There is no such thing as the body *before* context.

This said, however, de Beauvoir's 'solution' to the problem of women's otherness is suspect. She is convinced that women can become active and efficient like men when they engage in projects worthy of a human being[91] and so presents the male as the archetype of human 'being' – a problem which characterizes much liberal feminism. She consequently implies that projects such as childbearing, giving birth, housework and so on, are not worthy 'human' projects.[92] She also assumes that the body can be transcended and overcome and that this is in fact necessary and desirable for women to become as subjects. We have to ask then how those women wanting to *choose* maternity and housework as worthwhile projects would go about achieving subjectivity. De Beauvoir also assumes that the body is a drain on female becoming.[93] Periods are a curse and maternity prevents women from being free, independent subjects. But if women's bodies *are* a part of

87 De Beauvoir took the term 'bad faith' from Jean Paul Sartre. It connotes a state akin to 'false consciousness' or delusion. To live in 'bad faith' then is to fail to act consciously, to be oblivious, to compromise one's freedom. For more see de Beauvoir, *The Second Sex*, p. 233.

88 Ibid., p. 734.

89 Bauer, p. 201.

90 De Beauvoir, *The Second Sex*, p. 69.

91 Ibid., p. 615.

92 Ibid., p. 735.

93 Ibid., p. 61.

their situation and are tied up with their projects in the world, then in what sense can or should they actually be transcended?

There are, therefore, certain features missing in the theoretical apparatus supplied by de Beauvoir which need to be provided in our proposed model of subjectivity. First, admitting the existence of the female body demands that we work towards a more 'embodied' notion of subjectivity which is not founded on the desirability of bodily transcendence. Although it is important to avoid a recall back into essentialism, the body must be integral to notions of female subjectivity otherwise the concreteness of women's lived experience can be potentially denied.

Second, we have to consider the body's situatedness within language and thus revisit poststructuralist accounts of subjectivity. According to de Beauvoir, like most social constructionists, women *can* co-exist alongside men as subjects. This, however, is something which has been criticized heavily by poststructuralist theories on account that meaning is always constructed through opposition. According to this view, the arrival of the female 'other' within accounts of subjectivity will almost certainly always lead to hegemony and to the process of *saming*.[94] De Beauvoir, for example, certainly seems to be guilty of this since the subjectivity she encourages women to attain does in fact turn out to be *male* subjectivity. What post-structuralism commendably shows is that 'woman' as a socio-cultural invention is also a linguistic and discursive construction; that women's situations do not simply refer to their diverse positions within the world, but more than this, their bodies' positionality within language. Irigaray is particularly helpful in developing this point.

Luce Irigaray Like de Beauvoir, French feminist and literary theorist Luce Irigaray begins from the central idea that woman is the 'other'. Being influenced by both Derrida and Lacan, she recognizes that subjectivity is only posed through opposition; through that which is excluded or unheard. 'Woman' is only given meaning in opposition to what man is 'not', just as we might say 'low' is only meaningful in relation to what 'high' is not. What woman *is* cannot be heard.

This, however, is not all. Not only is subjectivity posed through opposition, but such differential relations, according to Irigaray, operate within a phallocentric[95] system where language serves the particular interests of the phallus, reinforcing his position as norm. Such a system is reflected in Western philosophy, in figures such as Freud and in his designation of women as 'little men'. Within this context, 'woman' only carries meaning in relation to the male as norm; she is either the

---

94 See Mary McClintock Fulkerson's discussion of post-structuralism in her essay 'Contesting the Gendered Subject: A Feminist Account of the *Imago Dei*', in Rebecca S. Chopp and Sheila Greeve Davaney (eds), *Horizons in Feminist Theology: Identity Tradition and Norms* (Minneapolis, 1997), pp. 99–115, esp. p. 107.

95 Elizabeth Grosz defines phallocentrism as 'the use of *one* model of subjectivity, the male, by which all others are positively or negatively defined.' See her *Sexual Subversions: Three French Feminists* (St. Leonards, 1989), p. 105.

same, too much or too less. 'He' is the standard against which 'she' is measured; if he is 'A', she is 'not-A'. Given this, Irigaray argues that understanding woman as 'other' within the phallocentric economy means that she is the other of the same,[96] always seen in comparison to the singular male, as lack, complementary or the same.[97] There can only be *one* subject position within phallocentrism – the position of the male phallus – so the apparent existence of difference is simply illusory. Where women are not the same as men, they fail to exist altogether.

What is important about Irigaray is that unlike de Beauvoir who advises women to reject their position as 'other' and go in search of 'equality' with men,[98] she suggests that women truly become the other through the assertion of sexual difference. This is to be the relative other (where women are also subjects and demand reciprocity) as opposed to the Absolute Other (where women are denied such subjectivity).[99] In short, she goes in search of a positive, although fluid and dynamic category of 'woman' that filters from women themselves as opposed to being constructed in relation to a male norm. Central to this task is the unearthing of the very foundation upon which phallocentrism is grounded – namely, the sameness, lack or non-existence of women and the apparent stability of the male phallus. If male subjectivity is only established through opposition to women then this is an insecure and unstable foundation. It rests upon the unheard and unsignifiable words of women. However, if women were to speak their words and bodies and thereby signify *difference*, then the phallocentric economy would be exploded. Irigaray's aim then is to deconstruct phallocentric accounts of otherness (such as de Beauvoir's) so as to allow women space to be different and, as such, to be as subjects.

The role of the female body in this agenda is key. Like de Beauvoir, Irigaray wants to admit the real materiality of the body, and so in agreement with her argues that the body exists, and that women are 'other' because of it. However, unlike de Beauvoir, Irigaray responds by redirecting otherness in a positive direction, claiming that women always already contain the other within themselves. For her, the female body is characterized by multiple points of desire[100] and by continuous touching, a point which she communicates through the image of the 'two lips'.

---

[96] Irigaray 'The Question of the Other', in Lynne Huffer (ed.), *Another Look, Another Woman: Retranslations of French Feminism*, Yale French Studies (vol. 8, New Haven, Connecticut and London, 1995), pp. 7–19, esp. p. 10.

[97] Irigaray, 'The Other: Woman', in Sandra Kemp and Judith Squires (eds), *Feminisms* (Oxford and New York, 1997), pp. 308–15, esp. p.310.

[98] See Luce Irigaray, 'The Power of Discourse and the Subordination of the Feminine', in Margaret Whitford (ed.), *The Irigaray Reader* (Oxford and Cambridge, Massachusetts, 1991), pp. 118–32. For Irigaray this is to make woman a 'potential man' (p. 130).

[99] Marilyn Frye, 'The Necessity of Differences: Constructing a Positive Category of Women', *Signs*, 21/4 (1996): 991–1010, esp. p. 993.

[100] See Luce Irigaray, *This Sex Which is Not One*, trans. Catherine Porter with Carolyn Burke (Ithaca, New York, 1985), p. 28. Also see p. 59 of her 'Volume without Contours',

Women do not need to look outside of themselves – their bodies – in order to establish their own subjectivity. Because 'she' is already *more* than one, she need only look to herself for self-definition.

For Irigaray, then, speaking the multiplicity of the female body (what Irigaray refers to as *parler-femme*) holds great potential for destabilizing phallocentric logic and for signifying two subject positions.[101] This indicates the importance of safeguarding transcendence between the two; so that the one can never be grasped or possessed by the other.[102] Her call for *parler-femme* (or speaking woman) is not, however, a call to speak female 'biology' for she does not suggest that the body precedes its locatedness within discourse. The female body Irigaray talks about is a constructed body which is contextualized within discourse and language; a body which is already coded, structured, inscribed, constituted and given meaning by culture and within history.[103] This is the *morphological* body as opposed to the anatomical body: the body which is discursively constructed.[104] However, that the female body cannot be 'spoken' within phallocentric language exposes the limits of language. The body, although constructed through language, cannot be collapsed into it.

Although more will be said about Irigaray in the next chapter, such insights serve to further those previously noted in relation to de Beauvoir's conception of the body as 'situation'. Whereas de Beauvoir's conception of female subjectivity seems to require the pre-requisite of disembodiment, Irigaray's firmly roots this within the discursive, morphological female body. This is not an essentialist move but a tactical one, establishing the female body as the locus of resistance to phallocentric logic. Such a model of subjectivity also makes clear its discursive position within phallocentric relations of opposition. This moves de Beauvoir's understanding of the body as 'situation' to a new level, identifying the body's situatedness within language. Hence although the body is a lived, historical body, it is 'always already' a body which is constructed through discourse. However, the body is not reducible to discourse; it reveals the limits of discourse and may be used to challenge phallocentric logic. Irigaray also provides a positive vision of female otherness which compensates for de Beauvoir's, which does not reduce 'women' to the binary opposite of 'men' (what men are 'not') and thus to a position

---

in Margaret Whitford (ed.), *The Irigaray Reader* (Oxford and Cambridge, Massachusetts, 1991), pp. 53–68.

101 According to Irigaray, difference enables the becoming of a 'dialectic' of two subjects. See *The Way of Love*, trans. Heidi Bostic and Stephen Pluháček (London, New York, 2002), p. 100 and 'The Question of the Other', p. 11.

102 See Luce Irigaray, 'The Wedding Between the Body and Language' in Luce Irigaray (ed.), *Luce Irigaray: Key Writings* (London, New York, 2004), pp. 13–22, esp. p. 14.

103 Grosz, p. 111. Also see Grace M. Jantzen's article, 'What's the Difference? Knowledge and Gender in (Post) Modern Philosophy of Religion', *Religious Studies*, 32 (1996): 431–48, esp. p. 440.

104 Grosz, pp. 111–13.

which is to be overcome. For Irigaray, women's otherness lies at the heart of their subjectivity.

There are, of course, problems with Irigaray's reading of female subjectivity. Most significantly she appears to establish sexual difference as the most fundamental difference and appears to be guilty of minimizing the importance of other areas of difference such as class, race, and sexuality. Her vision of two positive subject positions alludes to a heterosexist framing of subjectivity and this is problematic in light of the problems already discussed above: such problems will be addressed in more detail in the next chapter. However, her central contention that female subjectivity cannot and should not be theorized outside of the female body is, I believe, important for two significant reasons: first, because it identifies that the body is an inevitable part of a woman's situation within the world, and second, because it claims that this is the means by which women's nothingness is constructed within the symbolic order and thus the means by which women's subjectivity is tactically produced.

How then are we to combine the useful features of de Beauvoir's contribution with Irigaray's proposal in such a way that takes account of the difficulties already identified? One response is to understand subjectivity in terms of what I call 'positionality'. This draws on de Beauvoir's notion of the female body as 'situation' and Irigaray's understanding of 'woman' as a symbolic position within language without repeating difficulties already highlighted with these views. It also avoids the universalism and essentialism detectable within earlier appeals to women's experience and the generalizing tendencies of feminist standpoint epistemology.

What is 'Woman'? Embracing the notion of 'Positionality'

Essentially, the notion of positionality communicates that women are all positioned differently and do not inhabit only *one* cultural tradition. It is not simply that different women are constructed by different influencing cultural forces (such as class, gender, geographical location, race and so on) but that these forces themselves may vary, shift and change as individual women go through life. Positionality then admits both the complexity and fluidity of (female) subjectivity and selfhood. It recognizes that women are embodied within particular dynamic, shifting contexts; that women each embody a matrix of differences and that each individual woman may be embodied differently at different times. Within this setting, there can be no room for essentialist readings of 'woman'.

Second, and related to this, it says that there is 'no view from nowhere' but also that there is no 'dream of everywhere'.[105] The body *is* a real historical body which cannot be erased through the recognition of other discursive or social influences. Thus, although a woman's position may change, with her class, for example, taking a more prominent role than say sexual difference at certain times and in certain contexts, these shifts are always embodied. The body is not free to go anywhere

[105] Bordo, p. 218.

and change its shape as it so wishes – a postmodern dream which Susan Bordo links with the concept of 'cultural plastic'.[106] There are real, concrete limitations to human bodies.

This brings to the fore the importance of 'embodiment'. Indeed, positionality does not erase the body or collapse the body into discourse because it says that the body *exists*. This, however, is not to say that the body determines gender, or that all women have the exact same body. The body is never just a biological body. Thus, rather than speaking about the 'body' as though there is some 'thing' which exists before culture and language, we more accurately speak about *embodiment* – the body in the world and, as such, the body which is 'positioned' or 'located' within language and culture. This is not to reduce the body to text. Although Butler is right in saying that materiality is a function of discourse, materiality can also challenge discourse and give rise to new discourses.

Such a stress on embodiment also carries significant implications for understanding women's experience. Although appeals to women's experience have been criticized for assuming that there is such a thing as pre-linguistic, immediate experience, a focus on positionality not only admits the materiality of the body but also the concreteness of experience. As Sheila Greeve Davaney notes, we literally 'feel our way through life'[107], hence even though experience may not constitute a stable, innocent, pre-linguistic foundation in feminist theology, it, like the body, cannot be collapsed completely into language. Experience is real for all who experience. This is one of the main contributions of contemporary historicism. As an embodied and materially embedded reality, the body experiences the world. But language informs our feeling and thinking.[108] Indeed, language cannot be separated from experience or 'feeling', however, this is not to call into question the actuality of experience itself, women *do* experience; it simply undermines any understanding of (women's) experience as immediate and self-evident. To say that women are *embodied* within different positions then recognizes the reality of women's experiences without assuming these to be a stable foundation.

Positionality also recognizes that sexual difference is not the only difference within women and men's 'situations', hence there can be no generic female essence or uniform way of seeing or experiencing the world which filters from gender. A white, middle-class woman living in North America may find that she has far more in common with a white, middle-class man living in North America than with a black woman living in South Africa. However, just because there is no 'woman's way of knowing the world' on account of gender does not mean that women do not share experiences or similar conditions in the lived world. It is true that some women will share more in common with particular women than with others. The notion of positionality allows for this without assuming such

[106] Ibid., p. 246.

[107] Sheila Greeve Davaney, *Pragmatic Historicism: A Theology for the Twenty-First Century* (New York, 2000), p. 24.

[108] Ibid.

commonalities reduce women to the same or testify to the existence of a shared female essence.

There may also be cross-cultural agreement between women (on the basis of experience) that certain acts, practices, behaviour are oppressive. Jennifer Beste, for example, convincingly argues that significant social scientific cross-cultural research on the effects of trauma on persons and society indicates that individuals share certain vulnerabilities and experience particular events (such as rape, torture and the violence of war) as damaging.[109] Hence, she argues that women's experience can offer reliable knowledge about reality, not on the basis of essentialism but on the basis of overlapping experiences. Indeed, Beste's point is a good one. Although women *need not* share experience, feminist theology must operate on the basis that commonalities between women's experiences are possible and must be recognized. Feminist theologians must be free to make such claims without being accused of essentialism. The notion of positionality allows for this. Although experiences are particular and informed by culture and discourse, women's positions within the world may overlap and intersect at different points. This does not slip into false universalism because no two women's embodiments are ever identical; if we take individual women's contexts seriously, essentialism will be avoided. Positionality then admits that identity is constructed in relation to others as well as in relation to cultural and historic factors.[110] As positioned bodies, we are who we are because of other bodies (as well as other factors).

Admitting that women are diversely embodied then need not collapse women into an endless sea of difference. On the contrary, the category 'women' carries meaning at three significant levels. First, it serves as an identifier of possible commonalities between women which have been discovered across a range of differing contexts. Such commonalities do not provide evidence of a universal female essence or set of experiences but testify to overlapping strands of historical circumstance. Second, the term can find meaning in relation to its identification with certain physical features common to may women, such as breasts, the vagina and clitoris. However, although women might be *identified* by the body they can never be *defined* in relation to it. Of course some women may not identify or be identified in this way so we must embrace this only as a partial, tentative and pragmatic descriptor. Third, it identifies the female body's position within language. The notion of positionality says that the body is a body positioned within a symbolic, linguistic context where identity is formed through opposition. Here, women can be identified in relation to their position as 'lack' or '*not*-man' within phallocentric discourse. This, however, is not a pre-determined, essential position for women, but a constructed symbolic position. Women can actively claim subjectivity but only by exploding the phallocentric system through the

---

[109] See Jennifer Beste's article, 'Limits of the Appeal to Women's Experience Reconsidered', *Horizons*, 33/1 (2006): 54–77, esp. pp. 61–2.

[110] Linda Alcoff makes this point on p. 433 of her article, 'Cultural Feminism Versus Post-structuralism: The Identity Crisis in Feminist Theory', *Signs*, 13/3 (1988): 405–36.

exposure of difference and thus by revealing a *different* position within language: I will address this point in the next chapter.

Such a rendering of subjectivity is, I believe, deeply important if feminist theology is to make a meaningful appeal to 'women's experience' in its doing of theology. It prevents women from being collapsed into the body whilst recognizing the body's concreteness. It prevents the body from being collapsed into 'text' and women's diverse experiences form being reduced to abstraction but does not overlook difference nor the body's locatedness within language. However, despite this, there are still a number of questions surrounding the use of women's experience in theological method which need to be answered, namely why *women's* experience in particular should be privileged in theological method, *whose* experience should operate as normative and on *what* grounds this should be established.

Justifying the Use of Women's Experience in Theological Method

Why women's experience? In light of the difficulties already considered, many feminists today choose to establish an appeal to women's experience on historical-pragmatic grounds. Linda Hogan provides one example, insisting that feminist theological insights (which filter from women's experiences) can claim an ethical-pragmatic as opposed to ontological priority on the basis of the type of commitments they inspire. Because feminist theologies are committed to right relationship and justice they can claim priority over patriarchal theologies.[111] Sheila Davaney provides a less optimistic view arguing that women's experience cannot claim any epistemological privilege. Theological claims, she proposes, must be judged according to their pragmatic consequences – that is, in terms of the consequences we anticipate might result from adopting one set of values and visions over another – rather than in relation to a feminist standpoint or an ontological foundation.[112] Because all knowledge is perspectival, the most we can say, she argues, is that feminist visions of the world provide *alternative* interpretations of reality as opposed to ontologically truer glimpses of the way the world *is*.[113] There can be no sure and certain knowledge applicable for all times and in all places which is grounded on unquestionable foundations.[114]

Whilst I am sympathetic to Davaney's views and attracted to her historicist-pragmatic approach, I do think (along with Hogan) that women's experience can continue to operate as source and norm without suggesting that women have a monopoly on truth as a result of being women. Indeed, I think that beginning

---

111 Hogan, p. 171.

112 Davaney, 'Continuing the Story', p. 212.

113 Sheila Greeve Davaney, 'The Limits of the Appeal to Women's Experience', in Clarissa W. Atkinson, Constance H. Buchanan and Margaret R. Miles (eds), *Shaping New Vision: Gender and Values in American Culture* (London, 1987), pp. 31–50, esp. p. 47.

114 Davaney, *Pragmatic Historicism*, p. 23.

with women's experience is a way to expose the contextual nature of all theology, to expose the differences women make to theology and to affirm in light of this that women's lives and experiences matter. If women's experiences have been rendered invisible in the past then beginning with these experiences provides a more accurate view of the landscape – not in terms of professing to know how the world *really* is and/or should be on account of gender, but in terms of revealing the existence of a plurality of voices, perspectives and differences which theology has, in the past, overlooked. Such experiences do not provide an infallible, self-evident, pre-linguistic, timeless or universal account of reality, but they do contribute to a *clearer* vision of the world (that is, the world as constructed and known through discourse), on account of their exposure of difference.

Women's experience then claims its privilege on methodological as opposed to ontological grounds. This is similar to Hogan's account of pragmatism[115] and Sandra Harding's account of 'strong objectivity'.[116] In keeping with previous chapters it does not say that we have access to a pre-linguistic and pre-contextual reality but it does say that there are more and less useful resources for learning about the world. It recognizes also that although different women experience oppression in different ways and different experiences as oppressive, the shared principles which feminist critical reflection on such experiences inspire within feminist communities (namely principles of resistance to oppression and a commitment to liberating praxis) make 'feminist' standpoints possible and ensure that feminist visions are attentive to difference. Solidarity here is fostered through experience and through the sharing of experience in dialogue. It is not a reducing of difference to sameness or an essentializing of women's experience because different feminists will invariably produce different knowledges from their own particular positions: I will develop this point in the final section of this chapter. However, insofar as these visions welcome experiences which have previously been silenced, they are rendered more effective than patriarchal visions at facilitating a clearer view of the world. Although we can never know the Truth about the world or access reality as it *realty* is, a *better* understanding of the world is one which takes account of difference.[117]

In saying this then, I believe there is an ethical-pragmatic imperative for beginning theology with women's experiences. Not denying that there are a plethora of differences within the feminist-Christian community (because of a diversity of experience), most if not all feminists seek to resist oppression and work towards liberating praxis. Inherent within these commitments are concerns for justice, right

---

115 See Hogan, p. 171.

116 See previous discussion in this chapter and Harding, 'Rethinking Standpoint Epistemology'.

117 For a similar argument, see Nancy J. Hirschmann, 'Feminist Standpoint as Postmodern Strategy', in Sandra Harding (ed.), *The Feminist Standpoint Theory Reader: Intellectual and Political Controversies* (London and New York, 2004), pp. 317–32, esp. p. 320.

relationship,[118] and liberation for all oppressed peoples. Certainly feminists may and often do disagree on what these commitments and concerns tangibly mean, but they do nevertheless form a shared ethical and pragmatic focus in relation to which the normativeness of women's experience can be established. Rather than signalling an ontological core within feminist visions which transcends experience or language, these principles and commitments are firmly rooted in experience and provide a reference point in relation to which women's diverse experiences might be critically assessed.

Whose experience is to be privileged? The final question for us to answer then is whose experience is to be privileged in feminist theology? In seeking to respond to this question, a firm distinction must first be made between women's experience and critical *feminist* reflection on women's experience. As we have already seen, one of the most common criticisms of feminist standpoint epistemology has been the assumption that all women share feminist values and are committed to the same feminist goals. To say that women have a clearer understanding of the world and how it should be assumes that all women are looking at the world through the same spectacles and are committed to the same ethics. Clearly this is not the case. I therefore propose that it is women's experiences as shared and critically reflected upon within the Christian *feminist* community which are to be prioritized in theological method.

At one level, this avoids subjectivism and relativism since it is not women's *individual* experiences which are normative (as suggested by Stanley and Wise), but the experiences of women which are shared and reflected upon within the Christian feminist *community*. Thus, if a woman experiences patriarchy as fruitful or as her lot in life, this experience, although heard, is not embraced as normative. Of course, this assumes a level of consensus within the Christian feminist community, specifically a shared understanding that patriarchy is oppressive and that liberation should be sought after, however I have already suggested that this exists, at least at a general ethical and pragmatic level. It is, therefore, experiences which are critically reflected upon in relation to feminist commitments to resist oppression and work towards liberating praxis which are privileged.

Such an understanding of the feminist community owes a considerable amount to Elisabeth Schüssler Fiorenza's notion of the *ekklesia gynaikon* or 'women-church'.[119] For Fiorenza, it is the historical experiences of women as shared and critically reflected upon within the *ekklesia* of wo/men[120] which provide the criteria against which to judge theological claims. The *ekklesia*, she argues, has the

---

118 These are characteristics also highlighted by Linda Hogan, see p. 171.

119 I have discussed Fiorenza's model of *ekklesia* elsewhere in a chapter co-authored with J'annine Jobling, 'Why Feminists Should Still be Liberals', *Theological Liberalism: Creative and Critical* (London, 2000), pp. 91–113.

120 Fiorenza uses the term 'wo/men' because she wants to transcend the sex/gender polarity. The term may refer to all women and also marginalized men.

authority to choose or reject biblical texts on the basis of a systematic exploration of women's experiences of oppression and liberation.[121] Its goal is not simply the full humanity of women (see Ruether and her 'critical principle')[122] since 'humanity' is often defined in relation to a male ideal, as is evident in the case of de Beauvoir. Instead, it seeks to promote women's religious self-affirmation, power and liberation from all patriarchal structures, including racism, classism and colonialism.[123]

For Fiorenza, the *ekklesia* is a movement made up of self-identified women and women-identified men. It constitutes a congress of full decision-making citizens, a discipleship of equals which seeks to give voice to the oppressed and gain solidarity with them. The *ekklesia* is a radically democratic community in which difference is welcomed but not at the expense of particularity; where diversity is knitted together so as to form a strong base from which feminism might take its root. Within this movement, solidarity is gained through the self-identification of women; by women identifying themselves in distinction from the self-alienation encouraged by patriarchy.[124] It is because those within the *ekklesia* are committed to living what Fiorenza calls 'the option for our women selves',[125] of struggling for liberation, that community can be maintained within the context of vast differences. Indeed, Fiorenza argues that solidarity is gained through accountability and, therefore, through women getting alongside one another in friendship, respecting diverse experiences and placing them within a shared ethical perspective which is in counter distinction from kyriarchal structures.[126]

This shared vision is, however, according to Fiorenza, deeply Christian. She notes that there is a shared conviction within the *ekklesia* that 'kyriarchy'[127] stands outside God's intentions for the world: a vision of a time when God's justice will prevail, when the marginalized and outcast will be vindicated and when God's kingdom will, at last, be established.[128] In this sense the *ekklesia* is liberation bound. It does not stop at *understanding* oppression (as do Stanley and Wise on the whole) but is actually loaded with political force and committed to changing the status quo through an appeal to women's diverse experiences.

---

121 Fiorenza, 'The Will to Choose', p. 131.

122 Ruether, *Sexism*, p. 18.

123 Fiorenza maintains that she does not define patriarchy in a general sense as a social system in which men have power over women but in a 'classical' sense as 'a social, economic and political system of graded subjugations and oppressions'. See 'The Will To Choose', p. 127.

124 Ibid., p. 128.

125 Ibid.

126 Fiorenza, *Discipleship of Equals: A Critical Feminist Ekklesia-ology of Liberation* (London, 1993), p. 200.

127 Fiorenza's uses this term to signify multiplicative axes of oppression.

128 Fiorenza, *Discipleship of Equals*, p. 67.

Fiorenza's notion of *ekklesia* or women-church is useful here then because it does not assume that sexism is the most fundamental form of oppression on top of which other forms rest. This resonates well with the notion of positionality previously outlined. Indeed, for Fiorenza, the *ekklesia* speaks of the multiplicity of oppression across a range of co-ordinates – whether racism, sexism, classism, colonialism and so on – all of which, according to Fiorenza, constitute the workings of 'kyriarchy'. Women-church then is a place where differences are embraced and welcomed and where oppression is not ultimately reduced to sexism. Such a concept allows space for a more complex understanding of oppression which does not simply operate along the lines of sexual differences, although admittedly, Fiorenza seems to pay more attention to sexual difference than any other. Women-church can signify the global (as opposed to white-Western) Christian-feminist community working towards the liberation of all who are oppressed.

Fiorenza's articulation of the *ekklesia* is also useful because it is not relativist. Although different women have different experiences, the *ekklesia* is united in its struggle against multiplicative forces of oppression and in its shared vision of the kingdom of God. It is through this shared Christian vision, which Fiorenza aligns with a feminist ethical commitment to resisting oppression and working towards liberating praxis, that solidarity is gained and transformation rendered possible.

However, there are a number of problems with appealing to the *ekklesia* as normative in this way. Perhaps most obviously, experiences within the global community of women-church are not uniform. As Linda Hogan notes: 'Texts and traditions which are experienced as oppressive by some may not be so experienced by others.'[129] Feminists may disagree on *which* texts and traditions contribute to women's wholeness and liberation because their experiences of what make for wholeness and liberation may differ. Although there may be overlap, there is in no sense a universal agreement between all feminists on what makes for justice, liberation and right relationship. If this is so, then how does the feminist community of women-church actually provide a consistent set of norms and criteria which filter from experience?

This tension between upholding difference and maintaining solidarity between women is clearly present within Fiorenza's notion of *ekklesia*, although she provides little guidance as to how it might realistically be resolved. The way forward I propose, is by viewing the feminist community in more fluid terms, at both a general and particular level. At a general level the feminist community upholds a commitment to liberation, justice and right relationship. These are generalized norms which operate cross-culturally to provide a common, although not fixed, interpretative framework for the discussion of women's diverse experiences. As I have already argued, such norms filter from the specifics of context and are established on non-foundational grounds; they do, however, serve to direct the praxis of particular local communities. At a more particular level, the feminist community is broken down into many diverse communities and it is at this

[129] Hogan, p. 91.

level that generalized norms are given their specific meaning. Individuals may be members of various communities on the basis of different, fluctuating factors which influence their sense of identity (such as sexuality, class, race, physical ability and others). Thus, although most, if not all feminists will be committed to the values of liberation, justice and right relationship, different women will experience patriarchy in different ways and will interpret these general values in ways congruent with their own historical and discursive positions. What may constitute grounds for solidarity at one point in time or in one context (for example shared experience about sexual difference or class) may divide women at another time or in another context.

In this sense, the Christian-feminist community is composed of various different fluid communities; a concept which echoes (to a point) Rita Felski's notion of the 'feminist public sphere' which she suggests is composed of 'loose and contingent coalitions of diverse groups'.[130] It is from the basis of these loose and contingent communities that more specific norms are sketched and more specific knowledges produced. There will be 'family resemblances'[131] between the norms and assumptions produced by different groups on account of the generalized framework to which all feminist communities contribute and on account of the inter-cultural dialogue which takes place between communities. Of course, because any one individual may be part of a range of communities at the same time, these 'coalitions' are interconnected and in no sense water tight. Norms produced within community then need not be just local and particular – they are related to one another just as communities are related to one another. Because of the interconnectivity of communities and the potential for highlighting shared experience through dialogue, communities may build greater consensus.

We may ask how useful this is for feminist theology. It certainly asserts, in keeping with more postmodern accounts, that communities are the primary generators of knowledge. It says that knowledge is produced (rather than found) by embedded and embodied individuals who live in relation to one another[132] and that experience and reality are socially shaped. It does, therefore, propose a more flexible and less stable conceptualization of community than Fiorenza appears to suggest. Because we participate in a number of social communities, we contribute to a range of knowledges produced by them.[133] This identifies feminist knowledges as historical, limited and discursive – 'they hold out the vision of certain goods and values but are always incomplete, contingent, fallible and hence vulnerable to challenge and open to revision or replacement'.[134]

---

130 Felski, p. 201.

131 Ibid.

132 See Barbara J. Thayer-Bacon's outline of 'relational epistemology' presented in *Transforming Critical Thinking: Thinking Constructively* (New York and London, 2000), p. 2.

133 See Lynn Hankinson Nelson's chapter, 'Epistemological Communities', in Linda Alcoff and Elizabeth Potter (eds), *Feminist Epistemologies: Thinking Gender* (London and New York, 1993), pp. 121–60.

134 Davaney, 'Continuing the Story', p. 211.

This, however, is not to collapse women-church into endless difference and theological claims into a sea of relativity. There *are* norms and criteria established by women's multiple and diverse experiences, and so there *are* better and worse ways to think and speak about God. These are determined at a general level (in relation to the general norms of liberation, justice and right relationship shared by the feminist community) and at a particular level (in relation to the particular norms produced by specific communities).

Fiorenza is therefore right to assert a sense of solidarity which characterizes women-church, namely a commitment to transformative and liberative praxis which is both a Christian as well as feminist vision. Women-church understood as a collection of communities of knowers, although characterized by multiple experiences, confesses a commitment to liberating the oppressed and producing knowledge which contributes to this. What this means is that Christian feminist theologians must engage in global, inter-cultural dialogue in order to prevent feminist theology from becoming ghettoized and so that knowledge and norms are shared and learnt from. Indeed, the appeal of the *ekklesia* is that it seeks to embrace difference whilst retaining a shared vision of resistance. Here, experiences can be shared (between individuals and between communities) without such experiences being colonized by the 'other'. Because knowledge is contextual, it is always in danger of excluding and reflecting the particularities of particular groups, hence feminist theology's openness to dialogue is its biggest asset and is essential. It is the means by which overlapping experiences are made apparent and the means by which a stronger objectivity is produced. Dialogue here is not a way of mitigating difference, but serves the interests of 'coalition-building'.[135]

Women's Experience as a Realistic Starting Point?

Such an argument, however, implies that 'women's experience' is a realistic starting point in the first place; that it is indeed possible to begin from this position so long as an adequate case can be presented in its favour. To be sure, beginning from women's experience assumes that women are able to articulate their *own* experiences. The next chapter questions this assumption. If, as we have argued, women are positioned within a symbolic system which necessarily defines them as 'lack' in relation to a male norm then this carries significant implications for the use of women's experience in theological method. It is not simply that women have no *subjectivity* of their own but that they consequently have no *experience* of their own, hence appeals to *women's* experience become vacant and unrealizable in actuality. The next chapter considers this problem in more detail. Essentially it argues that in order for women to claim their *own* experiences they must be able

[135] Beatrice Hanssen, 'What Happened to Feminist Theory?' in Elisabeth Bronfen and Misha Kavka (eds), *Feminist Consequences: Theory for the New Century* (New York, 2001), pp. 58–98, esp. p. 63.

to speak as *subjects* and this requires a transformation of the logic of the current symbolic order. In order for women's experience to operate as a meaningful starting point, women must be able to speak *as* subjects. It is in relation to this final concern that I call upon Irigaray and her notion of *parler-femme*.

Chapter 5
From Women's Experience to 'Speaking (as) Woman':
Luce Irigaray and *Parler-Femme*

'*Parler-femme*' is a term used by Luce Irigaray to connote a distinctive style of female exchange and speech which is grounded in the morphology of the female body.[1] For her, *parler-femme* (or 'speaking (as) woman'[2]) is essential to the undermining of phallocentric logic and the arrival of women as subjects. It signals a place for women in language and so points towards the transformation of the current phallocentric order. This chapter considers the opportunities *parler-femme* raises for a feminist theological method which seeks to take women's experience seriously. Essentially it argues that this theoretical model helps establish women's experience as a realistic starting point by insisting on *subjectivity* as a pre-requisite for *experience*. Women can only claim their *own* experiences if they claim their *own* positions as subjects. 'Women's experience' then only constitutes a meaningful starting point for feminist theology when women are able to speak (as) themselves and claim their *own* place within language. To this extent Irigaray's notion of *parler-femme* helps inform and map the final stage of the feminist theological method developed so far.

'Women's Experience' as a Phallocentric Construct

In the opening to *An Ethics of Sexual Difference*, Irigaray states that, 'Sexual difference is one of the major philosophical issues, if not the issue, of our age. … [It] is probably the issue in our time which could be our "salvation" if we thought it through.'[3] Thus, for Irigaray, sexual difference lies at the very heart of women's subjectivity. Such a strong conviction comes as a response to Irigaray's observation that there is, as of yet, no sign of sexual difference within the current Western symbolic order. The 'symbolic' – which refers to 'the pure system of

1 See Alison Stone, *Luce Irigaray and the Philosophy of Sexual Difference* (Cambridge, New York, Melbourne, Madrid, Cape Town, Singapore, Sao Paulo, 2006), p. 22.

2 See for example Luce Irigaray's use of this term in *This Sex Which is Not One*, trans. Catherine Porter with Carolyn Burke (Ithaca, New York, 1985), p. 135.

3 Luce Irigaray, *An Ethics of Sexual Difference*, trans. Carolyn Burke and Gillian C. Gill (London, 1993), p. 5.

signifiers'[4], namely to our necessary submission to language and culture[5] – erases the female-feminine. Reason, language and subjectivity are all established on the basis of a mono-sexual economy, only recognizing the *male* sex and consequently rendering language, logic and subjectivity inherently male. As a result, women are unknowable within the representational world of the symbolic for as soon as they submit to language, they fail to speak and signify as women.

This is Irigaray's central contention. Women cannot speak their own sex because as soon as they speak, they fail to speak as women. Following Lacan, she argues that subjectivity can only be acquired through the process of using and becoming subject to language; by submitting to what Lacan calls the 'Name of the Father'. However, because the only language available for women within the present symbolic order is that which is owned and controlled by men for the purpose of their own self-affection and autoeroticism,[6] women can only ever find meaning in relation to what the male is *not*. As soon as a woman submits to language, she loses her-'self'. Irigaray thus follows other poststructuralists in arguing that language does not so much *express* meaning as *produce* meaning in relation to that which is other. Freud, she argues, epitomizes this logic defining 'woman' as lack; as the absence or negation of the male norm. The result, Irigaray maintains, is that women constantly find themselves in *masquerades*, acting like men in order to try and claim some degree of identity but always inevitably submitting to the dominant economy of (male) desire.[7]

This phallocentric symbolic order is therefore characterized by a process of *saming*. Here, 'woman' constitutes the mirror (or speculum) through which the male reflects himself and establishes his own subjectivity, 'giving man back "his" image and repeating it as the "same"'.[8] She provides the ground upon which the male establishes his own subjectivity and as such, fails to exist as subject in her own right. Within this phallocentric economy, male subjectivity is achieved by a return in and through the female. According to Irigaray, the male is nostalgic about the loss of his original home in the woman and so establishes his own subjectivity by a return to and through her. This return, however, according to Irigaray, operates to control, possess, and appropriate the woman. The man uses the woman as an instrument (and therefore 'object') by which to secure and establish his own transcendence. She has no space or being of her own and is a place from which the male cannot separate himself. She cannot return to herself and so cannot establish her own identity.

---

4 Claire Colebrook, *Gender* (Hampshire, New York, 2004), p. 199.

5 Ibid.

6 Jane Flax presents a critique of this perspective in her chapter, 'Postmodernism and Gender Relations in Feminist Theory', in Linda J. Nicholson (ed.), *Signs*, 12/4 (1987): 621–43.

7 Irigaray, *This Sex*, p. 133.

8 Luce Irigaray, *Speculum of the Other Woman*, trans. Gillian C. Gill (New York, 1985), p. 54.

For Irigaray, this process of *saming* infects the whole of Western philosophy and culture.[9] As we have already seen, she exposes Freud specifically as both following and promoting such a phallocentric logic, preaching a mono-sexual economy in which the woman fails to exist except as lack in relation to the male. Irigaray shows how for Freud, the girl is the 'little man', the clitoris a penis equivalent,[10] and her sex the epitome of 'nothing to see'.[11] Irigaray therefore criticizes Freud for theorizing sexual difference in terms of the ocular (that is in terms of what is visible) and for establishing a phallocentric economy in which the male sex organ is viewed as normative. In this sexual imaginary, woman's sexual desire cannot be signified. The main problem with the symbolic then, according to Irigaray, is that it produces the myth of the genderless subject – the false view that 'I' is a generic and neutral term when in fact the truth is that the only legitimate 'I' within this representational system is the male.

Such a critique of Western language and culture seems both plausible and important. Aristotelian thought as well as ancient Greek thought in general, demonstrates a dichotomous, oppositional ordering of the world which is reflected in Western culture, even today. The Pythagorean table of opposites which posits the male, good, light, right side against the female, evil, dark, left side evidences the way in which the symbolic world of representation has been divided in relation to sexual difference and structured so that the male always claims priority *over* the female. According to this logic, God is associated with the male, defining women in relation to what the male is not as not-man and not-God. For Aristotle, such a logic is evidenced in his understanding of women as misbegotten males. Such ideas have subsequently been taken forward by the likes of Augustine in the Patristic period and Aquinas in the Middle Ages,[12] reflecting and further establishing the dualistic nature of Western thought. The implications such a logic raises, however, for the use of women's experience in theological method are serious.

If women cannot signify as themselves within language and this is necessary in order for women to be subjects, then women have no subjectivity of their own. If they have no subjectivity of their own then they have no experience of their own since both are only ever given meaning in relation to what the male is not. This fails to recognize difference between men as well as difference between women and women's experiences. This consequently 'puts woman in the position of experiencing herself only fragmentarily, in the little-structured margins of a dominant ideology, as waste, or excess, what is left of a mirror invested by the (masculine) "subject" to reflect himself, to copy himself'.[13] In other words,

---

9 She cites many examples of which Plato, Nietzsche and Hegel are but a few.

10 Irigaray, *Speculum*, p. 25.

11 Such a critique of Freud can be found in the opening section of *Speculum* and is cited by Irigaray in the second chapter of *This Sex*, p. 26.

12 For further consideration of this point see Nancy Jay, 'Gender and Dichotomy', *Feminist Studies*, 7, 1 (Spring, 1981): 38–56, esp. p. 46.

13 Irigaray, *This Sex*, p. 30.

women experience themselves as objects of the male gaze – as less than, or the same as, him. To this extent, appeals to 'women's experience' are exposed as not strictly appeals to *women's* experience at all. Because 'woman has not yet taken (a) place[14] and 'for her part, remains unrealized potentiality – unrealized, at least, for/by herself',[15] 'women's experience' is exposed as a phallocentric construct and as a contentious starting point for feminist theology.

Irigaray's proposed solution to this problem is *parler-femme* and, thus, that women should begin to speak as women and speak their 'sex'. For Irigaray, speaking (as) woman enables women to establish their *own* subjectivity and serves to develop a feminine imaginary (or 'logic'/way of thinking) that has its roots in the female body rather than in the oneness of the male libido. For her, *parler-femme* holds the key to an imaginary which is not structured by phallocentric logic, and it is therefore only by speaking (as) women that women, she believes, are able to claim their own subjectivity. Before we assess the usefulness of this theoretical model for securing female subjectivity and for, therefore, completing the theological method developed in this book, it is important to unpack the meaning of *parler-femme* in more detail.

A Place for Women's Experience: The Importance of 'Speaking (as) Woman'

Parler-femme *and the Female Body*

For Irigaray, speaking (as) woman is related analogously to the female body and female pleasure. Just as female pleasure and sexuality are multiple and diverse, so is female speech and the female imaginary. Towards the beginning of *This Sex*, Irigaray argues that a woman's autoeroticism is deeply different from a man's making female language incongruous with phallocentric discourse. Whereas man requires an instrument to touch himself, woman does not;[16] whereas man has one sexual organ, woman has sexual organs '*more or less everywhere*.'[17] Masculine language, as analogous to the man's body, is determined by the logic and law of oneness and sameness whereas feminine language, as analogous to the female body, is characterized by plurality. 'He' uses language like he uses woman – as an instrument through which to secure his own transcendence and return. 'She', however, need not use language in this way since she already contains the other *within* herself. Her body is made up of two lips 'in continuous contact'[18] so she does not need to posses the 'other' in order to secure her own subjectivity. Irigaray therefore argues that female sexuality has the power to destabilize phallocentrism

[14] Irigaray, *Speculum*, p. 227.

[15] Ibid., p. 165.

[16] Irigaray, *This Sex*, p. 24.

[17] Ibid., p. 28.

[18] Ibid., p. 24.

because it does not reflect the logic of the same. 'Within herself, she is already two – but not divisible into one(s) – that caress each other.'[19]

Irigaray therefore uses the image of the 'two lips' touching as a metaphor for the plurality and irreducibility of female sexuality and female language (*parler-femme*). Just as the two lips are in continuous contact, so *parler-femme* favours an economy of 'touch' over an economy of the 'gaze'.[20] Just as female sexuality cannot be reduced to oneness, so female speech is characterized by multiplicity and cannot be reduced to the logic of sameness. Indeed, Irigaray argues that when woman speaks, her language is not recognizable within the present symbolic order. Her words, she says, seem 'contradictory ... somewhat mad from the standpoint of reason, inaudible for whoever listens to them, with ready-made grids, with a fully elaborated code in hand'.[21] Her speech is fluid, multiple and diverse,[22] setting off in all directions,[23] failing to fit into the univocal framework of the masculine symbolic. It does not rely on the A/not-A binary system of the Western phallocentric imaginary, but instead enables room for two subjects, for 'more' than one, and as such, for exchange and reciprocity between the *two*.[24]

The two lips then, as a metaphor for *parler-femme*, signal a female imaginary in which ownership and property are foreign concepts.[25] The image speaks about an economy founded on the reality of sexual difference where two subject positions are recognized. This twoness, however, is not a two reducible to ones, but like the two lips, a two which is typified by irreducible relations of closeness rather than consummation and appropriation. Within this economy, subject relations are not hierarchical but characterized by love and proximity. Difference is recognized and respected rather than disintegrated or annihilated. Rather than perpetuating a logic grounded on the oneness of the male libido, *parler-femme* signals a new economy (or culture) grounded on the reality of sexual difference, making possible a dialogical encounter between subjects.

'Speaking' and 'Speaking "to"': Parler-femme *as the Place of 'Encounter' Between Subjects*

Dialogue lies at the heart of the feminine imaginary. Indeed, for Irigaray, a second subject of discourse can only be established if the dialogical nature of language is secured; if there is space *between* 'me' and 'you' for a language of exchange to be made possible. Indeed, for Irigaray a central distinction must be

---

19 Ibid.

20 Ibid., pp. 26 and 79.

21 Ibid., p. 29.

22 Ibid., p. 79.

23 Ibid., p. 29.

24 For more on this see Susan Sellers, *Language and Sexual Difference: Feminist Writing in France* (London, 1991), pp. 135–8.

25 Irigaray, *This Sex*, p. 31.

made between 'speaking' and 'speaking *to*' for these are not the same.[26] Whereas 'speaking' connotes a language of need, 'including the need to master nature, objects and others',[27] an information model of transmission or instruction which operates by way of objectifying and appropriating the other, speaking *to* connotes a more horizontal model of communication which operates by way of reciprocal listening.[28] The 'to' indicates a space and place for genuine encounter between subjects and it is speaking *to* that Irigaray associates with *parler-femme*.

Irigaray uses her linguistic research to show that the desire for communication is more typical of women and is therefore a distinct characteristic of women's speech.[29] She does, however, argue that such communication is deeply hindered because there are no 'real partners'[30] at present within the dialogue/conversation – thus, although women may seek communication through their speech this is nevertheless defeated because women do not embody a separate space or place from the male subject. Indeed, Irigaray argues that language is not neuter because it always privileges the male subject. Drawing on her research, she argues that a typical sentence produced by the male is, 'I wonder if I am loved or: I tell myself that perhaps I am loved' whereas a typical sentence produced by a woman is, 'Do you love me?'.[31] Whereas the first statement makes use of 'I', is self-referential and addresses no other, the only subject in the second sentence is the 'you' to whom the woman (object) refers. Within this system, there is no room for dialogue between the sexes because the masculine is dominant within culture and within language. Speaking *to*, however, according to Irigaray, signals a different culture – a culture where an encounter between the sexes is made possible and 'where no man or woman can become master or slave for fear of destroying the given objective'.[32] The language of 'I love you', which reproduces a culture of possession and allows no space for love *between* subjects, is thus replaced by the language of 'I love *to* you' allowing space for genuine encounter.[33] Whereas the former utilizes a language of need and instruction, 'I love *to* you' connotes a language of personal relations characterized by communication and exchange.[34] *Parler-femme* then, as a language of communication, offers a glimpse of a different culture and form of speech which allows space for women to claim their *own* place as subjects of language/discourse.

---

[26] Luce Irigaray, *I Love to You: Sketch of a Possible Felicity in History*, trans. Alison Martin (London, New York, 1996), p. 45.

[27] Ibid., pp. 43–4.

[28] Ibid., p. 46.

[29] Ibid., p. 97.

[30] Ibid., p. 98.

[31] Irigaray, *An Ethics*, p. 134.

[32] Irigaray, *I Love to You*, p. 46.

[33] Ibid., p. 102.

[34] Ibid., p. 113.

Parler-Femme *and the Feminine Divine*[35]

Such a speaking position however, according to Irigaray, necessitates the construction of a feminine divine. Women can only speak their sex if they create a God of their own, a transcendental horizon, that will secure and confirm their own identity as sexed subjects. According to Irigaray, women must become *divine women* so that they are no longer overtaken as objects of male desire. Up until now, it is the male, according to Irigaray, who has constructed God in his own image in order to accomplish and realize his own subjectivity. By projecting himself onto the divine, the male has used God (like the woman, language, and other external instruments) as a tool by which and through which to secure his own return. Women, however, have not been able to claim subjectivity in the same way. Women, she says, 'lack a God to share, a word to share and to become'.[36]

In response, Irigaray encourages women to become divine themselves – 'Divinity is what we need to become free, autonomous, sovereign' she says.[37] 'It is essential that we become gods *for ourselves* so that we can be divine for the other, not idols, fetishes, symbols that have already been outlined or determined.'[38] For Irigaray then, becoming divine holds the key to attaining the subjectivity and relations of encounter signalled by *parler-femme*. By repeating the phallocentric logic of return in and through the other, women are able to accomplish and confirm their *own* sex. Indeed, she states quite firmly that the only God that can save women is a God of their *own* creation, a God who is the other for women, who can support and encourage female becoming; in short, a God who represents the self-love of women and their own subjectivity *apart* from the male gaze.

This, however, clearly raises problems for a feminist theological methodology which seeks to be orthodox as well as contextual. Collapsing God into female subjectivity destroys the objective reality of God and reproduces difficulties already addressed in relation to Schleiermacher. It collapses theology into anthropology and God becomes nothing more than a projection of the female self. This critique will be developed further when we return to a consideration of the Trinity in the following chapter, however, it is sufficient to say that such an understanding of the divine can never be sufficient for a theological method which wishes to preserve the ontological reality of God.

---

35 For more in this see my article, 'What's Right with the Trinity? Thinking the Trinity in relation to Irigaray's Notions of Self-love and Wonder', *Feminist Theology*, 15/2 (2007): 220–35.

36 Luce Irigaray, *Sexes and Genealogies*, trans. Gillian C. Gill (New York, 1993), p. 71.

37 Ibid., p. 62.

38 Ibid., p. 71.

Parler-Femme *and the Tactical Strategy of Mimesis*

Parler-femme then connotes the arrival of a new female imaginary. It signals a female culture which is analogous with female morphology and which is consequently characterized by dialogue and encounter between the sexes. It represents a distinctly female language which is itself made possible by the becoming of women as 'divine women' and by their own 'self-love'. But how exactly is *parler-femme* made possible within the current phallocentric imaginary?

According to Irigaray, the way to bring about *parler-femme* is through the tactical strategy of *mimesis*. It is only by deliberately repeating the logic of the same that such a logic can itself be undone. Because women have no existence or language of their own, their only option is to work within the present system, using (and submitting to) the language and logic of the oppressor. Irigaray is, however, clear that such a tactical submission will enable women to find their *own* voice within discourse as it will unveil the contradiction speaking as a woman actually entails. Once this contradiction is exposed, the reality of sexual difference becomes visible and the grounds upon which phallocentrism is established become shaky. Indeed, she argues that it is only through this process that woman will be exposed as being castrated of words.[39] If women assume the role of the feminine deliberately, acting as a mirror which reflects the man, they have the potential to reflect back the hidden (or repressed) gaps and spaces which lie dormant within the symbolic order, thus posing a threat to the stability of the phallus.[40]

At first such a strategy may seem strange, for in what sense is mimicking the logic of the same really going to help women break free from this logic and speak their *own* sex? In answering this it is important to keep in mind Irigaray's distinction between 'reproductive' and 'productive' forms of *mimesis*.[41] For Irigaray, *mimesis* is more than simply copying the status quo for such a 'reproductive' strategy would certainly maintain women within their non-existence. Instead, Irigaray claims to employ a more 'productive' *mimesis*, one which always has the intention of creating and producing something different.[42] This mimics the status quo, not to reinforce it but to expose it, opening up new possibilities so as to make clear the instability and inconsistency of the phallocentric order. Whereas the former constitutes a passive surrender to phallocentrism the latter constitutes an active search for fresh possibilities, hence the horizons and intentions are different.

The metaphor of the 'two lips' previously considered reveals the potentially subversive nature of *mimesis* as a strategy for exposing and exploding the logic of the same. As we have seen, Irigaray uses this image in order to communicate the diverse nature of female sexuality and desire. Now if phallocentric logic relies on the logic of 'saming' and uses the woman as a stable mirror through which

---

39 Irigaray, *Speculum*, p. 142.

40 See Irigaray, *This Sex*, p. 76.

41 Ibid., p. 130.

42 Ibid.

to reflect the male's oneness, the diverse nature of women's sexuality and desire stands to upset the logic of phallocentrism considerably. Because woman is always *more* than one, she cannot be used to reflect a stable image of the male back at himself. The plurality of the female sex causes the male to be thrown off centre. As Irigaray puts it, 'For if she ... were at once to be two but not divisible into one(s), how would he find his bearings?'[43] He is left without a stable mirror through which to secure his transcendence and the reality of sexual difference is exposed.

Deliberately assuming the role of 'not-A' then, according to Irigaray, gives women the chance to assert themselves positively as different. In this way, speaking (as) women filters from a sense that something still remains to be said that resists all speech; that there is something else 'other' than the singular male voice.[44] It signals that there is not only *one* possible space for women (as lack, as man's other) and that another alternative is in fact possible. Hence, it has the potential to place 'woman' outside phallocentric discourse as other – as something 'more' than can be said[45] and as such, to expose 'speaking' as not generic, universal, objective or neutral but as sexed, and more importantly, as sexed male. It is this *mimesis* then that, according to Irigaray, makes the idea of woman-speak a real possibility, rather than constituting a contradiction in terms. Of course, there are obvious difficulties with this strategy since it seems to reproduce rather than challenge an essentialist account of sexual difference, assuming women share the *same* subject space. We will deal with this later, however, the point which is useful for us here is that by women strategically occupying the place of the 'feminine', difference is exposed.

Parler-Femme *and Women's Experience*

Before critiquing the notion of *parler-femme*, let us pause to consider the implications such a female imaginary raises for articulating women's experience as a realistic starting point for feminist theology. We have already noted that if phallocentrism reduces women's experience to the 'same' as male experience, then it cannot operate as a realistic starting point in feminist theology. What is termed 'women's experience' turns out to be women's experience as viewed through the male gaze and so does nothing to secure the subjectivity of women as speaking subjects. *Parler-femme*, however, as a vision of a space which is truly 'different' and a culture which allows women to be themselves and to speak (as) women as opposed to masquerade as men, shows that the arrival of female subjectivity is key to the articulation of women's experience as a realistic starting point in feminist theology. In this sense, to establish women's experience as source and norm in theology means placing women back in 'touch' with their own bodies.[46]

---

43 Irigaray, *Speculum*, p. 239.

44 Ibid., p. 193.

45 Irigaray, *This Sex*, p. 89.

46 See Dani Cavallaro, *French Feminist Theory: An Introduction* (London, New York, 2003), p. 119. Also see Morny Joy, 'Equality or Divinity: A False Dichotomy?', *Journal of*

However, although Irigaray's theory is helpful in establishing women's experience as a realistic starting point it does, nevertheless, raise a series of major concerns. First, her notion of *parler-femme* seems to assume that sexual difference is the most fundamental and universal difference and as such, seems to ignore or at least play down the significance of other axes of difference, including race, class and sexuality. Second, and related to this, Irigaray's linking of female language with the female body could be seen as an essentialist move which threatens to reduce women once more to their bodies. Irigaray has been frequently criticized on this front and not, I believe, without good reason. Third, the notion of *parler-femme* may be seen as being overly utopian and idealistic. Although it provides a vision of a new language and culture, we must ask how realizable this is within the current symbolic order. Clearly, these criticisms raise important questions about the value of *parler-femme* for our own thinking about women's experience. We must therefore address these difficulties further, making clear the place of *parler-femme* within a feminist theological method which takes women's experience seriously.

Assessing the Usefulness of *Parler-Femme* for Feminist Theological Method

Sexual Difference as Primary

A major difficulty with Irigaray's articulation of *parler-femme* is her insistence that sexual difference constitutes the most universal difference between subjects. In *I Love to You* she writes:

> Without doubt, the most appropriate content for the universal is sexual difference. Indeed, this content is both real and universal. Sexual difference is an immediate natural given and it is a real and irreducible component of the universal. The whole of humankind is composed of women and men and of nothing else. The problem of race is, in fact, a secondary problem – except from a geographical point of view? – which means we cannot see the wood for the trees, and the same goes for other cultural diversities – religious, economic and political ones.[47]

Thus, it seems that for Irigaray difference between men and women is both 'natural' and elementary. In order for men and women to speak *to* one another – to engage in the language of dialogue and communication indicated by *parler-femme* – the universal of sexual difference must be acknowledged. Indeed, Irigaray is clear that in the end, there are only women and men. Other 'cultural diversities' are secondary.

Such a framing of sexual difference is, however, deeply problematic when viewed through the lens of 'positionality' as outlined in Chapter 4. This argued

Feminist Studies in Religion, 6/1 (1990): 9–24.

[47] Irigaray, *I Love to You*, p. 47.

strongly for a view of subjectivity which does not prioritize sexual difference over other forms of difference. Indeed, we have to ask why race should be viewed as a 'secondary problem' and sexual difference seen as primary. Surely this assumes that all women are essentially the same and that race, sexuality and class (amongst other things) do not influence what it means to be a woman. From what has already been argued, it should be clear that I do not embrace such a line of argument. Sexual difference is not to be understood in essentialist terms but is socially and discursively produced.

Some commentators, however, suggest that Irigaray's prioritization of sexual difference is political, strategic and, therefore, deliberate. Rosi Braidotti, for example, argues that Irigaray priorities sexual difference because this is a central point of reference for power relations in the phallocentric world. Because identity is always defined and assigned in relation to the polarized cultural categories of 'masculine' and 'feminine', we cannot escape the importance of this social and morphological point of departure.[48] For Claire Colebrook, Irigaray's reproduction of the male-female binary as primary provides another example of how Irigaray's strategy of *mimesis* serves to undermine phallocentrism. 'If it is the gender binary that has been metaphysical thought's primary trope, then only the radicalization of *this* binary can begin a rethinking of oppositional logics.'[49] For her, Irigaray's prioritization of sexual difference constitutes an attempt to play phallocentrism at its own game.

Not withholding these readings of Irigaray, her prioritization of sexual difference still remains hard to justify. If we are to say, as I have argued before, that commonalities between women should be *discovered* rather than assumed, and that race, class and sexuality (amongst other areas of difference) *do* influence how an individual experiences their body in the world, then it does not make sense to cite sexual difference as primary in the way that Irigaray does. We cannot insist that sexual difference is ontological or universal. Indeed, even if Western culture (and therefore philosophy) uses sexual difference as its structuring motif (which is hard to deny), it is debateable how far Irigaray's mimicking of this binary serves to successfully subvert phallocentrism. Indeed, the main problem with Irigaray is that her *mimesis* does not go far enough in challenging and transcending the male-female binary. Even though she may *intend* to utilize phallocentric logic in order to undermine it, her sustained exclusive emphasis on sexual difference places limits on what actually counts as difference. This undermines the notion of difference itself and reproduces rather than challenges a logic of sameness. In order to truly undermine this, *mimesis* must be used in order to signal an understanding of subjectivity which explodes even a binary view of difference and which pays attention to the multiplicity of subjectivity and difference.

---

48 Rosi Braidotti, 'Feminist Philosophies', in Mary Eagleton (ed.), *A Concise Companion to Feminist Theory* (Malden, Oxford, Melbourne, Berlin, 2003), pp. 195–214, esp. p. 207.

49 Colebrook, p. 204.

An Essentialist Connection Between the Body and Language?

Related to this, Irigaray also seems guilty of essentialism – of upholding the female body as an unmediated corporeality and of implying that female biology determines female language. Indeed, this is an area in relation to which Irigaray's work has experienced frequent criticism. How then are we to read her?

In her earlier work (such as *Speculum* and *This Sex*), Irigaray seems to advocate a form of 'political' essentialism[50] – an essentialism which is adopted deliberately and tactically in order to subvert phallocentric logic. According to this reading, Irigaray's attempt to root female language within the female body is not intended to suggest that woman is determined by her body or that there is such a thing as a distinctly female essence which determines a distinctly female way of speaking. Instead, such a move is intended to subvert phallocentric logic through a deliberate adoption of traditional representations of the female. Indeed, in *This Sex*, Irigaray responds to the question 'What is a woman?' by saying, 'there is no way I would "answer" that question',[51] seemingly affirming that women cannot be defined.

This approach to Irigaray's rooting of *parler-femme* within the female body interprets her reference to the 'two lips' as a non-literal, non-referential metaphor. For those who endorse this reading, such as myself and others like Elizabeth Grosz,[52] the image is used strategically to combat dominant phallocentric representations. Through its use, Irigaray reiterates women's traditional connection with the body but in a way that redefines the body in positive terms, outside the logic of the same.[53] She deliberately assumes the role of the (specular) feminine so as to expose the contradictions inherent within it.

Within this setting, *parler-femme* is understood as a constructed language which exists in close proximity to, but is not determined by, the constructed, morphological body. Because it is the way the female body is *constructed* that reduces women to silence and therefore the way the female body is *reconstructed* that, according to Irigaray, leads to women having voices of their own, *parler-femme* is not determined by a feminine essence connected to the female genitalia but instead relates to a constructed position within discourse.[54]

In her later work, however, Irigaray seems to adopt a more 'realist' form of essentialism.[55] Here Irigaray appears to suggest that there *are* certain universal commonalities shared by *all* women; commonalities which are actively determined

---

50 Alison Stone (p. 19) makes a distinction between 'political' and 'realist' forms of essentialism.

51 Irigaray, *This Sex*, p. 122.

52 Elizabeth Grosz, *Sexual Subversions: Three French Feminists* (St. Leonards, 1989), p. 116.

53 Stone, p. 31.

54 For more on this see Diana Fuss, *Essentially Speaking: Feminism, Nature and Difference* (London, 1989), pp. 62–3.

55 See Stone, p. 19.

by the female body and which exist outside culture and outside language. She thus seems to suggest that matter develops in line with its inherent character – that there *is* an ontology of man and an ontology of woman. In *I Love to You*, for example, Irigaray argues: 'The natural is at least two: male and female.'[56] She thus maintains that to recognize that there are *two* ways of being in the world, *two* cultures, *two* natures would lead to a revolution in ethics and sexual relations and would help safeguard against racism, war and ecological ruin. And yet the problem here is obvious: such a model once again implies that all women share a nature and essence which is distinct from men and which informs female language and culture. It assumes that matter is naturally determinate and that this can be separated from cultural representations of the body. We are thus thrown back into problems already discussed in the previous chapter and in the previous section of this chapter.

Given these difficulties, it seems to me that the most useful reading of Irigaray is one which proposes a political (rather than realist) essentialism. Although it is hard to deny the fact that her more recent work has moved significantly away from this emphasis, such a reading does arguably fit better with Irigaray's own proposed understanding of *parler-femme* as a dialogical and communicative language as opposed to a referential language of information, transmission and need. *Parler-femme* is a constructed, fluid and dynamic language and can be used to undo phallocentric logic. According to this reading, although women are defined by phallocentric discourse, they *can* actively use this language in order to construct another place for themselves within the symbolic order. This place need not be a position of sameness shared by all women in opposition to all men, as seems to be implied by Irigaray, but can connote the signification of multiplicity beyond the confines of sexual difference.

This is the subversive message of *parler-femme* and the message which holds so much promise for a feminist theological method which seeks to take women's experience as its starting point. Indeed, if women's experience is a phallocentric construct, then constructing a place for women within language – a place of encounter – not only seems useful for securing female subjectivity in all its variety, but for securing difference beyond the contours of sexual difference. Irigaray's notion of *parler-femme* is, however, only helpful if understood as a constructed female language as opposed to an unmediated language which filters directly from the female body. If sexual difference is considered to be universal and natural then this threatens to place limits on who and what women can 'be' reducing women to the 'same' as one another. This reproduces rather than challenges the logic of the same. If, however, we maintain that women are free to culturally determine their *own* subjectivity then women may be able to deliberately use phallocentric language and logic in order to purposefully and actively explode Irigaray's own binary logic of twoness as well as phallocentrism's logic of oneness and sameness.

---

56 Irigaray, *I Love to You*, p. 35.

In other words, *parler-femme* need not lead to the exposure of 'sexual' difference but of difference in a multiplicity of forms.

Parler-Femme *as Unachievable Goal?*

Finally, we must assess whether Irigaray's vision of a female imaginary is in fact realizable or whether this simply amounts to a mere utopian vision. Margaret Whitford, for example, argues that 'we have to act as though the ideal future is both impossible and possible, while knowing that the ideal is both incoherent and unrealistic, and in any case, subject to metamorphosis on route'.[57] For Whitford then, Irigaray's notion of a female imaginary can only ever be read at an ambiguous level – it is both realisable and unrealisable at the same time. Although the notion of speaking (as) woman might be theoretically necessary, it may not be wholly possible given the force and weight of phallocentrism within Western culture. Despite this however, Whitford is clear that for Irigaray, the theoretical concept nevertheless provides the impetus for practically working towards the vision of a female economy.

Yet the question of practical application is an important one for a feminist method that wishes to take women's experience seriously. Since beginning with 'women's experience' does not seek to merely signify a theoretical category but to actually affirm and give voice to the concrete and tangible experiences of women within the *ekklesia*, that women be able to speak (as) themselves in practice is of the utmost importance. However, Irigaray is clear that the new culture signalled by *parler-femme* is realizable only through the gradual destabilization and deconstruction of the phallocentric economy. Indeed, she says: 'It is not a matter of toppling that order so as to replace it – that amounts to the same thing in the end – but of displacing and modifying it, starting from an "outside" that is exempt, in part, from phallocentric law.'[58] This 'outside' may constitute the excess and hidden spaces previously referred to which have no voice within the symbolic. It is by starting here that the unity and exclusivity of the symbolic order is exposed as fictitious.

The female imaginary to which Irigaray refers then does not constitute a separate pre-packaged order which can be slotted in at the soonest available point, for such an understanding would simply recreate the A/not-A binary system of the current symbolic thereby failing to fulfil Irigaray's own goal of sexual difference. Instead, it connotes an economy in a process of *becoming,* and, thus, an economy whose *being* is always undecided.[59]

---

[57] Margaret Whitford, *Luce Irigaray: Philosophy in the Feminine* (London, New York, 1991), p. 24.

[58] Irigaray, *This Sex*, p. 68.

[59] For more on this see Alison Anley, 'Luce Irigaray: Divine Spirit and Feminine Space', in Philip Blond (ed.), *Post-Secular Philosophy: Between Philosophy and Theology* (London, New York, 1998), pp. 334–45, esp. p. 342.

Moving Beyond Irigaray's Binary Rhetoric

Such a vision raises interesting implications for a feminist theological methodology which wishes to take women's experience as its starting point. It means that women's experience can be placed at the beginning of theological method without *parler-femme* being fully realized. So long as the tactical strategy of *mimesis* deconstructs and subverts phallocentrism, it allows more room for women to speak and as such, more room for them to articulate their *own* experiences. The problem is, however, as we have already noted, that Irigaray does not always successfully subvert the logic of the same. This is mainly because Irigaray confines talk of difference to a binary rhetoric which prioritizes *sexual* difference and which therefore frames subjectivity in relation to the male-female couple. It is this binary rhetoric which lies at the heart of problems surrounding Irigaray's modelling of subjectivity and which must be overcome if *parler-femme* is to make a positive contribution to feminist theological method.

Indeed, Irigaray's binary rhetoric threatens to compromise difference and thwarts her own efforts to destabilize the logic of the same. This is clearly seen through Irigaray's call for a feminine divine since such a rendering of divinity threatens to reduce God to the same. Gavin D'Costa commendably criticizes this move by Irigaray on the grounds that it: a) reintroduces sex into notions of divinity,[60] a measure challenged by Christian orthodoxy, and b) re-establishes a binary, and therefore essentialist, view of sexual difference. He claims that Irigaray's call for *two* separate divine horizons, one male and one female, tends to freeze associations of gender with the body so that 'male' and 'female' become essentialized.[61] Hence he argues that Irigaray's call for a divine 'couple' simply encourages Feuerbachian projectionism, collapsing God into what women and men desire to be, thereby reinforcing phallocentrism.[62] Articulating the divine and sexual difference through such a binary rhetoric then fails to adequately signify the difference and diversity previously emphasized by the notion of 'positionality' and falls into the trap of projectionism previously criticized in relation to Schleiermacher.

Such a difficulty is also apparent in Irigaray's discussion of subjectivity. Because *parler-femme* signals the arrival of women subjects through the use of a specifically female language, Irigaray is clear that *parler-femme* points towards an economy in which *two* speaking subjects are recognized; where 'dialogue' and 'encounter' are made possible and where difference can co-exist alongside subjectivity. Speaking of difference in terms of *twoness* however implies that difference can be categorized as *either* 'this' or 'that'; as 'A' *or* 'B' and this stands to potentially limit subjectivity once more. As Nancy Jay points out, 'A/B distinctions are necessarily limited; in themselves they do not encompass C, D,

---

60 Gavin D'Costa, *Sexing the Trinity: Gender, Culture and the Divine* (London, 2000), p. 36.

61 Ibid., pp. xv, 7–10 and p. 29.

62 Ibid., pp. 29 and 48.

and so forth.'[63] Although I have suggested that we read this stress on *twoness* as a tactical attempt by Irigaray to subvert the logic of the same, to the extent that multiplicity and diversity between persons fails to be adequately signified, such a rhetoric fails to communicate the plurality of difference articulated in the previous chapter and must be challenged. To this end, Irigaray fails to achieve the goals she sets in place. Although her aim is to mimic phallocentrism so as to expose an alternative economy, this economy is not different enough since it fails to take account of difference between women.

In order to make *parler-femme* a helpful tool within my own feminist theological method then, it is necessary to move away from Irigaray's binary rhetoric towards a rhetoric which stresses the *many* as opposed to the *two*. Placing an emphasis on the *many* as opposed to the *two* means that sameness between women, sameness between men, and sameness between women and men is not presumed but can be discovered without compromising difference. It allows space for men and women to express their own subjectivities without assuming sexual difference as the most fundamental point of difference. This coheres well with the understanding of positionality outlined in the previous chapter and responds well to the critique previously outlined. It recognizes that women do not experience the same things nor in the same way. Although we acknowledge the materiality of the body and of sexual difference, we also acknowledge the influence of other varieties of difference. Although women may share similar physical bodies, they do, nevertheless, live their bodies in different ways and in different contexts.

The presumption of universal sexual difference which underlies Irigaray's articulation of *parler-femme* then is dismissed on the basis that this *reproduces* rather than subverts phallocentrism and is replaced by a logic which embraces plurality and multiplicity rather than twoness. *Parler-femme* is not an essentialist language which filters directly from the female body but involves the tactical taking up of the 'feminine' within language so as to expose the reality and multiplicity of difference across a range of coordinates. It does not expose the reality of two subject positions (male and female) as Irigaray implies, but of many. Indeed, if sexual difference is not primary, then difference cannot adequately be signified through a binary rhetoric. If a woman's 'sex' is only part of her situation and differences between individuals is not pre-determined by an appeal to 'essence', then the man-woman/masculine-feminine dichotomy is contested and begins to break down. A logic of the many points away from the A/not-A economy of phallogocentrism (where woman is defined in terms of what man is *not*), and from the A/B logic presented by Irigaray, towards a more concentrated focus on the diversity and plurality of subjectivity. This can be seen in terms of the following diagram.

63 Jay, 'Gender and Dichotomy', p. 44.

Phallocentrism	Parler-Femme	Beyond the Two
A/not-A	A/B	A, B, C, D, E, F and so on
Male	Male-female	Difference
Subject	Subject-Subject	Subjects
One	Two	Many

Suggesting a logic which stresses the many is not, however, to overlook the significance of the body or commonalities between women. As Chapter 4 argued, the term 'woman' carries meaning in relation to the female body because this is the means by which women are often identified and the means by which women are defined in the current phallocentric order. A logic of the many then does not refute commonalities between women or even between men and women, what it does refute, however, are any essentialist readings of these commonalities. It is not that subjectivity is marked by endless difference, but that commonalities occur across a range of co-ordinates, not just at the level of sexual difference. Identity is complex and we must favour a rhetoric which reflects this.

Of course, the challenge is that talk of the 'many' carries no meaning within phallocentrism but this is exactly the point! This is where the real subversive potential lies. Because phallocentrism cannot speak about difference in these terms, such a logic (which can, as Irigaray shows, be metaphorically and tactically [rather than literally] demonstrated by the multiplicity of female embodiment and female desire) stands to destabilize phallocentrism to a far greater degree than a binary logic which often reproduces rather than subverts the logic of the same.

If we therefore follow Irigaray in suggesting that love is only possible through the realization of difference and through 'encounter', then it is only through recognizing the *plurality* and *multiplicity* of difference that the logic of the same will be destabilized and that love will actually prevail. In this sense love is not between the *two* but between the *many*. Since difference does not pose a threat to subjectivity but constitutes the means by which it is achieved, difference here enables subjects to speak 'to' one another and enables relationships of encounter.

Conclusion

Beginning theological reflection with women's experience then necessarily demands that women be able to speak as subjects and brings to the fore the importance of *parler-femme* and *mimesis*. In order for women's experience to operate as a meaningful starting point, subjectivity must be affirmed outside a non-phallocentric context, in relation to a logic which does not define women as 'lack' or suggest some kind of universal difference between men and women. Subjectivity must find voice outside a phallocentric and even binary rhetoric so that the multiple and diverse nature of women's experience might be better communicated. This still requires the tactical use of *mimesis* as the only way in which women might achieve subjectivity is through the utilization of language within the current symbolic order. However, the realization of difference which occurs as a result of this is better expressed through a rhetoric of the many as opposed to a rhetoric of the two since this allows the multiplicity of difference to be more effectively signified.

This chapter then completes the final stage of the proposed feminist theological methodology developed in the second part of this book. This process has passed through three important stages, beginning in Chapter 3 with an articulation of *experience* as the logical starting point of theological reflection, moving on in Chapter 4 to establish *women's* experience in particular as an important point of departure, then finally ending in Chapter 5 by arguing for a modified appeal to *parler-femme* and *mimesis* as a way of making women's experience a realistic starting point for feminist theology.

The final chapter now returns to a discussion of the Trinity, assessing this doctrine's usefulness on the basis of what has been argued so far in relation to women's experience. Essentially we ask to what extent thinking God as Trinity might help subvert and resist phallocentric accounts of difference and subjectivity and so provide a helpful theological tool by which women's diverse subjectivities (and therefore experiences) might be affirmed.

PART THREE
Thinking the Trinity in Light of Feminist Theological Methodology

Chapter 6
This God which is Not-One:
Thinking the Trinity in Light of Feminist Theological Methodology

This final chapter returns to a discussion of the doctrine of the Trinity. If using women's experience as starting point demands that women claim their *own* positions as subjects by engaging strategically in *mimesis*, using the language and logic of phallocentrism in order to open up a discursive space in which women, in all their diversity, might be able to assert their *own* multiple experiences outside the logic of the same, then this final chapter asks how far thinking God as Trinity helps support this agenda. How might a trinitarian understanding of God resist and subvert patriarchal, phallocentric tendencies to reduce women to sameness, providing a theological setting in which difference and subjectivity might be celebrated? How might thinking God as Trinity challenge rather than reproduce phallocentric understandings of God which tie God to the male and alienate women from the *imago Dei*? Can a trinitarian understanding of God provide a theological context in which female subjectivity might be affirmed beyond the binary rhetoric of Irigaray and the multiplicity and richness of women's experiences be acknowledged and embraced?

These are critical questions and they lie at the heart of this final chapter. My aim here is to consider the ways in which and extent to which thinking God as Trinity (as outlined in Chapters 1 and 2) might reflect the central values which underpin the use of women's experience in feminist theology (as it has been outlined in Chapters 3 to 5). This is a form of *mimesis* insofar as we ask how thinking God as Trinity might strategically mimic the values underpinning the use of women's experience. This is strategic, however, in that the aim is not one of saming the Trinity or of collapsing the triune God into women's experience (where God becomes nothing more than the sum of these values which are drawn out of this method). Instead, the aim is to expose a trinitarian logic as being inconsistent with a phallocentric one and thus to reveal the subversive power of thinking God in this way. Although the Trinity may be used to support the centrality of the phallus and seemingly serve to reinforce the non-existence of women and women's experience, it may also resist and transform this logic. Calls to speak God in *new* ways so as to avoid reinforcing associations between the divine and male dominance (through, for example, reference to the divine as God-She or as Goddess), need not be the only way forward since *thinking* God as Trinity can subvert this dynamic.

In seeking to establish this case, the following chapter identifies 'difference' and 'subjectivity' as two central values which underpin the use of women's experience in theological method. These values are clarified and further broken down through a reflection on what has already been argued in Chapters 3 to 5. Given that women's experience has been presented as the logical starting point for feminist theology, it follows that the values which underpin this model call for certain measures in our thinking about God. Certainly, our thinking must be consistent with them. As such, this final chapter seeks to set out the requirements such values call for when it comes to thinking 'rightly' about God. The task here, however, is not to *reconstruct* God in light of these values since this has never been part of my agenda. Instead, the aim is to consider how thinking God as Trinity serves to affirm, and is affirmed by them. Overall it is argued that as Trinity, God *always already* exists in such a way that supports a non-phallocentric account of difference and subjectivity. If God is diversity in communion, three-in-one and one-in-three, then thinking God as Trinity provides a theological logic which operates in contradistinction to phallocentrism and which celebrates rather than curtails difference.

Before we proceed with this argument, however, it is important to note that an emphasis on difference and subjectivity in relation to 'women' here is not meant to reinforce a dichotomy between men and women, reinstating an essentialist and binary view of difference. Such a focus simply recognizes that it is *women's* subjectivity and difference which have been marginalized and ignored in the past and so maintains this emphasis on the ethical and pragmatic grounds established in Chapter 4. Also, because women are structurally located as 'other' and as 'lack' within the current symbolic order, difference cannot be spoken. If women's 'sex' then is the means by which the oneness of the phallocentric economy is established and confirmed then it becomes the means by which it is strategically destabilized and undermined. Hence, a focus on women is necessary. However, what thinking God as Trinity affirms is the *multiplicity* of difference, and this challenges a reducing of difference to sexual difference, celebrating difference across a range of coordinates.

Key Values Underpinning the Use of Women's Experience

From our discussion so far we can say that there are two broad values which underpin the use of women's experience in feminist theology: first, an affirmation of *difference* and second, an affirmation of *subjectivity*. Difference is important because without its recognition, women's diverse experiences are collapsed into a false homogeneity. This leads to the silencing of women's voices and to the consequent negation of women's experience as a meaningful, authentic starting point for feminist theology. Subjectivity is important because without this women's experience fails to be *women's* experience at all. This again undermines women's experience as a realistic starting point. What then, more specifically, can we say about these values on the basis of what has been argued throughout the course of this book?

Difference

Beginning with the central value of difference, it should be clear that to assert women's experience as the starting point in the doing of feminist theology means to recognize and appreciate difference between women. In one way, this value is reflected by the notion of 'positionality' proposed in Chapter 4, communicating that women are situated differently according to a range of historical and social factors including race, class, sexuality and geographical location. Such a notion undermines any attempts to essentialize about women and their experience. Indeed, Chapter 4 argued that 'woman' and 'women's experience' were not homogenous categories but actually constitute sites of complexity and contestation. Here, the meaning of 'woman' was neither collapsed entirely into biological essentialism nor entirely into social constructionism. Instead, the notion of 'positionality' was suggested as a way of bringing together biological, social and discursive elements without posing distinctions between them.

On this basis, it was argued that there can be no such thing as a 'woman's' way of knowing or of experiencing the world. Because women are positioned differently, such consensus cannot be *assumed.* Women may not only experience different things but also the same things differently. However, although difference must be recognized, space must also be allowed for women to *discover* and identify commonalities for themselves between their own experiences. In this sense, although the notion of 'positionality' highlights difference as fundamental to understanding female subjectivity, it also allows space for self-identified solidarity between women. It recognizes the materiality and historicity of the female body and suggests that coalitions of solidarity can be forged.

In the second instance, the valuing of difference is reflected in my concern to make women's experience a *realistic* starting point for feminist theology. Because it has been argued in Chapter 5 that women can only claim their *own* experiences if they claim their *own* positions as subjects and that the attainment of subjectivity itself rests on the realization of difference in the symbolic order, then the affirmation of difference becomes key to the use of women's experience in feminist theological method. Difference here, however, is not simply seen in terms of *sexual* difference as is the case with Irigaray, but in terms of multiplicity. Because women are all positioned differently with any one woman occupying a range of different positions, difference should not be limited by a rhetoric which limits and reduces difference to a logic of 'twoness'. Instead, this is more accurately signified by a rhetoric which identifies subjectivity in terms of the 'many' as opposed to the male-female 'couple'.

What measures then does this call for in relation to our thinking about God? I suggest it calls for three particular measures: first, that God should be thought about in ways which affirm diversity, multiplicity and inclusivity; second, that God should be thought in ways which affirm embodiment rather than in ways which deny this or undervalue it; and third, that God should be thought in such a way as to promote a positive reading of otherness.

Diversity, multiplicity and inclusivity Beginning with the first point, thinking God in light of difference means thinking God in ways which affirm diversity, multiplicity and inclusivity. If we are to take difference seriously then we must be suspicious of any theological accounts which image God in ways that support phallocentric logic, for this logic simply reduces difference to sameness and conveniently serves to undermine differences between women. Thinking God in light of difference then calls for an understanding of God that recognizes, affirms and welcomes diversity and multiplicity; an understanding that operates in contradistinction to the logic of the same. It means thinking God in ways which support the subjectivity of all women without enforcing a logic of sameness and without negating coalitions of solidarity which have been forged.

Embodiment In addition to this, if we are to think God in light of difference then we also need to think God in ways which affirm a variety of female embodiments. Chapter 4 argued that doing theology from women's experience means to appreciate that all women are 'positioned' differently. It was then argued that this brings to the fore the importance of embodiment in the doing of theology since grounding understandings of 'woman' in the notion of positionality means to ground 'women's experience' in women's diverse embodiments. Such a concern for embodiment, it was argued, works out as a concern to uphold and admit the materiality of the body and the concreteness of women's experiences. This means that the female body is not simply reduced to text but is, instead, seen as a material body which is *always already* positioned within language and culture. To begin with women's experience means to begin with, and to value, women's diverse embodiments.

Thinking God in light of this requires that our doctrine of God reinforce the goodness of the body, specifically the goodness of the female body. It means breaking with the anti-body tendencies present within much of the Christian tradition and evidenced by thinkers like Augustine, Tertullian, Aquinas and Luther, no longer viewing the female body as 'anti-God' or God as 'anti-body'. Rather than promoting an oppositional, dualistic relationship between God and the material (where God is 'holy' and the [female] body 'sinful', where God is 'sacred' and the [female] body 'profane'), thinking God in such a way that affirms difference means thinking God in such a way that affirms and supports bodiliness and which does not reinforce an understanding of the female body as 'lack'.

More than this, however, it also means imaging God in ways that affirm the *diverse* nature of embodiment. This negates a phallocentric account of the female body where the affirmation of one female body may depend on the negation or appropriation of another. If God is inclusive of difference then God cannot be used to support a phallocentric account of embodiment which only recognizes the existence of the male body. If God includes difference then there is space for the affirmation of more than one body, for multiple bodies and so for *all* bodies. Understood this way, God can affirm bodiliness in all its richness and diversity.

Otherness Finally, thinking God in light of the central value of difference means to think God in ways that affirm the otherness of all subjects. Chapter 4 argued that in order for difference to be truly recognized and valued, otherness must be theorized outside a phallocentric framework. Otherness must be viewed in *positive* terms for it is only when such a positive account of otherness is affirmed and recognized that difference between women and women's experiences can be properly signified. Otherness must also be articulated outside the binary model Irigaray proposes.

On this basis, Chapters 4 and 5 suggested a move away from de Beauvoir's perception of otherness towards a more Irigaraian understanding. This, however, did not posit female otherness in opposition to male otherness. Because all are subjects, all are other. An affirmation of difference then means that otherness is not ordered hierarchically. Chapters 4 and 5 argued that a consideration of women's otherness becomes particularly significant, not because women are essentially different to men as a class in their own right (an essentialist reading of 'woman'), but because it is primarily those with female bodies who have failed to construct themselves positively as 'other' in contradistinction to phallocentric logic. Affirming the otherness of women then, it was suggested, constitutes an attempt to affirm the subjectivity of women outside the logic of the same and an attempt to invest positive value in difference.

In order for God to be consistent with such values, God should be thought in ways which promote otherness without this in any way compromising the subjectivity of individuals or the richness of difference between them. If God affirms a positive account of otherness (rather than a phallocentric account) then God can affirm differences between subjects without demanding that such differences be forced into the false homogenized categorizes of 'male' or 'female'. The multiplicity of difference can be both recognized and valued so that each individual is affirmed as 'other'. Within this setting, the otherness of women can identify with God, not as an otherness which is defined as 'lack' in relation to a male norm but as an otherness which finds its place in relation to a *network* of differences.

Subjectivity

Of course, difference is not the only value which underpins the use of women's experience in feminist theological method. Such a starting point also signals the need to affirm subjectivity, and a particular rendering of this. Chapter 4 proposed an understanding of subjectivity as 'positionality', brining to the fore the fact that all bodies are positioned differently in relation to biological, social and discursive influences. It is not simply that different women are constructed by different influencing cultural forces (such as class, gender, geographical location, race and so on) but that these forces themselves vary, shift and change as individual women go through life. Positionality then admits both the complexity and fluidity of subjectivity and selfhood. It also admits that there is 'no view from nowhere', no disembodied place or space from which women might know the world. The body cannot be escaped or reduced to text. The body is a body in the world and as such, a body which is 'positioned' or 'located' within language and culture. Women are diversely positioned, hence there can be no essentialist account of what it means to be a woman.

This said, the term 'woman', it has been argued, continues to be meaningful at three levels. First, it serves as an identifier of possible commonalities between women which have been discovered across a range of differing contexts; second, the term can find meaning in relation to its identification with certain physical features common to may women, such as breasts, the vagina and clitoris; and third, it identifies the female body's position as 'lack' within the current symbolic order. It is this final point which is of particular importance when seeking to identify the nature of women's subjectivity. Because there is no space for difference within the current symbolic order, there is only space for one subject, the male, hence women are unable to speak their difference. Because women are defined as either lack, complementary or the same, they fail to exist as subjects in their own right and lack a language of their own. Chapter 5 then clearly stated that in order for women's experience to be a realistic starting point, women must first occupy their *own* spaces within discourse so as to be able to speak their *own* experiences. This, however, does not establish women as a separate 'sex' in distinction from men (as is the danger with Irigaray's approach) but serves to expose the reality of difference across a range of axes. *Parler-femme* calls women to speak their *own* bodies so that dialogue *between* subjects, whether male or female, is made possible; so that there is space *between* 'me' and 'you' for a language of exchange to be made possible.

Subjectivity then brings to the fore the importance of three more particular values: self-love, (mutual) relationship and otherness. Whereas 'self-love' identifies the importance of women enveloping themselves as subjects in their own right, 'relationship' insists that it is only through doing this that mutuality can be established between subjects. Both require that otherness be theorized outside a phallocentric framework, since women can only love themselves and other subjects if otherness does not necessitate the erasure of their own subjectivity. Applying these insights to our thinking about God, I suggest, requires that God affirm the self-love of *all* women (in all their diversity). It also demands that God affirm mutual relations between subjects and that otherness be affirmed in terms of activity as opposed to passivity.

Self-love First, to value subjectivity is to value self-love.[1] If women must occupy their *own* spaces within language and secure their *own* positions as subjects outside reflection in the male gaze in order for women's experience to be a realistic starting point, then the value of subjectivity can be further clarified here through the adoption of Irigaray's notion of 'self-love'. Indeed, for Irigaray, 'love of self' (*amour de soi*) lies at the very heart of subjectivity and at the very heart of

[1] Comments here about Irigaray's notion of 'self-love' have been developed more fully in my article, 'What's Right with the Trinity? Thinking the Trinity in Relation to Irigaray's Notions of Self-love and Wonder', *Feminist Theology*, 15/2 (2007): 220–35.

relationship. According to her, male self-love is achieved by a return (*recour*) in and through the female. The male is nostalgic about the loss of his original home in the woman/maternal and so establishes his self-love by a return to and through the maternal feminine. Such a return, however, Irigaray argues, operates on the basis of the appropriation and control of women. The female serves as mirror through which the male confirms and secures his own identity as subject. She thus has no identity of her own and is prevented from becoming as subject in her own right. Because he relies on her for his subjectivity, she is a place from which he cannot separate himself.

Self-love for women, however, according to Irigaray, means something different than it does for men. For women, to love self is to envelop oneself rather than to depend on the subjectivity of the (male) other. It demands that a woman construct a 'protective house'[2] of her own, a space of her own within language[3] and a place outside the male imaginary where her own identity (as subject) can be realized. It is only by first loving herself that a woman, Irigaray argues, will be able to relate to the other (the male) in ways that do not undermine her identity (and difference) as subject. If she does not first love herself, she cannot then love the other.

The adoption of Irigaray's notion of self-love is helpful here then because it aligns well with the model of subjectivity developed previously in Chapters 4 and 5. Certainly, if *parler-femme* is important as a strategy for enabling a space for women within language as I have argued, then the value of self-love, as defined by Irigaray, filters nicely from this. It insists that women no longer depend on men's return for their own self-love[4] and communicates, in keeping with *parler-femme*, that female subjectivity can only be forged and protected if women occupy their *own* spaces as subjects. As such, Irigaray's notion enables us to outline in more specific terms the value of subjectivity. To value subjectivity means to value self-love.

There are, however, problems with adopting this particular value as Irigaray defines it. For Irigaray, the notion of self-love is closely tied to divinity. Women, she says, must claim their own self-love by constructing a transcendental horizon through which their *own* gender can be confirmed and this, she insists, requires that women become *divine women*. Chapter 5 noted how, according to Irigaray, God constitutes a horizon to work towards, a projection of human potential and as such, amounts to a reflection of human subjectivity. Indeed, for Irigaray, to be subject means to be divine; hence love of God equates to love of self. However, equating God with female self-love in this way is problematic. Although Irigaray may intend to 'productively' mimic the specular economy of phallocentrism by strategically constructing God along the same lines as the male in such a way as to subvert phallocentric accounts of female personhood, she does nevertheless run the

---

[2] Margaret Whitford, *Luce Irigaray: Philosophy in the Feminine* (London, New York, 1991), p. 143.

[3] Luce Irigaray, *An Ethics of Sexual Difference*, trans. Carolyn Burke and Gillian C. Gill (London, 1993), p. 66.

[4] Ibid., p. 65.

risk of 'reproducing' the logic of the same, collapsing God into female subjectivity, allowing God no space of God's own. Put simply, God becomes the *same* as the woman subject. Because of this, the value of self-love is in fact compromised with God either threatening to swallow female desire, or female desire threatening to swallow God. Indeed, Esther Reed rightly maintains that Irigaray's tendency towards sameness means that difference and relationality cannot thrive.[5] Because Irigaray allows no real difference between God and woman, there can be no real relationship between them, no real exchange, no real communion, and as such, no real love.[6] To this extent, 'the relationship between women and the divine … becomes one of sameness and utility-exchange rather than gift exchange … God is no real partner but a projection that arises because of lack within the self'.[7] God is not a power that liberates but a power identical to human desire.[8]

To this end, Irigaray's own understanding of the divine fails to fulfil her own agenda for female subjectivity. Collapsing God into female self-love must, therefore, be avoided. What then does this mean if we are to think God in light of this value? What measures does this call for in our thinking about God? Most obviously, it demands that God is not collapsed into female subjectivity. It requires that we think God in ways which *support* women's self-love rather than in a way which fully identifies God with this. God must remain distinct. If this is so, then it is helpful to think God as having God's *own* self-love; as enveloping Godself in order that relationship with the other (i.e. human subjects) is made possible and so this does not turn into appropriation or consummation of the other. Thinking God as 'self-love' means that difference between God and the female subject can be protected and the problems identified with Irigaray's definition potentially avoided.

Relationship Self-love paves the way for relationship with the other. In this sense, to value self-love means to value relationship. Both underpin the general value of subjectivity. However, it is a particular understanding of relationship which is of value here. If subjectivity signals the possibility of intimacy, encounter and dialogue between persons (as articulated previously through our discussion of *parler-femme and* the importance of 'speaking *to*'), then it is *mutual* relationship which is of importance here. What it means to be in mutual relationship and how this impacts subjectivity is well expressed through Irigaray's notion of 'wonder'.

In dialogue with René Descartes, Irigaray defines 'wonder' as 'the passion of the first encounter'.[9] It connotes a relationship between the male and female 'couple' in which one approaches the other always as if for the first time. This is a relationship characterized by surprise in the face of the unknowability of the

---

5 Esther Reed, 'Revelation in Feminist Theology and Philosophy', in Paul Avis (ed.), *Divine Revelation* (Grand Rapids, 1997), pp. 156–73, esp. p. 167.

6 Ibid., p. 171.

7 Ibid.

8 Ibid., p. 169.

9 Irigaray, *An Ethics*, p. 82.

other. To the extent that the other can never be fully known, she or he can never be appropriated as object by the other. It is in the space *between* the two subjects then that wonder takes place, causing the other to stop and glance at him or her inquisitively and to ask, 'Who art thou?'[10] Wonder then, for Irigaray, constitutes a meeting place between the two. Where wonder exists, the other is never taken for granted or taken advantage of. Instead, they are embraced by the caress of the other and invited to become what they have not yet become.[11] Love here is focused on the other, not in order to possess or utilize the other as external object, but in order to encourage the becoming of the other. For Irigaray, the notion of 'wonder' breaks with phallocentrism precisely because it relies on the existence of *two* subjects rather than one.

Irigaray's articulation of wonder here is useful for helping us think through what reciprocity and mutuality between subjects might mean. It aligns well with the model of subjectivity proposed in Chapters 4 and 5 and expresses effectively the dynamics or 'ethics' which lie at the heart of subject relations within a non-phallocentric setting. If women must claim their *own* subjectivity in order to claim their *own* experiences and if this requires women to envelop themselves and to occupy separate spaces in language, then at the heart of female subjectivity is the reciprocal relation of wonder between persons. Without wonder, relationship with the other threatens to repeat the dynamics of phallocentrism, using the other in order to establish the stability and subjectivity of the self. The value of relationship then signals here an ability to be *with* and *for* the other without becoming or appropriating the other. It supports the first general value of difference by affirming that relationship is only possible where difference is secured. It also communicates effectively what has been argued previously in Chapters 4 and 5, that difference *should* and *must* be held alongside subjectivity so that the former is not collapsed into a false homogeneity or universalism and the latter not compromised by an awareness of otherness. It is only in this context that women can claim their own identities. To value subjectivity means to value relations of wonder between subjects.

Of course, there are problems with adopting Irigaray's notion of wonder when seeking to clarify more clearly the value of relationship for our purposes. Unsurprisingly, Irigaray frames her discussion of wonder in relation to the male-female 'couple' and so is privy to the same charges of heterosexism and essentialism addressed in the previous chapter. She fails to pay sufficient attention to difference, favouring a rhetoric of the 'two' over that of the 'many'. In this sense, she fails to achieve the goals she sets in place, reducing relationship to a model of the 'two'. The principle of 'wonder' (as Irigaray outlines it) is, however, useful in highlighting the importance of a non-phallocentric model of relationship for the securing of subjectivity. It effectively reflects the argument made so far that the valuing of subjectivity is central to women's experience and successfully

---

10 Ibid., p. 74.

11 Ibid., p. 187.

communicates that subjectivity can only be secured if relationships between subjects are characterised by mutuality and reciprocity.

If the value of relationship is a central value which underpins the use of women's experience in feminist theological method, then the next question we must ask is what measures this value might call for in our thinking about God. In response, the first point to note is that thinking God in light of this presents God's self-love as the grounds upon which mutual relations (of wonder) with the world are established. This does not mean that God must exist first as God in Godself and *then* as God in relationship with the world for there is never a time when God is God without the world. It does, however, require that God envelop Godself in such a way that God is not collapsed into human subjectivity nor human subjectivity collapsed into God.

Of course, if God is in *mutual* relationship with others then the securing of difference between God and other subjects through mutuality means that God and human subjects cannot be reduced to sameness. Using the language of Irigaray, we can say that God enjoys relations of 'wonder' with humanity. This means that God and the individual can touch without either one posing a threat to the other's subjectivity. Always approaching as if for the first time, both God and the subject can give completely of themselves, not in order to gain as much as possible, but in order to encourage the other to become what they have not yet become. If thinking God in light of the central value of subjectivity means thinking God as one who envelops Godself and therefore as 'self-love', then this also means thinking God as one whose self-love enables mutual relationships of exchange with others. To be in relationship, according to this view, does not compromise God's own subjectivity, because both God and the individual are thought as occupying *different* subject positions. Because the subjectivity of God cannot be collapsed into the subjectivity of the individual, love and intimacy are made possible *between* them. This means that God and the woman subject cannot be reduced to one another as is the difficulty with Irigaray. Both are active in relationship.

Otherness (revisited) This clearly challenges traditional patriarchal associations of women with passivity and so calls for another consideration of the notion of otherness previously discussed. It is not only that otherness signals a positive signification of difference, challenging phallocentric accounts which seek to define women as other and as 'lack', but also an affirmation of *mutual* relations between subjects. Rather than polarizing men and women, affirming the former as active and the latter as passive, this articulation of otherness affirms all subjects as other, and so all as active in relationship. Of course, if both God and the individual are to be seen as subjects then this connotes an *active* partnership of mutuality and reciprocity.

This is to see God and the human subject as 'lovers', to use a turn of phrase developed again by Irigaray.[12] It is not to categorise human subjects as the 'beloved' and God as 'lover' because this pacifies humanity and compromises the value of

---

[12] Ibid., p. 199ff.

relationship. Humanity is not object and God subject. Because God and the human subject are both 'other' they are both lovers, hence God's identification with otherness is clearly affirmed. Also, because all are other, God is able to identify with an infinite number of others without becoming the *same* as them. Thinking God in this way then clearly avoids the problems previously discussed in relation to Irigaray's own understanding of the divine and retains the otherness of God in relation to humankind.

Towards a Way Forward: Thinking God as Trinity?

Of course, thinking God in light of these values is all well and good but if we are not to be guilty of projectionism and of creating a God in our own image then our task cannot be one of constructing God anew in light of these values. Indeed, this chapter began by stating clearly that the aim of this section was not to re-think God in light of these values but to consider the kind of measures such values might call for in our thinking about God. Having done this, the final and most important task before us is to consider the ways in which, and extent to which, these measures might be met by a specifically *trinitarian* understanding of God. We ask, how does thinking God as Trinity affirm the key values which underpin the use of women's experience in feminist theology put forward here and to what extent can we claim this doctrine to be useful for feminist theology today? In seeking to address these questions we return once more to a consideration of the central values of difference and subjectivity and consider the ways in which thinking God as Trinity might affirm and be affirmed by these.

Difference

Beginning with the value of difference, it should be apparent that thinking God as Trinity repositions the doctrine of God outside phallocentrism by subverting and undermining phallocentric accounts of difference. As we have already argued, to think God as Trinity means to image God as *not*-one. A 'trinitarian logic' draws attention to diversity in God, a diversity which is not compromised by God's unity, and so signals a view of God as irreducible to the same. Understood as diversity-in-communion, the triune God is both inwardly and outwardly diverse. Because there is no God behind the God revealed in the economy of salvation, that God is *not*-one in God's relation with the world means that God is *not*-one in Godself. To be God means to be diverse.

This, though, is not to retreat from Christian monotheism; it simply means that God cannot and should not be reduced to the 'abstract monotheism' Moltmann warns about. Thinking God as Trinity provides a theological way in which difference might be fully affirmed. How then might the Trinity affirm the specific values of diversity, multiplicity and inclusivity previously identified as integral to an affirmation of difference?

Diversity, multiplicity and inclusivity: the Trinity as diversity in communion In keeping with trends detectable within the trinitarian thought of Gregory of Nazianzus, Chapter 2 proposed that we locate the being of God within the *koinōnia* shared by all three *hypostases*. To 'be' for God means to be three, hence the oneness of God is located within the Godhead itself rather than in the person of God the Father specifically. It is the Godhead who is the unoriginate principle, substance and *monarchē* of God. According to this understanding, God the Father is not ontologically superior or different in 'rank' to the Son or Holy Spirit since all are equal and co-exist eternally with one another. Such an understanding also means to cite God's being in communion, in mutual relationship; in *perichoresis*. There is no underlying oneness underneath or outside of the threefold person of God; God is diverse in Godself as well as in relation to the world. God's unity then does not constitute a disintegration of difference but is rather constitutive of it.

Chapter 2 then argued that the unity of God is cited within the community and inter-relationality of the Godhead. This, however, does not mean that all three *hypostases* are the same, for if this were so, there would be no room for relationship *between* them – a point on which Irigaray's understanding of the divine has already been criticized. Although the three *hypostases* are in perfect mutual relationship with one another, they remain distinct in terms of their operations. The Father is Creator, the Son Redeemer and the Holy Spirit Sustainer/Restorer. To confess faith in *one* God then is not to assert that God is numerically one, a point made well by Leonardo Boff,[13] but that each divine *hypostasis* acts in perfect harmony with the others, laying themselves down for one another so as to seek the glory of one another. Unity in God is achieved through perfect communion and perfect relationship; through reciprocity, mutuality and exchange.

Difference then, it is suggested here, lies at the very centre of God's trinitarian being. As Trinity, God encapsulates difference and as such, affirms and welcomes it. Difference does not stand in opposition to God as phallocentric logic dictates, difference *is* God and is *in* God. Certainly, God is not aligned with the phallus as a self-identical monad. Because the Trinity confirms that God is not-one, God does not constitute a mirror through which the stability and singularity of the phallus are reflected. As a community of difference, the Trinity reflects back an image of diversity rather than sameness and so exposes the oneness of the male subject as fiction.

Previously it has been argued that within the triune community diversity is non-hierarchical. Although Father, Son and Spirit are distinct, they are co-equal. The Father is not *more* God than the Son, nor the Son *more* God than the Holy Spirit. All are fully God, and yet all are different. Difference thus exists alongside mutuality, freedom and love. Hence, whereas with phallocentrism, difference is only ever

---

[13] Boff argues that when Jesus says 'The Father and I are one' in John 10.30, he is not suggesting that he and the Father are numerically one but that they are *together*. Hence he says, 'The union of Father and Son does not blot out the difference and individuality of each.' See *Trinity and Society*, trans. Paul Burns (Eugene, Oregon, 1988), p. 5.

organized according to the logic of A/not-A, rendering that which is other as 'lack', complementary or the same, the logic of the Trinity allows difference to co-exist simultaneously alongside mutuality. Thinking God as Trinity is thus exposed to be deeply useful for feminist theology on the grounds that it provides a theological logic by which we might signify a non-phallocentric account of difference.

This is further reinforced by previous discussion concerning God's association with temporality, suffering and change. If to think God as Trinity is to see temporality, suffering and change as integral to the trinitarian life of God but without reducing God to these, then this helps affirm a logic which allows difference to thrive. Chapter 2, for example, argued that whilst God certainly does suffer, suffering is not the whole extent of God. '*[B]ecause God is God, it means that suffering is not all that God does.*'[14] God suffers but suffering is also restored and redeemed by God. It is only when redemption is complete that God will be 'all in all'. The argument here then is that whereas phallocentrism insists on a reducible logic of A/not-A, a trinitarian logic is inclusive, allowing scope for *both* this *and* that; for suffering *and* redemption. Of course, if difference is welcomed within the triune God, constituting the ground upon which unity is actually fostered in the first place, then holding such seemingly antithetical principles as suffering/healing, temporality/eternity together in the life of God need in no way compromise the integrity of God. If God contains difference then it would be nonsensical to reduce God to either one of these principles as this would reinforce a more phallocentric understanding of the divine, reducing God once more to oneness and sameness. That God as Trinity models diversity, multiplicity and inclusivity thus means that the Trinity need not be used to support a phallocentric account of difference.

Indeed, aligning the Trinity with the central value of difference is extremely worthwhile for feminist theology. It can both support, and be supported by, a trinitarian understanding of God and thus enable all subjects, including all women in all their difference, to identify with God as Trinity. It means that differences between women and between women's experiences can find a point of identification with the trinitarian God, thus enabling all women to claim their place as *full* participants in the *imago Dei*.

It is also true that thinking God as Trinity helps theologically affirm connections between women, a point of considerable significance for establishing solidarity between women. It also, however, affirms connections between women and men. To be sure, such an understanding of God neither imposes a logic of sameness nor a logic of *absolute* difference, for both amount to the same in the end. Although no one of the three *hypostases* can take the place of another, there is mutual sharing between them. Insofar as this is the case, thinking God as Trinity invests theological value in the dialogue and mutual sharing of experiences which takes place between women within the *ekklesia* and reinforces the significance of solidarity through community.

[14] Mary Grey, *Introducing Feminist Images of God* (Sheffield, 2001), p. 60.

The affirmation of embodiment: another look at the incarnation Of course, if the trinitarian God is welcoming of diversity and difference, drawing temporality and change into the divine life through the incarnation, then thinking God as Trinity helps also affirm embodiment as good. To be sure, feminist theologians have been clear in outlining the problems posed by the *maleness* of Jesus for the affirmation of the *female* body, however Chapter 1 argued that incarnation need not be interpreted in this way. Jesus' maleness need not be the insurmountable barrier it is considered to be by the likes of Daphne Hampson and Mary Daly because it is not Jesus' maleness which is important in the incarnation but God becoming a body and taking on particularity.[15]

This is not to throw the body into abstraction since it is impossible to deny that Jesus of Nazareth was a *human* body and a *male* human body at that. However, Jesus was also more than this. Jesus was able-bodied, Jewish and from Galilee. Chapter 1 thus argued that it would be ridiculous to insist that Jesus' embodiment only affirmed Galileans, Jews and the able-bodied. In other words, it is not the specifics of Jesus' particularity which are important in the incarnation – that Jesus is male and not female, for example – but that God takes on *particularity* in the first place; that God chooses to become a body in the world and to be limited by the restrictions of such particularity. Particularity then, when understood in this way, does not serve to exclude bodies from being *like* Christ but instead functions to include *all* bodies on the basis that *all* bodies are particular. Female bodies, rather than being marginalized in relation to Christ (through virtue of Jesus' maleness) are now fully able to identify with Christ on the basis of their own embodied particularity.

It has also been argued previously that the incarnation of God in Christ reveals the sacramentality of all material things and establishes the principle of incarnation as a cosmic principle. Jesus establishes this principle through the historical incarnation but since incarnation is part of the eternal self-identity of God, the association between matter and divinity is established as part of the trinitarian identity. Jesus does not establish the sacramentality of bodies *in time* but *eternally* through always being the Word made flesh, the second person of the trinitarian Godhead. All material things have the capacity to communicate the divine because God becomes flesh and becomes particular.

What all this means is that embodiment and particularity are affirmed through the incarnate Christ who finds a co-equal place within the trinitarian Godhead. Incarnation reveals that bodiliness is not opposed to God but actually participates in God and is integral to the self-identity of God. More than this, however, incarnation affirms the particularities of 'positionality'. If particularity is affirmed by incarnation, then the positionality of all persons is affirmed and so with this, the

---

[15] For more on this, see my chapter, 'A Very Particular Body': Assessing the Doctrine of Incarnation for Affirming the Sacramentality of Female Embodiment', in J'annine Jobling and Gillian Howie (eds), *Women and the Divine: Touching Transcendence* (New York, 2009), pp. 227–52.

multiplicity of female embodiment. Because all women are particular, multiplicity finds space to live and breathe in relation to the triune God.

Of course, if we are to see the Church also as the body of Christ then this goes one step further revealing Christ as a trans-gendered, communal and inclusive body. Chapter 1 argued that the body of Christ is a body in which male and female both participate. Following Gavin D'Costa then we can say that the communal body becomes the place where relations between embodied individuals come to reflect and thereby participate in the relations of the Trinity. In the communal body, love is generated *between* (gendered) bodies rather than being located *in* the body.[16] On this basis, we can argue that the body of Christ should not be used to establish the maleness of God or to exclude women from participating in the *imago Dei*. Because the body of Christ is a communal body, it is an inclusive body that welcomes and affirms *all* embodiments. It is a body that cannot be reduced to oneness and a body that cannot be reduced to maleness. The variety of gendered people who make up the church 'fill out' Christ, signalling a refusal to allow closure on the incarnation.[17] That God is incarnate then means that *all* bodies participate in God, through Christ, without exclusion.

Subjectivity

Turning now to the second general value which was identified in relation to women's experience, we draw our focus towards 'subjectivity'. Earlier in the chapter, it was argued that since women must establish their own 'self-love' in order to be subjects and in order to relate to the 'other' (whether male or female), so God must also establish God's own 'self-love' and envelop Godself so that the other is not appropriated or consumed by God, or indeed God by the other. If women's subjectivity and otherness are to be affirmed by God, there must be space enough for difference *between* God and women to exist. How then does thinking God as Trinity align with this?

Self-love: The Trinity as self-love As Trinity, God envelops Godself in three ways, traditionally identified as Father, Son and Holy Spirit. This is what it means for God to be God and thus, what it means for God to be subject. As Trinity, however, God is not-one. God does not envelop Godself as a single monad but always in relation to the other trinitarian persons. The self-love of God then finds its place within the context of community rather than in isolation or solitariness. God envelops Godself as a community of love and as diversity in communion, hence the self-love of God (to use Irigaray's language) is a love that takes place *between* the trinitarian persons. To love self for the triune community means to be with and for the other divine *hypostases*.

[16] Gavin D'Costa, *Sexing the Trinity: Gender, Culture and the Divine* (London, 2000), p. 35.

[17] Ibid., p. 196.

Such a rendering of self-love and subjectivity carries important implications for the affirmation of female subjectivity. At a basic level, the self-love of God encourages women to go in search of their own self-love and subjectivity. As well as this, however, the self-love of God also reflects the model of mutual subject relations previously outlined in this chapter and in relation to *parler-femme*. Just as subjectivity is only possible where there is space *between* subjects for dialogue and encounter, so the triune relations engage in mutual relations of encounter through virtue of being distinct from one another. As Trinity, God is understood as interpersonal communion (*koinōnia*) and as a circle of love typified by *perichoresis*. Relations within the Trinity are non-hierarchical, with each person occupying a *different* space within the Godhead in perfect relation to the others. As such, there is space *between* the divine *hypostases* so as to enable relationship within the community. Thinking God as Trinity thus establishes that relationship can co-exist alongside difference and mutuality. Although the three persons are distinct, difference is not swallowed up nor is relationship forfeited. The dynamics of *parler-femme* and the logic of speaking 'to' can, therefore, find a point of identification with the triune relations because the space *between* Father, Son and Spirit provides the basis for relationship *between* them. Insofar as this is the case, the Trinity models the importance of retaining difference in relationship. Of course, if difference in God does not compromise the equal importance of each divine *hypostasis*, then this demonstrates that difference need not lead to the possession or appropriation of the other but may in fact go hand in hand with subjectivity. Thinking God as Trinity thus provides a means by which difference between women and between women's experiences might be theologically acknowledged and celebrated. Moreover, because God is subject but also includes difference, a trinitarian understanding of God fails to support the myth that subjectivity is necessarily defined by sameness (and therefore maleness). If God is more than one, then God can support more than one subject position.

Of course, we should not be so crude as to think that because God is diverse in three ways, God can only ever support a model of subjectivity which only recognizes three subject positions. To be sure, this would be of little help in subverting or undermining a phallocentric reading of subjectivity since it would still limit subjectivity and pay insufficient attention to difference. Chapter 5 outlined how Irigaray's articulation of subjectivity in relation to the sexed 'couple' was insufficient on the grounds that it threatened to reduce subjectivity to *sexual* difference and to a seemingly limited model of twoness. Favouring a rhetoric which speaks about subjectivity in terms of the 'many' and in terms of irreducible and multiple difference thus moves beyond an articulation of sexual difference as the most universal type of difference. Thinking God as Trinity affirms *more* than three subjects because the Trinity does not constitute a closed community of love. As Trinity, God is three, and as three, God 'avoids solitude, overcomes separation and surpasses exclusion.'[18] As Trinity, God also includes humanity and

[18] Boff, p. 3.

relationship with the world through the election of Jesus Christ. Because there is no God behind the God revealed in and through the world and thus, in and through the person and work of Jesus, the triune community cannot properly be seen as a closed community, sealed in upon itself. In this sense, the Trinity is not restricted to a static model of threeness but opens out to invite others into communion.[19]

I will return to this later, however the point for us here is that thinking God as Trinity allows God to affirm a limitless array of subjects without promoting one subject at the expense of another. This, therefore, reinforces the value of 'mutuality' talked about previously in relation to Irigaray's notion of 'wonder'. Indeed, we can adopt Irigaray's articulation of wonder in order to describe relations between the triune persons without compromising how these have been talked about previously in relation to the Christian tradition. As a community of 'wonder', Father, Son and Spirit can be seen as giving to one another without holding anything back. Neither person takes the others for advantage but always approaches as if for the first time. The Trinity then can be viewed as an economy of desire, since there is space enough *between* each person for love to exist and for desire to be made possible. As a community of wonder, the Trinity constitutes a relationship of nearness which makes all forms of property, impossible.[20] It comprises a mutual partnership of love which always beckons others into relationship without becoming, possessing or suffocating them. Characterized by reciprocal living, sharing and the overflowing of boundaries, the Trinity provides a model of mutuality in which the other is no longer at the mercy of the one,[21] with the one never seizing the other as object.[22] Within this setting, mutuality means that boundaries can be crossed without the 'other' disappearing.[23]

Such relations of mutuality and wonder then are demonstrated perfectly through and in the trinitarian God. Here, love of other and respect for difference do not simply constitute convenient ideals but form the very being of God. They form the basis on which divine unity is established for it is 'Through love and through reciprocal communion [that] they [the trinitarian *hypostases*] are one single thing, the one God-love.'[24] Of course, if God already exists in this way then to be in the image of God means to be in forgiving, loving relationships of mutuality and exchange with one another; that individuals find their place within the *imago Dei* exactly by claiming and respecting subjectivity in this way. To image God then is

---

19 This is not to say that humanity *become* God but that they *participate* in God through virtue of Christ's election by God.

20 Luce Irigaray, *This Sex Which is Not One*, trans. Catherine Porter with Carolyn Burke (Ithaca, New York, 1985), p. 31.

21 Susan Sellers, *Language and Sexual Difference: Feminist Writing in France* (London, 1991), p. 138.

22 Luce Irigaray, 'Sexual Difference', in Margaret Whitford (ed.), *The Irigaray Reader* (Oxford and Cambridge, Massachusetts, 1991), pp. 165–77, esp. p. 172.

23 Taken from Irigaray, *An Ethics*, p. 187.

24 Boff, p. 5.

not to obliterate difference but to knit differences together so as to establish unity in the face of community. Indeed, because God envelops Godself as always already other-ward, the triune God constitutes a direct challenge to the economy of the same. Here, God need not be used to support a phallocentric system in which the other is downtrodden or unrealized, but can instead support and affirm difference without this in any way compromising subjectivity and relationship. Whereas a phallocentric logic establishes subjectivity on the basis of the annihilation of difference, a trinitarian logic sees love fulfilled in the coming together of differences. Whereas a phallocentric logic orders difference hierarchically erasing the existence of women, a trinitarian logic supports mutuality and otherness and affirms the subjectivity of all women.

Relationship: the Trinity as subject-in-relationship Understanding God as Trinity, however, does not simply raise important implications for how we as subjects should approach one another, but also for how God engages with humanity and humanity with God. If we are to insist, as has been the case throughout this book, that God's relation with the world forms part of God's very identity – that for God to *be* means for God to be in relationship as Father, Son and Spirit and with the world – then we cannot speak about God's self-love without mentioning God's relation with humankind.

If God's very being is relational and other-ward then the love shared within the triune community should not be viewed as something separate from God's love for the world. The love shared within the Trinity reaches out to embrace humanity also. We have already noted how John Zizioulas presents this relationship in terms of *ekstasis*, signifying that God as love creates an immanent relationship of love outside Godself.[25] Because God reveals God's being as communion, as one who freely chooses to be immanently relational, then the same *ekstatic* love that exists within the triune community can be understood as extending to embrace humanity. As such, that God is Trinity means that relationship cannot stop with Father, Son and Holy Spirit but must beckon all humanity into communion. This clearly resonates with the understanding of the Trinity articulated in Chapter 2, specifically with the qualities of community, relationality and inclusivity which were identified partly through discussion of Zizioulas' trinitarian thought. Within this setting, it is not only trinitarian relations that are mutual, sharing a sense of wonder, but divine-human relations also.

Thinking God as Trinity thus allows for an understanding of God as subject in mutual relationship with humankind. If we can speak about the Trinity as self-love on the grounds that God envelops Godself as three distinct persons in community, then we can also speak about God as subject in relationship. This establishes both God and humankind as subjects and confirms that God's self-love is a love which is inclusive of otherness. Because both God and the individual occupy different subject positions, mutual relationship, love and intimacy can be fully actualized,

---

[25] John D. Zizioulas, *Being as Communion* (New York, 1993), p. 91.

with both encouraging one another to give as well as to receive. Within this setting, God does not threaten to swallow female subjectivity nor female subjectivity God's. This carries important implications for female self-love since it is not only the self-love of God which makes relationship possible but also the self-love of women. Without enveloping themselves as subjects, there is insufficient space for a relationship of wonder and encounter between women and the divine. As Serene Jones rightly notes, 'For the relations between women and God to be wonderous there must be the division of two worlds, two definite universes, two space-times, two others, for it is only in the difference that passage is possible.'[26]

Asserting mutuality between God and humanity, however, does not mean that God and humanity are the *same*. If we are to insist on the ontological priority of God in revelation as I have suggested in Chapter 3, then human subjects and God do not occupy the same space. God cannot be reduced to humanity because God exists as an objective reality apart from human desire and selfhood. However, because relationship with humankind is integral to God's self identity, relationship with humankind cannot be separated from God. It is, however, chosen by God and so the partnership which exists between humankind and God is one established on the basis of God's free decision to be this kind of God. As Barth comments, God's deity comprises God's freedom to be in and for Godself as well as with and for humankind.[27] God is the kind of God who opens out to include humanity also without this in any way compromising God's divinity.

God's self-love then secures God's freedom to be with as opposed to without, for as opposed to against the world. It is not that God, as self-love, exists separately from God as subject in relationship, but that God in Godself is free and in this freedom eternally chooses to be subject in relationship with the world. God, then, is *different* from humankind because it is God's free decision to relate to humanity not vice versa. God elects humankind; humankind does not elect itself. To this extent, the mutuality of the God-human relationship operates at a different level to that between humans. However, insofar as there can be no meaningful distinction between the *Logos asarkos* (the Logos 'without the flesh') and the *Logos ensarkos* (the Logos 'within the flesh'), we cannot speak about God's free decision (and so God's own self-love) without making reference to God's relationship with the world through the incarnation.

Thinking God as Trinity affirms both God's distinctiveness from humanity as well as God's togetherness with it. Although God's decision to embrace humanity logically precedes God's relationship with humankind, because this is an *eternal* decision, there is never a time when this decision has not been so. Thus, God's self-love exists alongside God's relationship with humanity; God's distinctiveness from humankind alongside God's togetherness with it. Because there is difference,

---

26 Serene Jones, 'Divining Women: Irigaray and Feminist Theologies', in Lynne Huffer (ed.), *Another Look, Another Woman: Retranslations of French Feminism*, Yale French Studies (vol. 8, New Haven, Connecticut and London, 1995), pp. 42–67, esp. p. 66.

27 See Karl Barth, *The Humanity of God* (London, 1961), p. 49.

there can be togetherness. Difference, thus, paves the way for a mutual relationship of wonder between God and humanity.

Applied to the triune God, 'wonder' points towards an understanding of God as caressing each subject, not in order to make them disappear but so as to invite them all to become what they have not yet become.[28] Through this lens, the triune God can be seen as encouraging *all* women to grow and establish their *own* becoming as subjects. As humankind's mutual partner, the triune God is always already other-ward, never taking the other for advantage, always enjoying loving exchange with them. Such love is self-giving, not out for what it can gain but for what it can give, not wanting to own or possess but to embrace and to encourage. Understood this way, love constitutes 'an attraction towards the other that nevertheless allows the other to remain her or himself'.[29] Here both the Trinity and the female subject are understood as sharing a desire for the other and a desire to be with the other without actually wanting to become or consume the other.[30] Within this context, the triune God can approach the female subject, not through any need to possess or overtake, nor through a need to reflect or stabilize God's own identity, but through the desire to be with and for her.

In this sense, thinking God as Trinity provides an important voice of resistance to phallocentric accounts of divinity and indeed subjectivity. As self-love, God encourages women to develop their *own* self-love outside the male gaze and to be in relationships of mutuality and exchange with other subjects and with God.

Otherness: the Trinity as community of lovers Finally, thinking God as Trinity can affirm a positive concept of otherness which challenges phallocentric associations of this value with 'lack' and passivity. At a basic level thinking God as Trinity supports this value because God is always *more* than one. Because God is always in relationship with Godself and with humankind, God is always already in relationship with more than one other. Within this context, otherness is never reduced to sameness and so is affirmed outside the A/not-A logic of phallocentrism and outside the A/B model presented by Irigaray. To be sure, a trinitarian view of God provides a theological context in which otherness can be celebrated in all its multiplicity rather than forced into false homogeneity. It allows space for the affirmation of multiple subjectivities and thus, for the affirmation of women and women's experiences.

It is also the case that the *active* nature of God's otherness affirms the active nature of human otherness. Returning once more to Irigaray's notion of the 'lover', we may refer to the Trinity as a community of lovers. Indeed, the Trinity affirms the active role of all subjects in relationship. Here, it is not only the Father who is active but also the Son and Holy Spirit. Indeed, the triune operations although distinct are, at the same time, inseparable – the Father never acts alone, nor does

28 Taken from Irigaray, *An Ethics*, p. 187.

29 Alison Martin, *Luce Irigaray and the Question of the Divine* (London, 2000), p. 133.

30 Ibid., p. 134.

the Son or the Holy Spirit. Imaging each person as 'lover' then demonstrates how the Trinity affirms this value. Also, as a community of lovers, the Trinity exposes the true dynamics of love as those of mutuality, reciprocity and openness and so challenges hierarchical relations. 'Between lovers, there is no first and last, no greater and smaller. Lovers give because they delight and adore.'[31] As Trinity then, each *hypostasis* gives to the others with no 'one' being the object of another's desire. A trinitarian understanding of God thus need not be used to affirm hierarchical relations between subjects (or between the sexes). Difference can provide no justification for inequality because in God difference exists alongside mutuality. If active, mutual and reciprocal relations are displayed between the triune persons and between God and humanity, then thinking God as Trinity can reinforce and affirm such relations between individuals.

Saming the Trinity?

It has already been mentioned briefly at the start of this chapter that affirming a trinitarian understanding of God on the basis of values inherent within feminist appeals to women's experience is not meant to repeat the 'sins' of phallocentrism by *manufacturing* a God who is identical with such values. The intention here is not to fabricate a God who massages the values of feminist theology but to show how the orthodox Christian confession of God as Trinity supports and is supported by such values.

Of course, the problem here, however, is that such an agenda seems to assume that such values need to be validated by God in the first place and thus appears to rest on the phallocentric assumption that value is only achieved in and through reflection in a transcendental other. The argument presented here, however, does not propose that such values are *only* validated when aligned with the triune God. They are validated first on the grounds that they are necessary in order for women to claim and articulate their *own* experiences and then *confirmed* and further *affirmed* by a trinitarian understanding of God. This is the direction of the methodological flow proposed in this chapter. However, insofar as the ontological priority of God as Trinity is also integral to my theological method, reflection on the Trinity does indeed expose God as the kind of God who has *always* existed in such a way as to affirm and confirm difference and subjectivity. Insofar as this is the case, the difference and subjectivity modelled by the Trinity can provide the ontological base for a theological acknowledgment of, and identification with, these values. To be made in the image of the Trinity means that we are made for communion and togetherness which welcomes the other into relationship rather than seeking to become the other.

---

31 Mioslav Volf, 'Being as God Is: Trinity and Generosity', in Mioslav Volf and Michael Welker (eds), *God's Life in Trinity* (Minneapolis, 2006), 3–12, esp. p. 11.

A second potential difficulty with this agenda is that it also assumes that God can *only* affirm difference, inclusivity, multiplicity, otherness, embodiment, self-love and relationship if God is revealed to be the *same* as these values. This again appears to rely on the phallocentric assumption that worth is only achieved through an assertion of sameness (rather than difference). In one sense, this kind of approach has dominated Christian theology through the ages, as God has been frequently cast in the image of the male and has often served to confirm his place at the centre of the symbolic order. This, however, provides little solace. If God can only demonstrate solidarity with human experience by being shown to be (or by being constructed in such a way as to be) identical to this experience then God becomes nothing more than a projection of ourselves and this kind of projectionism has been criticized at various points throughout this book, both in relation to discussion on Irigaray and in relation to earlier discussion on contextualization. How then do we avoid it?

Of specific importance here is to uphold a distinction between God and humankind. What it means for the triune God to be diverse, for example, is not the *same* as what it means for women subjects to be diverse. Although both reflect the same value, the specific meaning ascribed to this varies in relation to both contexts. The diversity of God means that God exists as three divine persons in mutual relationship with one another; diversity between women means that each woman embodies a different position and that the category 'woman' can no longer be defined in essentialist terms. The way the triune persons reflect the principle of self-love is not the same as the way in which women articulate their self-love. For God, to love self means to envelop Godself as three in one, for a woman to love herself means for her to create a discursive space which is not defined by the male gaze. The way that the triune persons mutually give to one another and involve the world in this mutual relationship of love is not the *same* as the way humankind relate mutually to one another or to God. Mutuality between God and humankind rests on God's prior decision to be with as opposed to without humankind and thus relies on the ontological priority of God. That humanity participates in God then is not to say that humanity is the same as God or is co-equal with the trinitarian Godhead, it is, however, to say that God cannot be straightforwardly separated from humanity. In other words, it is not the *ways* in which God and humankind demonstrate these values which are the same but the fact that both reflect these values.

This secures space between the triune God and human subjects and so makes possible a relationship of intimacy and encounter previously articulated through the notion of 'wonder'. To think God as Trinity then is to assert a degree of *likeness* between God and humankind but it is not to collapse either into sameness. Humanity is both *like* and *unlike* God and it is this tension which is held together when we confess God as Trinity. Certainly thinking God as Trinity means to engage in a *productive* and transformative form of *mimesis*. Because God is here both like and unlike human subjects, what appears at first glance as a mere reproduction of the logic of the same is now exposed as a subversion of it. Although aligning the triune God with the values of difference and subjectivity seems to reduce God to the same as women, that these values actually confirm rather than stifle the independence of God and the multiplicity of subjectivity means that phallocentric accounts of difference and subjectivity are resisted. Consequently thinking God as Trinity can provide a subversive logic through which the existence and value of women's diverse experiences might be theologically affirmed and phallocentric accounts of difference and subjectivity undermined.

Conclusion: The Trinity and Feminist Theology Today

Thinking God as Trinity then holds tremendous significance for feminist theology today. The values underpinning the use of women's experience in feminist theology strongly identify with the values affirmed by a specifically trinitarian understanding of God enabling women to claim their own place as fully *imago Dei*. If to understand God as Trinity means to understand God as ontologically diverse and communal, then this means that God eternally exists in such a way that explodes phallocentric accounts of difference and subjectivity and in such a way that, therefore, enables women to identify with God as *subjects*. Because difference is not reduced to sameness nor is it ordered hierarchically, women can take up their places as different (from other subjects) but as full participants in the image of God.

In this sense, thinking God as Trinity provides a theological support for women's attempts to speak their own bodies in the symbolic order and to establish genuine relationship *between* themselves and other subjects, whether male or female. It provides a theological endorsement of *parler-femme* and a theological mandate for a new ethics of relationship which operate in contradistinction to phallocentrism. Rather than reinforcing and reproducing patriarchal values of male domination and female non-being, thinking God as Trinity exposes mutuality and reciprocity, difference and community as at the heart of Christian thinking about God. To think God as Trinity then is to subvert dominant phallocentric accounts of difference and subjectivity and to replace this with a logic which enables the fullness and richness of women's experiences to find theological significance. Here, God is not a giant phallus who functions to confirm the subjectivity of the male and the otherness of woman as 'lack', but a God who identifies with the particularities (and complexities) of embodiment, who affirms the female body as good and as sacramental; a God who models difference alongside subjectivity and who, therefore, affirms female desire without seeking to appropriate or extinguish this for the sake of securing God's own identity and the identity of the male. Because God is diversity in communion, God welcomes mutual relationship and calls phallocentrism into repentance. This carries implications for men as well as for women since it undermines the male's position at the centre of the symbolic and exposes the oneness of male subjectivity as a fiction.

Such an understanding of God clearly carries important implication for Christian and feminist praxis. If *thinking* God as Trinity models a new ethics of relationship in which women's subjectivities are recognized and theologically affirmed and in which the multi-textured nature of women's experiences are therefore also theologically affirmed, then thinking God in this way must empower us towards action. It is not enough to affirm these values at an intellectual/theoretical level, they must be practiced through relationship with one another and with God. Thinking God as Trinity thus provides a theological support for feminist praxis which seeks to take these values seriously and offers a Christian, as well as feminist, mandate for change in the here and now. It means that we image God by welcoming difference and by supporting rather than suffocating subjectivity.

God then need not be reimaged in *new* ways in order to resist and subvert the reproduction of male dominance in our thinking about God because thinking God as Trinity claims that God already eternally exists in such a way as to challenge and subvert these dynamics. This can operate as a radical tool of resistance within feminist theological thinking about God. It need not connote an uncritical adoption of 'orthodox' Christian doctrine for this book has engaged in dialogue with a series of critiques and theological voices in order to avoid this. Instead, it demonstrates how a 'generous orthodoxy', which takes seriously the tradition of the Christian community whilst remaining open to difference and *fully* attentive to the challenges posed by the feminist community, can affirm the self-respect and dignity of women.

Conclusion
What's Right with the Trinity?

It is undeniable that the doctrine of the Trinity raises a series of difficulties for the feminist Christian. The obvious androcentric nature of trinitarian language ideologically reinforces the male as the archetype of humanity and as closer to the divine, with the language of 'Father' and 'Son' often operating to justify rather than subvert male power and male dominance. It is, therefore, no surprise that this doctrine has been targeted by feminist theologians for investing the dynamics of patriarchy with theological credence.

However, the task of feminist theology is not simply to articulate new ways in which to speak the trinitarian mystery (as worthwhile as this is), but to assess the value of thinking God in this way for the undermining of patriarchy and the subversion of phallocentrism. This has been the task of this book. Indeed, I have argued that understanding God as Trinity need not align God with maleness, aloofness, coerciveness, dominance or self-sufficiency but can in fact serve to challenge and subvert such associations. Thinking God as Trinity can be deeply worthwhile for feminist theology because it celebrates, reinforces and affirms the central values of difference and subjectivity which underpin feminist appeals to women's experience. Indeed, thinking God as Trinity provides a theological logic by which diversity between individuals can be acknowledged and through which women can identify with God as subjects and as full participants within the *imago Dei*. Rather than confirming the male as the centre of the symbolic order, the Trinity disrupts this logic, promoting a view of difference and subjectivity which destabilizes the male's place at the centre. As such, thinking God as Trinity provides a theological context in which difference and subjectivity can be affirmed and women's *own* diverse experiences be both acknowledged and validated. Because God is diversity in communion, the rich, complex, multi-faceted and multi-textured nature of 'woman' and 'women's experience' can be theologically acknowledged and celebrated through identification with God as Trinity.

Importantly, however, thinking God as Trinity also provides a theological mandate for the *practising* and *implementation* of these values. If difference and subjectivity are values which communicate something meaningful about what God is like and are therefore identified as *Christian* as well as *feminist* values, then feminist calls for liberative praxis are in fact informed and supported (rather than undermined) by this understanding of God. If taken seriously, this doctrine has the potential to revolutionize the way in which we relate to other bodies and the world as a whole. If we truly accept that the trinitarian God is a God who is both *with* and *for* us, not distant and aloof but involved in the world at the level of the particular as revealed through the particularity of God's revelation in Jesus Christ, then this would mean valuing the particularities and contexts of others. It would mean living in such a way that recognized the sacramentality of all material things and the place of bodiliness in the trinitarian identity of God. It would mean living in solidarity with others rather than seeking to control or govern those who are different from us, in full recognition that God has eternally decided to be humanity's partner and to engage in mutual relations of love and exchange with us.[1] If Christ represents God's movement towards humanity and humanity's movement towards God (as Barth suggests) then to be in solidarity with God is, in one very important sense, to join ourselves to others.[2] Such solidarity however is not established on the basis of rule or control, but on the basis of mutuality and service.

Indeed, taking seriously the difference and relationality which characterize what it means for God to *be* as Trinity means letting go of any false sense of self-sufficiency, peeling back any desire to control and exert power *over* the other, and confessing our togetherness with God, with one another and with the rest of the created order. If the triune community is characterized by mutual sharing and the indwelling of love, then this divine community calls us also to not only participate in this love but also to make it present in the world through the way we relate and act. In this sense thinking God as Trinity confirms that humanity is not passive in God's eternal work of salvation but active agents in establishing God's reign of justice and peace here on earth. The journey towards wholeness which compromises God's work of salvation within us is not simply a private spiritual matter in which God is the only active agent, but a social and collective responsibility in which we are invited to work alongside God as co-redeemers. Matthew 25.31–46 makes clear that our actions and behaviour towards others cannot be separated form our actions and behaviour towards Christ. If we welcome the stranger then we welcome Christ, if we renounce the stranger then we renounce Christ. The work of salvation then is the responsibility of the Christian community and those who seek to follow Christ and one which is fulfilled through the practising of mutual, loving, sharing relationships. Such relationships do not seek to take the other for advantage or erase the other in order to establish the existence of ourselves. Instead, they seek the becoming of the other and approach with 'wonder' as if the first time.

Giving and generosity are, therefore, at the centre of the trinitarian life. 'God gives without self-seeking and for the benefit of others. That kind of giving is at the heart of who God is.'[3] This is not a kind of giving which gives in order to receive from others, whether praise, goods or forgiveness,[4] for this is self-seeking

---

1 I note the influence here of Cynthia L. Rigby and her closing comments in her chapter, 'Scandalous Presence: Incarnation and Trinity', in Amy Plantinga Pauw and Serene Jones (eds), *Feminist and Womanist Essays in Reformed Dogmatics* (Louisville, London, 2006), pp. 58–74, esp. pp. 72–3.

2 Ibid., p. 73.

3 Mioslav Volf, 'Being as God Is: Trinity and Generosity', in Mioslav Volf and Michael Welker (eds), *God's Life in Trinity* (Minneapolis, 2006), pp. 3–12, esp. p. 8.

4 Ibid.

and is contrary to the logic of the Trinity. God gives for the other's benefit; because it is good to give and because God, in God's *ekstatic* love, cannot help but be generous. The triune life is characterized by mutual giving in a circle of loving exchange. Within this setting, giving does not establish hierarchies – the giver is not greater than the one who receives because all give and all receive.[5]

Seen within a trinitarian context, relationship and love do not necessitate the eradication of difference but are established on the basis of it. As Leonardo Boff remarks in relation to the trinitarian relations, 'The union of Father and Son does not blot out the difference and individuality of each. Union rather supposes differentiation.'[6] Indeed, without difference there can be no mutual relationship between the triune *hypostases* and without difference there can be no mutual relationship between humankind and God or between one human subject and another. Difference between the *hypostases* ensures that loving relationship with the other does not turn into consummation of the other; difference between God and humankind ensures that God is not collapsed into humankind whilst also establishing God's eternal relationship with it; difference between individual persons ensures that relationship is not collapsed into sameness or subjectivity thwarted through a desire to control or posses the other for one's own ends. Thinking God as Trinity thus reflects the importance of difference and subjectivity and of practising behaviour which preserves and reinforces, rather than dissolves and undermines, these central values.

At the beginning of this book I asked the question, 'what's *wrong* with the Trinity?'. It is true that many answers can still be provided in relation to this question, even after the discussion provided here, hence this book in no way claims to 'solve' the plethora of feminist contentions identified in relation to this. What should be apparent, however, is that although thinking God as Trinity can serve the agenda of male dominance, it need not. In fact, thinking God as Trinity can be of great use for feminist theology today. Reframing the question from 'what's *wrong* with the Trinity' to 'what's *right* with the Trinity?' can thus provoke some extremely valuable responses and I have tried to offer one such response here. Essentially, thinking God as Trinity not only provides a theological context in which the feminist values of difference and subjectivity might be celebrated and the diversity of women's experiences therefore affirmed but also provides a theological mandate for the *practising* of these values, for the safeguarding of difference and subjectivity and for the realization and celebration of diversity within contexts of relationship, solidarity and togetherness.

---

5 Ibid., p. 10.

6 Leonardo Boff, *Trinity and Society*, trans. Paul Burns (Eugene, Oregon, 1988), p. 5.

Bibliography

Biblical quotations taken from: *Holy Bible. New Revised Standard Version* (New York: Oxford University Press, 1989), unless otherwise stated.

Achtiemer, Elizabeth, 'Exchanging God for "no Gods": A Discussion of Female Language for God', in Alvin F. Kimel (ed.), *Speaking the Christian God: The Holy Trinity and the Challenge of Feminism* (Grand Rapids, Michigan: William B. Eerdmans Publishing Company, Leominster: Gracewing, 1992), pp. 1–16.

Alcoff, Linda, 'Cultural Feminism Versus Post-structuralism: The Identity Crisis in Feminist Theory', *Signs*, 13/3 (1988): 405–36.

Anley, Alison, 'Luce Irigaray: Divine Spirit and Feminine Space', in Philip Blond (ed.), *Post-Secular Philosophy: Between Philosophy and Theology* (London, New York: Routledge, 1998), pp. 334–45.

Aquino, María Pilar, 'Theological Method in U.S. Latino/a Theology: Toward an Intercultural Theology for the Third Millennium', in Orlando O. Espín and Miguel H. Díaz (eds), *From the Heart of Our People: Latino/a Explorations in Catholic Systematic Theology* (Maryknoll, New York: Orbis Books, 1999), pp. 6–48.

——, *Our Cry for Life: Feminist Theology From Latin America* (Maryknoll, New York: Orbis Books, 1993).

Augustine, *On the Trinity*, ed. M. Dods and trans. Rev. Arthur West Hadden, B.D. (Edinburgh: T & T Clark, 1873).

——, *Sermons*, III, 51–94 on the New Testament, trans. Edmund Hill, ed. John E. Rostelle (New York: New City Press, 1991).

——, 'Answer to the Arian Sermon', in John E. Rotelle (ed.), *Arianism and Other Heresies*, I/18, trans. Roland Teske (New York: New York City Press, 1995).

——, *Letters*, 100–155, II/2, trans. Roland Teske, ed. Boniface Ramsey (New York: New York City Press, 2003).

Awad, Najeeb G., 'Between Subordination and Koinonia: Toward a New Reading of the Cappadocian Theology', *Modern Theology* (2007): 181–204.

——, 'Should We Dispense with *Sola Scripture?* Scripture, Tradition and Postmodern Theology', *Dialog: A Journal of Theology*, 47/1 (2008): 64–79.

Ayres, Lewis, '"Remember That You are Catholic" (ser. 52.2): Augustine on the Unity of the Triune God', *Journal of Early Christian Studies*, 8/1 (2000): 39–82.

——, 'The Fundamental Grammar of Augustine's Trinitarian Theology', in Robert Dodaro and George Lawless (eds), *Augustine and His Critics* (New York: Routledge, 2000).

——, *Nicaea and It's Legacy: An Approach to Fourth-Century Trinitarian Theology* (Oxford, Oxford University Press, 2004).

——, 'Nicaea and Its Legacy: An Introduction', *Harvard Theological Review*, 100/2 (2007): 141–4.

Bacon, Hannah and Jobling, J'annine, *'Why Feminists Should Still be Liberals', Theological Liberalism: Creative and Critical* (London: SPCK, 2000), pp. 91–113.

Bacon, Hannah, 'What's Right with the Trinity? Thinking the Trinity in Relation to Irigaray's Notions of Self-love and Wonder', *Feminist Theology*, 15/2 (2007): 220–35.

——, 'A Very Particular Body: Assessing the Doctrine of Incarnation for Affirming the Sacramentality of Female Embodiment', in J'annine Jobling and Gillian Howie (eds), *Women and the Divine: Touching Transcendence* (New York: Palgrave Macmillan, 2009), pp. 227–52.

——, 'Contextual Theologies' in M. Davie, T. Grass, S. Holmes, J. McDowel and T. Noble (eds), *New Dictionary of Theology* (InterVarsity Press, forthcoming).

Baker-Fletcher, Karen, *Dancing with God: The Trinity from a Womanist Perspective* (St Louis, Missouri: Chalice Press, 2006).

Barrigar, Christian J., 'Protecting God: The Lexical Formation of Trinitarian Language', *Modern Theology*, 7/4 (July 1991): 299–310.

Barth, Karl, *Church Dogmatics*, I/1, The Doctrine of the Word of God, trans. and ed. G.T. Thomson (Edinburgh: T & T Clark, 1936).

——, *Church Dogmatics*, II/1, The Doctrine of God, ed. G.W. Bromiley and T.F. Torrance, trans. T.H.L. Parker, W.B. Johnston, Harold Knight and J.L.M. Haire (Edinburgh: T & T Clark, 1957).

——, *Church Dogmatics*, II/2, The Doctrine of God, ed. G.W. Bromiley and T.F. Torrance, trans. T.H.L. Parker, W.B. Johnston, Harold Knight and J.L.M. Haire (Edinburgh: T & T Clark, 1957).

——, *Church Dogmatics*, III/2, The Doctrine of Creation, ed. G.W. Bromiley and T.F. Torrance, trans. H. Knight, G.W. Bromiley, J.K.S. Reid, R.H. Fuller (Edinburgh: T & T Clark, 1960).

——, *Church Dogmatics*, IV/1, The Doctrine of Reconciliation, ed. G.W. Bromiley and T.F. Torrance, trans. G.W. Bromiley (Edinburgh: T & T Clark, 1956).

——, *Church Dogmatics*, IV/2, The Doctrine of Reconciliation, ed. G.W. Bromiley and T.F. Torrance, trans. G.W. Bromiley (Edinburgh: T & T Clark, 1958).

——, *The Humanity of God* (London: John Knox Press, 1961).

——, *The Word of God and the Word of Man* (New York: Harper Torchbooks, 1957).

Bauer, Nancy, *Simone Beauvoir: Philosophy, and Feminism* (New York: Columbia University Press, 2001).

Bell Hooks, *Ain't I a Woman? Black Women and Feminism* (Boston: South End Press, 1981).

Beste, Jennifer, 'Limits of the Appeal to Women's Experience Reconsidered', *Horizons*, 33/1 (2006): 54–77.

Bevans, S.B., *Models of Contextual Theology*, revised and expanded edn (Maryknoll, New York: Orbis Books, 2002).

Bloesch, Donald, *The Battle for the Trinity: The Debate Over Inclusive Language* (Michigan: Vine Books, Servant Publications, 1985).

Bloomquist, Karen, '"Let God be God": The Theological Necessity of Depatriarchalizing God', in Carl E. Braaten (ed.), *Our Naming of God: Problems and Prospects of God-Talk Today* (Minneapolis: Fortress Press, 1985), pp. 45–60.

Boff, Leonardo, *Trinity and Society*, trans. Paul Burns (Eugene, Oregon: Wipf & Stock, 1988).

Bordo, Susan, *Unbearable Weight: Feminism, Western Culture, and the Body* (Berkeley, Los Angeles, London: University of California Press, 1999).

Braaten, Carl E., 'The Problem of God Language Today', in Carl E. Braaten (ed.), *Our Naming of God: Problems and Prospects of God-Talk Today* (Minneapolis: Fortress Press, 1989), pp. 11–33.

Braidotti, Rosi, 'Feminist Philosophies', in Mary Eagleton (ed.), *A Concise Companion to Feminist Theory* (Malden, Oxford, Melbourne, Berlin: Blackwell Publishing Ltd, 2003), pp. 195–214.

Brenner, Drayton C., 'Augustine and Karl Rahner on the Relationship between the Immanent Trinity and the Economic Trinity', *International Journal of Systematic Theology*, 9/1 (2007): 24–38.

Brown, Joanne Carlson and Parker, Rebecca, 'For God so Loved the World?' in Joanne Carlson Brown and Carole R. Bohn (eds), *Christianity, Patriarchy and Abuse* (New York: Pilgrim Press, 1989), pp. 1–30.

Butler, Judith, *Gender Trouble: Feminism and the Subversion of Identity* (New York and London: Routledge, 1990).

——, *Bodies that Matter: On the Discursive Limits of 'Sex'* (New York and London: Routledge, 1993).

——, *Excitable Speech: A Politics of the Performative* (New York and London: Routledge, 1997).

——, 'Critically Queer' in Paul du Gay, Jessica Evans and Peter Redman (eds), *Identity: A Reader* (London: Thousand Oaks and New Delhi: Sage Publishers, 2000), pp. 108–10.

Carmody, Denise, *Christian Feminist Theology* (Oxford: Blackwell, 1996).

Carras, Costa, 'The Holy Trinity, the Church and Politics in a Secular World', in Andrew Walker and Costa Carras (eds), *Living Orthodoxy in the Modern World: Orthodox Christianity and Society* (New York: St Vladimir's Seminary Press, 1996), pp. 189–216.

Cavallaro, Dani, *French Feminist Theory: An Introduction* (London, New York: Continuum, 2003).

Chodorow, Nancy, *The Reproduction of Mothering: Psychoanalysis and the Sociology of Gender* (Berkeley, Los Angeles and London: University of California Press, 1978).

Chopp, Rebecca, *The Power to Speak: Feminism, Language, God* (New York: Crossroad, 1989).

Christ, Carol P., 'The New Feminist Theology: A Review of the Literature', *Religious Studies Review*, 3 (1977): 203–12.

——, 'Theology and Political Implications of Imaging the Divine as Female', *Political Theology*, 8/2 (2007): 157–70.

Clements, Keith W., *Friedrich Schleiermacher: Pioneer of Modern Theology* (London: Collins Liturgical Publications, 1987).

Coakley, Sarah, 'The Trinity and Gender Reconsidered' in Miroslav Volf and Michael Welker (eds), *God's Life in Trinity* (Minneapolis: Fortress, 2006), pp. 133–42.

——, 'Introduction: Disputed Questions in Patristic Trinitarianism', *Harvard Theological Review*, 100/2 (2007): 125–38.

Colebrook, Claire, *Gender* (Hampshire, New York: Palgrave Macmillan, 2004).

Collins, Mary, 'Naming God in Public Prayer', *Worship*, 59 (1985): 291–304.

Cone, James, 'The Story of Black Theology', *Theology Today*, 32/2 (July 1975): 144–50.

——, *God of the Oppressed* (Maryknoll, New York: Orbis Books, 1975).

Congar, Yves, *I Believe in the Holy Spirit*, trans. D. Smith (3 vols, New York: The Seabury Press, London: Geoffrey Chapman, 1983).

Cunningham, D., *These Three are One: The Practice of Trinitarian Theology* (Malden, MA and Oxford: Blackwell, 1998).

D'Costa, Gavin, *Sexing the Trinity: Gender, Culture and the Divine* (London: SCM Press, 2000).

Daly, Mary, *Pure Lust: Elemental Feminist Philosophy* (London: Women's Press, 1984).

——, *Beyond God the Father: Towards a Philosophy of Women's Liberation* (London: Women's Press, 1991).

Davaney, Sheila Greeve, 'The Limits of the Appeal to Women's Experience', in Clarissa W. Atkinson, Constance H. Buchanan and Margaret R. Miles (eds), *Shaping New Vision: Gender and Values in American Culture* (London: UMI Research Press, 1987), pp. 31–50.

——, 'Continuing the Story but Departing the Text: A Historicist Interpretation of Feminist Norms in Theology', in Rebecca S. Chopp and Sheila Greeve Davaney (eds), *Horizons in Feminist Theology: Identity Tradition and Norms* (Minneapolis: Fortress Press, 1997), pp. 198–214.

——, *Pragmatic Historicism: A Theology for the Twenty-First Century* (New York: State University of New York Press, 2000).

Davis, Angela, *Women, Race and Class* (New York: Random House, 1981).

De Beauvoir, Simone, *The Second Sex*, trans. and ed. H.M. Parshley (London, Australia, New Zealand, South Africa: Vintage, 1949).

Diller, Kevin, 'Does Contemporary Theology Require a Postfoundational Way of Knowing?', *Scottish Journal of Theology*, 60/3 (2007): 271–93.

DiNoia, J.A., 'Knowing and Naming the Triune God: The Grammar of Trinitarian Confession', in Alvin F. Kimel (ed.), *Speaking the Christian God: The Holy*

Trinity and the Challenge of Feminism (Grand Rapids, Michigan: William B. Eerdmans Publishing Company, Leominster: Gracewing, 1992), pp. 162–87.

Drever, Matthew, 'The Self Before God? Rethinking Augustine's Trinitarian Thought', *Harvard Theological Review*, 100/2 (2007): 233–42.

Duck, Ruth, Gender and the Name of God: The Trinitarian Baptismal Formula (New York: Pilgrim Press, 1991).

Dulles, Avery, *Models of Revelation* (Dublin: Gill and Macmillan, 1983).

Eiesland, Nancy L., The Disabled God: Towards a Liberatory Theology of Disability (Nashville: Abingdon Press, 1994).

Fee, Gordon D., 'Paul and the Trinity: The Experience of Christ and the Spirit for Paul's Understanding of God', in Stephen Davis, Daniel Kendall, Gerald O'Collins (eds), *The Trinity: An Interdisciplinary Symposium on the Trinity* (Oxford: Oxford University Press), pp. 49–72.

Felski, Rita, *Doing Time: Feminist Theory and Postmodern Culture* (New York and London: New York University Press, 2000).

Fiddes, Paul, *Participating in God: A Pastoral Doctrine of the Trinity* (London: Darton, Longman & Todd, 2000).

Fiorenza, Elisabeth Schüssler, *In Memory of Her: A Feminist Theological Reconstruction of Christian Origins* (London: SCM, 1984).

——, *Foundational Theology: Jesus and the Church* (New York: Crossroad, 1984).

——, 'The Will to Choose or to Reject', in Letty M. Russell (ed.), *Feminist Interpretation of the Bible* (Louisville, London, Leiden: Westminster Press, 1985), pp. 125–36.

——, *Discipleship of Equals: A Critical Feminist Ekklesia-ology of Liberation* (London: SCM, 1993).

Flax, Jane, 'Postmodernism and Gender Relations in Feminist Theory', Signs, 12/4 (1987): 621–43.

Fox, Patricia A., *God as Communion: John Zizioulas, Elizabeth Johnson and the Retrieval of the Symbol of the Triune God* (Collegeville, Minnesota: The Liturgical Press, 2001).

Fraser, Nancy, 'Pragmatism, Feminism, and the Linguistic Turn' in Seyla Benhabib, Judith Butler, Drucilla Cornell, Nancy Fraser (eds), *Feminist Contentions: A Philosophical Exchange* (London, New York: Routledge, 1995), pp. 157–72.

Frei, Hans, *Theology and Narrative*, ed. George Hunsinger and William Packer (New York: Oxford University Press, 1993).

Friedan, Betty, *The Feminine Mystique* (London: Penguin, 1963).

Frye, Marilyn M., 'The Necessity of Differences: Constructing a Positive Category of Women', *Signs*, 21/4 (1996): 991–1010.

Frye, Roland, *Language for God and Feminist Language* (Edinburgh: The Handsel Press, 1988).

Fulkerson, Mary McClintock, *Changing the Subject: Women's Discourses and Feminist Theology* (Minneapolis: Fortress Press, 1994).

——, 'Contesting the Gendered Subject: A Feminist Account of the Imago Dei', in Rebecca S. Chopp and Sheila Greeve Davaney (eds), *Horizons in Feminist*

Theology: Identity Tradition and Norms (Minneapolis: Fortress Press, 1997), pp. 99–115

Fuss, Diana, *Essentially Speaking: Feminism, Nature and Difference* (London: Routledge Kegan Paul, 1989).

Gebara, Ivone, 'Women Doing Theology in Latin America', in Elsa Tamez (ed.), *Through Her Eyes: Women's Theology from Latin America* (Maryknoll, New York: Orbis Books, 1989), pp. 37–48.

Geffré, Claude, '"Father" as the Proper Name of God', in Johannes-Baptist Metz and Edward Schillebeeckx (eds), *God as Father?* (Edinburgh: T & T Clark, New York: The Seabury Press, 1981), pp. 43–50.

Giles, Kevin, *The Trinity and Subordinationism: The Doctrine of God and the Contemporary Gender Debate* (Downers Grove, Illinois: InterVarsity Press, 2002).

——, *Jesus and the Father* (Grand Rapids, Michigan: Zondervan, 2006).

Grant, Jacqueline, 'Black Theology and the Black Woman', in Gayraud S. Wilmore and James H. Cone (eds), *Black Theology: A Documentary History 1966–1979* (Maryknoll, New York: Orbis Books, 1979), pp. 418–33.

——, *White Women's Christ and Black Women's Jesus* (Atlanta, Georgia: Scholars Press, 1989).

——, 'The Challenge of the Darker Sister', in Janet Martin Soskice and Diana Lipton (eds), *Feminism and Theology* (Oxford: Oxford University Press, 2003), pp. 302–11.

Green, Garrett, 'The Gender of God and the Theology of Metaphor', in Alvin F. Kimel (ed.), *Speaking the Christian God: The Holy Trinity and the Challenge of* Feminism (Grand Rapids, Michigan: William B. Eerdmans Publishing Company, Leominster: Gracewing, 1992), pp. 44–64.

Greene-McCreight, Kathryn, 'Feminist Theology and a Generous Orthodoxy', *Scottish Journal of Theology*, 57/1 (2004): 95–108.

Gregory of Nazianzus, 'Select Orations of Gregory Nazianzen', in Philip Schaff and Henry Wace (eds), *A Select Library of Nicene and Post-Nicene Fathers of the Christian Church*, trans. Gordon Browne and James Edward Swallow (Edinburgh: T & T Clark, Grand Rapids, Michigan: WM Eerdmans Publishing Company, 1989), pp. 203–436.

Grey, Mary, 'The Core of Our Desire: Re-imaging the Trinity', *Theology*, 93 (1990): 362–72.

——, *Introducing Feminist Images of God* (Sheffield: Sheffield Academic Press, 2001).

Grosz, Elizabeth, *Sexual Subversions: Three French Feminists* (St. Leonards: Allen & Unwin, 1989).

Gunton, Colin, 'Proteus and Procrustes: A Study in the Dialectic of Language in Disagreement with Sallie McFague', in Alvin F. Kimel (ed.), *The Triune God and the Challenge of Feminism* (Grand Rapids: Eerdmans, 1992), pp. 65–80.

——, *The Promise of Trinitarian Theology* (Edinburgh: T & T Clark, 1997).

Gustavsson, Roger, 'Hauerwas's With The Grain of the Universe and The Barthian Outlook', *Journal of Religious Ethics*, 35/1 (2007): 25–86

Hampson, Daphne, *Theology and Feminism* (Oxford: Basil Blackwell, 1990).

Hannaford, Robert, 'Gender and the Person God Is', in Robert Hannaford and J'annine Jobling (eds), *Theology and the Body: Gender, Text and Ideology* (Leominster: Gracewing, 1999), pp. 30–46.

Hanssen, Beatrice, 'What Happened to Feminist Theory?' in Elisabeth Bronfen and Misha Kavka (eds), *Feminist Consequences: Theory for the New Century* (New York: Columbia University Press, 2001), pp. 58–98.

Harding, Sandra, *The Science Question in Feminism* (Milton Keynes: Open University Press, 1986).

——, 'Rethinking Standpoint Epistemology: What is Strong Objectivity?', in Sandra Harding (ed.), *The Feminist Standpoint Theory Reader: Intellectual and Political Controversies* (London and New York: Routledge, 2004), pp. 127–40.

Hart, Trevor, 'Revelation' in John Webster (ed.), *The Cambridge Companion to Karl Barth* (Cambridge: Cambridge University Press, 2000), pp. 37–56.

Hartsock, Nancy C.M., *Money, Sex and Power: Toward a Feminist Historical Materialism* (New York, London: Longman, 1983).

——, 'The Feminist Standpoint: Developing the Ground for a Specifically Feminist Historical Materialism', in Sandra Harding (ed.), *The Feminist Standpoint Theory Reader: Intellectual and Political Controversies* (London and New York: Routledge, 2004), pp. 35–54.

Hawkesworth, Mary, 'Knowers, Knowing, Known: Feminist Theory and Claims of Truth', *Signs*, 14/3 (1989): 533–7.

Hayter, Mary, *The New Eve in Christ* (London: SPCK, 1987).

Hector, Kevin W., 'Actualism and Incarnation: The High Christology of Friedrich Schleiermacher', *International Journal of Scottish Theology*, 8/3 (2006): 307–22.

Hekman, Susan, *The Future of Differences: Truth and Method in Feminist Theory* (Cambridge: Polity Press, 1999).

Heron, Alasdair, 'The Biblical Basis for the Trinity', in Alasdair Heron (ed.), *The Forgotten Trinity: A Selection of Papers presented to the BCC Study Commission on Trinitarian Doctrine Today* (London: BCC/CCB, 1991), 15–41.

Hirschmann, Nancy J., 'Feminist Standpoint as Postmodern Strategy', in Sandra Harding (ed.), *The Feminist Standpoint Theory Reader: Intellectual and Political Controversies* (London and New York: Routledge, 2004), pp. 317–32.

Hogan, Linda, *From Women's Experience to Feminist Theology* (Sheffield: Sheffield Academic Press, 1995).

Hopkins, Julie, *Towards a Feminist Christology: Jesus of Nazareth, European Women and the Christological Crisis* (Grand Rapids: Eerdmans, 1995).

Hunsinger, George, 'Election and the Trinity: Twenty-five theses on the Theology of Karl Barth', *Modern Theology*, 24/2 (2008): 179–98.

Irigaray, Luce, *Speculum of the Other Woman*, trans. Gillian C. Gill (Ithaca, New York: Cornell University Press, 1985).

——, *This Sex Which is Not One*, trans. Catherine Porter with Carolyn Burke (Ithaca, New York: Cornell University Press, 1985).

——, 'Sexual Difference', in Margaret Whitford (ed.), *The Irigaray Reader* (Oxford and Cambridge, Massachusetts: Basil Blackwell Ltd, 1991), pp. 165–77.

——, 'The Power of Discourse and the Subordination of the Feminine', in Margaret Whitford (ed.), *The Irigaray Reader* (Oxford and Cambridge, Massachusetts: Basil Blackwell Ltd, 1991), pp. 118–32.

——, 'Volume without Contours', in Margaret Whitford (ed.), *The Irigaray Reader* (Oxford and Cambridge, Massachusetts: Basil Blackwell Ltd, 1991), pp. 53–68.

——, *An Ethics of Sexual Difference*, trans. Carolyn Burke and Gillian C. Gill (London: Athlone Press, 1993).

——, *Sexes and Genealogies*, trans. Gillian C. Gill (New York: Columbia University Press, 1993).

——, 'The Question of the Other', in Lynne Huffer (ed.), *Another Look, Another Woman: Retranslations of French Feminism, Yale French Studies* (vol. 8, New Haven, Connecticut and London: Yale University Press, 1995), pp. 7–19.

——, *I Love to You: Sketch of a Possible Felicity in History*, trans. Alison Martin (London, New York: Routledge, 1996).

——, 'The Other: Woman', in Sandra Kemp and Judith Squires (eds), *Feminisms* (Oxford and New York: Oxford University Press, 1997), pp. 308–15.

——, *The Way of Love*, trans. Heidi Bostic and Stephen Pluháček (London, New York: Continuum, 2002).

——, 'The Wedding Between the Body and Language', in Luce Irigaray (ed.), *Luce Irigaray: Key Writings* (London, New York: Continuum, 2004), pp. 13–22.

Isasi-Diaz, Ada María, *Mujerista Theology: A Theology for the Twenty-First Century* (Maryknoll, New York: Orbis Books, 1996).

——, *La Lucha Continues: Mujerista Theology* (Maryknoll, New York: Orbis Books, 2004).

Jantzen, Grace M., 'What's the Difference? Knowledge and Gender in (Post) Modern Philosophy of Religion', *Religious Studies*, 32 (1996): 431–48.

Janz, Paul D., 'Divine Causality and the Nature of Theological Questioning', *Modern Theology*, 23/3 (July 2007): 317–48.

Jay, Nancy, 'Gender and Dichotomy', *Feminist Studies*, 7/1 (Spring 1981): 38–56.

Johnson, Elizabeth, 'Redeeming the Name of Christ: Christology', in Catherine Mowry LaCugna (ed.), *Freeing Theology: The Essential Theology in Feminist Perspective* (San Francisco: HarperCollins Publishers, 1993), pp. 115–27.

——, 'The Incomprehensibility of God and the Image of God Male and Female,' *Theological Studies*, 45 (1984): 441–65.

——, *Consider Jesus: Waves of Renewal in Christology* (London: Geoffrey Chapman, 1990).

——, *She Who Is: The Mystery of God in Feminist Theological Discourse* (New York: Crossroad, 1992).

Jones, Serene, 'Divining Women: Irigaray and Feminist Theologies', in Lynne Huffer (ed.), *Another Look, Another Woman: Retranslations of French Feminism*, Yale French Studies (vol. 8, New Haven, Connecticut and London: Yale University Press, 1995), pp. 42–67.

Joy, Morny, 'Equality or Divinity: A False Dichotomy?', *Journal of Feminist Studies in Religion*, 6/1 (1990): 9–24.

Julian of Norwich, *The Revelations of Divine Love*, trans. James Walsh, S.J. (Tenbury Wells: Fowler Wright Books Ltd, 1961).

Kaufman, Gordon D., *In Face of Mystery: A Constructive Theology* (Cambridge, Massachusetts, London: Harvard University Press, 1995).

Kimel, Alvin, 'The God Who Likes His Name: Holy Trinity, Feminism and the Language of Faith', in Alvin F. Kimel (ed.), *Speaking the Christian God: The Holy Trinity and the Challenge of Feminism* (Grand Rapids, Michigan: William B. Eerdmans Publishing Company, Leominster: Gracewing, 1992), pp. 188–208.

Kwok Pui-Lan, *Introducing Asian Feminist Theology* (Sheffield: Sheffield Academic Press, 2000).

——, 'Feminist Theology as Intercultural Discourse', in Susan Frank Parsons (ed.), *The Cambridge Companion to Feminist Theology* (Cambridge: Cambridge University Press, 2002), p. 23–39.

Kyung, Chung Hyun, *Struggle to Be the Sun Again: Introducing Asian Women's Theology* (Maryknoll, New York: Orbis Books, 1990).

LaCugna, Catherine Mowry, Mowry, 'Returning from "The Far Country": Thesis for a Contemporary Trinitarian Theology', *Scottish Journal of Theology*, 41/2 (1988): 191–215.

——, *God for Us: The Trinity & Christian Life (*New York: HarperCollins Publisher, 1991).

——, 'God in Communion with Us – The Trinity', in Catherine Mowry LaCugna (ed.), *Freeing Theology: The Essentials of Theology in Feminist Perspective* (New York: HarperCollins, 1993), pp. 83–114.

Lindbeck, George, *The Nature of Doctrine: Religion and Theology in a Postliberal Age* (Louisville, Kentucky: Westminster John Knox Press, 1984).

Lossky, Vladimir, *The Mystical Theology of the Eastern Church* (New York: St Vladimir's Seminary Press, 1997).

Luther, Martin, 'Disputations held at Heidelberg, 1518', in J. Atkinson (trans. and ed.), *Luther: Early Theological Works, Library of Christian Classics*, XVI (London: SCM, 1962), pp. 274–307.

Lyotard, Jean-François, *The Postmodern Condition: A Report on Knowledge* (Manchester: Manchester University Press, 1984).

Marshall, Bruce, *Trinity and Truth* (Cambridge: Cambridge University Press, 2000).

——, 'Trinity' in Gareth Jones (ed.), *The Blackwell Companion to Modern Theology* (Malden, MA, Oxford, UK, Victoria, Australia: Blackwell, 2004) pp. 183–203.

Martin, Alison, *Luce Irigaray and the Question of the Divine* (London: Maney Publishing for the Modern Humanities Research Association, 2000).
Martin, Jane Roland, 'Methodological Essentialism, False Difference and Other Dangerous Traps', *Signs*, 19/3 (1994): 630–57.
McCormack, Bruce, 'Grace and Being: The Role of God's Gracious Elements in Karl Barth's Theological Ontology', in John Webster (ed.), *The Cambridge Companion to Karl Barth* (Cambridge: Cambridge University Press, 2000), pp. 92–110.
——, 'Seek God Where He May be Found: A Response to Edwin Chr. Van Driel', *Scottish Journal of Theology*, 60/1 (2007): 62–79.
McFague, Sallie, *Models of God: Theology for an Ecological, Nuclear Age* (Philadelphia: Fortress Press, 1987).
——, *The Body of God: An Ecological Theology* (Minneapolis: Fortress Press, 1993).
——, *A New Climate for Theology: God, the World, and Global Warming* (Minneapolis: Fortress Press, 2008).
Migliore, Daniel L., 'The Trinity and the Theology of Religions', in Miroslav Volf and Michael Walker (eds), *God's Life in Trinity* (Minneapolis: Fortress Press, 2006), pp. 101–17.
Molnar, Paul D., *Divine Freedom and the Doctrine of the Immanent Trinity: A Dialogue with Karl Barth and Cotemporary Theology* (London, New York: T & T Clark, 2002).
Moltmann, Jürgen, 'The Crucified God', *Theology Today*, 31/1 (1974): 6–18.
——, *The Crucified God: The Cross of Christ as the Foundation and Criticism of Christian Theology*, trans. R.A. Wilson and John Bowden (London: SCM, 1974).
——, *The Church in the Life of the Spirit* (New York: Harper and Row, 1977).
——, *The Trinity and the Kingdom of God: The Doctrine of God* (Munich: SCM, 1981).
——, 'The Motherly Father: Is Trinitarian Patripassionism Replacing Theological Patriarchalism?', in Johannes-Baptist Metz and Edward Schillebeeckx (eds), *God as Father?* (Edinburgh: T & T Clark, New York: The Seabury Press, 1981), pp. 51–6.
——, *Experiences of Theology* (Minneapolis: Fortress Press, 2000).
Moulaison, Jane Barter, '"Our Bodies, Our Selves?" The Body as Source in Feminist Theology', *Scottish Journal of Theology*, 60/3 (2007): 341–59.
Nelson, Lynn Hankinson, 'Epistemological Communities', in Linda Alcoff and Elizabeth Potter (eds), *Feminist Epistemologies: Thinking Gender* (London and New York: Routledge, 1993), pp. 121–60.
Newlands, George, *God in Christian Perspective* (Edinburgh: T & T Clark, 1994).
——, *Trinitarian Perspectives* (Edinburgh: T & T Clark, 1994).
O'Collins, G., 'The Holy Trinity: The State of the Question', in Stephen Davis, Daniel Kendall, Gerald O'Collins (eds), *The Trinity: An Interdisciplinary Symposium on the Trinity* (Oxford: Oxford University Press, 1999), pp. 1–25.

O'Donnell, J., *Trinity and Temporality: The Christian Doctrine of God in the Light of Process Theology and the Theology of Hope* (Oxford: Oxford University Press, 1983).

Oakes, Kenneth, 'The Question of Nature and Grace in Karl Barth: Humanity as Creature and as Covenant Partner', *Modern Theology*, 23/4 (2007): 595–616.

Oduyoye, Mercy Amba, *Introducing African Women's Theology* (Sheffield: Sheffield Academic Press, 2001).

——, 'Jesus Christ', in Susan Frank Parsons (ed.), *The Cambridge Companion to Feminist Theology* (Cambridge: Cambridge University Press, 2002), pp. 151–70.

——, *Beads and Strands: Reflections of an African Woman on Christianity in Africa* (Maryknoll, New York: Orbis Books, 2004).

Oxford-Carpenter, Rebecca, 'Gender and the Trinity,' *Theology Today*, 41/1 (April 1984): 7–25.

Pannenberg, Wolfhart, *Basic Questions in Theology: Collected Essays* (Philadelphia: Fortress Press, 1970).

Papanikolaou, Aristotle, *Being with God: Trinity, Apophaticism and Divine-Human Communion* (Notre Dame, Indiana: University of Notre Dame, 2006).

Pecknold, C.C., 'How Augustine used the Trinity: Functionalism and the Development of Doctrine', *Anglican Theological Review*, 85/1 (Winter 2003): 127–41.

Peters, Ted, *God as Trinity: Relationality and Temporality in Divine Life* (Louisville, Westminster, Kentucky: John Knox Press, 1993).

Placher, William C., 'Believing in the Triune God: Three in One', *Christian Century* (17 April 2007): 28–32.

Polkinghorne, John, 'Jürgen Moltmann's Engagement with the Natural Sciences', in Miroslav Volf and Michael Walker (eds), *God's Life in Trinity* (Minneapolis: Fortress Press, 2006), pp. 61–70.

Prestige, G.L., *God in Patristic Thought* (London: SPCK, 1964).

Rahner, Karl, *The Trinity*, trans. Joseph Donceel (London and New York: Burns and Oates, 1970).

Ramshaw, Gail, 'De Divinis Nominibus: The Gender of God', *Worship*, 56 (1982): 117–36.

——, 'Naming the Trinity: Orthodoxy and Inclusivity', *Worship*, 60 (1986): 491–8.

——, *Under the Tree of Life: The Religion of a Feminist Christian* (New York, The Continuum Publishing Company, 1998).

Reed, Esther, 'Revelation in Feminist Theology and Philosophy', in Paul Avis (ed.), *Divine Revelation* (Grand Rapids: Eerdmans, 1997), pp. 156–73.

Rigby, Cynthia L., 'Scandalous Presence: Incarnation and Trinity', in Amy Plantinga Pauw and Serene Jones (eds), *Feminist and Womanist Essays in Reformed Dogmatics* (Louisville, London: Westminster John Knox Press, 2006), pp. 58–74.

Ronan, Marian, 'Reclaiming Women's Experience: A Reading of Selected Christian Feminist Theologies', *Cross Currents* (1998): 218–29.

Rousseau, Jacques, *Discourse on the Origin of Inequality. Discourse on the Origin and Foundation of Inequality Among Men*, trans. Donald A. Crex (Indianapolis, Cambridge: Hackett Publishing Company, 1992).

Ruether, Rosemary Radford, *Sexism and God-talk: Toward a Feminist Theology* (Boston: Boston Press, 1983).

——, *Introducing Redemption in Christian Feminism* (Ohio: The Pilgrim Press, 2000).

——, 'Methodology in Women's Studies and Feminist Theology', in Arvind Sharma (ed.), *Methodology of Religious Studies: The Interface with Women's Studies* (Albany: State University of New York Press, 2002), pp. 179–206.

Russell, Letty, *Human Liberation in a Feminist Perspective – A Theology* (Philadelphia: The Westminster Press, 1974).

——, *The Future of Partnership* (Philadelphia: Westminster Press, 1979).

Saiving, Valerie, 'The Human Situation: A Feminine View' in Judth Plaskow and Carol P. Christ (eds), *Womanspirit Rising: a Feminist in Reliogion* (New York: Harper Collins, 1992), pp. 25–42.

Sanders, Fred, 'Trinity Talk, Again', *Dialog: A Journal of Theology*, 44/3 (2005): 264–72.

Schillebeeckx, Edward, *Christ the Sacrament of the Encounter with God* (Maryland: Sheed and Ward, 1963).

Schleiermacher, Friedrich, 'On the Discrepancy Between the Sabellian and Athanasian Methods of Representing the Doctrine of the Trinity', trans. with notes and illustration by M. Stuart, *The Biblical Repository and Quarterly Observer*, XVIII (April 1936): 316–17.

——, *On Religion: Speeches to its Cultural Despisers*, trans. John Oman (New York: Harper and Row Publishers, 1958).

——, *The Christian Faith*, trans. and ed. H.R. Mackintosh and J.S. Stewart, second edn (Edinburgh: T & T Clark, 1999).

Schluter, M., *Christianity in a Changing World: Biblical Insight on Contemporary Issues* (London: Marshall Pickering, 2000).

Scirghi, Thomas J., *An Examination of the Problems of Inclusive Language in the Trinitarian Formula of Baptism. Studies in Religion and Society* (New York: Edwin Mellen, 2000).

Scott, David, 'Creation as Christ: A Problematic Theme in Some Feminist Theology', in Alvin F. Kimel (ed.), *Speaking the Christian God: The Holy Trinity and the Challenge of Feminism* (Grand Rapids, Michigan: William B. Eerdmans Publishing Company, Leominster: Gracewing, 1992), pp. 237–57.

Sellers, Susan, *Language and Sexual Difference: Feminist Writings in France* (London: Macmillan Education, 1991).

Sherman, Franklin, 'Reticence and Exuberance in Speaking of God', in Carl E. Braaten (ed.), *Our Naming of God: Problems and Prospects of God-Talk Today* (Minneapolis: Fortress, 1989), pp. 35–43.

Slee, Nicola, 'The Holy Spirit and Spirituality', in Susan Frank Parsons (ed.), *The Cambridge Companion to Feminist Theology* (Cambridge: Cambridge University Press, 2002), pp. 171–89.

Soskice, Janet Martin, *Metaphor and Religious Language* (Oxford: Clarendon Press, 1985).

——, 'Theological Realism', in William J. Abraham and Steven W. Holtzer (eds), *The Rationality of Religious Belief* (Oxford: Clarendon Press, 1987): 105–20.

——, 'Trinity and Feminism', in Susan Frank Parsons (ed.), *The Cambridge Companion to Feminist Theology* (Cambridge: Cambridge University Press, 2002), pp. 135–50.

Stanley, Liz, 'Method, Methodology and Epistemology', in Liz Stanley (ed.), *Feminist Praxis: Research Theory and Epistemology in Feminist Sociology* (London and New York: Routledge, 1990).

Stanley, Liz and Wise, Sue, *Breaking Out: Feminist Consciousness and Feminist Research* (London, Boston, Melbourne and Henley: Routledge and Kegan Paul, 1983).

——, *Breaking Out Again: Feminist Ontology and Epistemology*, second edn (London and New York: Routledge & Kegan Paul, 1993).

Stone, Alison, *Luce Irigaray and the Philosophy of Sexual Difference* (Cambridge, New York, Melbourne, Madrid, Cape Town, Singapore, Sao Paulo: Cambridge University Press, 2006).

Streufert, Mary J., 'Reclaiming Schleiermacher for Twenty-first Century Atonement Theory: The Human and the Divine in Feminist Christology', *Feminist Theology*, 15/1 (2006): 98–120.

Sykes, Stephen, *Friedrich Schleiermacher* (Working: Lutterworth Press, 1971).

——, *The Identity of Christianity: Theologians and the Essence of Christianity from Schleiermacher to Barth* (London: SPCK, 1984).

Tamez, Elsa, 'Cultural Violence Against Women in Latin America', in Mary John Manazan, Mercy Amba Oduyoye and Elsa Tamez (eds), *Women Resisting Violence: Spirituality for Life* (Maryknoll, New York: Orbis Books, 1996), pp. 11–19.

Taylor, Iain, 'In Defence of Karl Barth's Doctrine of the Trinity', *International Journal of Systematic Theology*, 5/1 (2003): 33–46.

Teevan, Donna, 'Challenges to the Role of Theological Anthropology in Feminist Theologies', *Theological Studies*, 64 (2003): 582–97.

Tennis, Diane, *Is God the Only Reliable Father?* (Philadelphia: Westminster Press, 1985).

Thayer-Bacon, Barbara J., *Transforming Critical Thinking: Thinking Constructively* (New York and London: Teacher's College Press, 2000).

Thiemann, Ronald F. 'Beyond Exclusive and Absolutism: A Trinitarian Theology of the Cross' in Miroslav Volf and Michael Walker (eds) *God's Life in the Trinity* (Minneapolis, 2006), pp. 118–29.

Toon, Peter and Spiceland, James D., *One God in Trinity* (London: Samuel Bagster, 1980).

Toon, Tarmo, *Classical Trinitarian Thought: A Textbook* (London and New York: T & T Clark, 2007).

Torrance, Alan, 'Trinity', in John Webster (ed.), *The Cambridge Companion to Karl Barth* (Cambridge: Cambridge University Press, 2000), pp. 72–91.

Torrance, Thomas F., *Karl Barth: Biblical and Evangelical Theologian* (Edinburgh: T & T Clark, 1990).

Van Driel, Edwin Chr., 'Karl Barth on the Eternal Existence of Jesus Christ', *Scottish Journal of Theology*, 60/1 (2007): 45–61.

——, 'Schleiermacher's Supralapsarian Christology', *Scottish Journal of Theology*, 60/3 (2007): 251–70.

Volf, Mioslav, 'Being as God Is: Trinity and Generosity', in Mioslav Volf and Michael Welker (eds), *God's Life in Trinity* (Minneapolis, 2006), 3–12.

Wainwright, Arthur W., *The Trinity in the New Testament* (London: SPCK, 1962).

Wainwright, Geoffrey, 'A Language in Which we Speak of God', *Worship*, 57 (1983): 309–21.

——, 'Trinitarian Worship', in Alvin F. Kimel (ed.), *Speaking the Christian God: The Holy Trinity and the Challenge of Feminism* (Grand Rapids, Michigan: William B. Eerdmans Publishing Company, Leominster: Gracewing, 1992), pp. 209–21.

Ward, Graham, 'Bodies: The Displaced Body of Jesus', in J. Milbank, C. Pickstock and G. Ward (eds), *Radical Orthodoxy: A New Theology* (London: Routledge, 1999), pp. 163–81.

Webster, John, *Karl Barth*, second edn (London, New York: Continuum, 2004).

Wells, David F., 'The Nature and Function of Theology,' in R.K. Johnston (ed.), *The Use of the Bible in Theology: Evangelical Options* (Atlanta: John Knox, 1985), pp. 175–99.

Whitford, Margaret, *Luce Irigaray: Philosophy in the Feminine* (London, New York: Routledge, 1991).

Wilkinson, Loren, '"Post-Christian" Feminism and the Fatherhood of God,' in Maxine Hancock (ed.), *Christian Perspectives on Gender, Sexuality and Community* (Vancouver, British Columbia: Regent College Publishing, 2003), pp. 103–26.

Williams, Delores, *Sisters in the Wilderness: The Challenge of Womanist God-Talk* (Maryknoll, New York: Orbis, 1993).

——, 'Black Women's Surrogacy Experience and the Christian Notion of Redemption', in Marit Trelstad (ed.), *Cross Examinations: Readings on the Meaning of the Cross Today* (Minneapolis: Fortress Press, 2006), pp. 19–32.

Williams, Jane, 'The Doctrine of the Trinity: A Way Forward for Feminists?', in Teresa Elwes (ed.), *Women's Voices: Essays in Contemporary Feminist Theology* (London: Marshall Pickering, 1992), pp. 31–43.

Williams, Jay G. 'Yahweh, Women and the Trinity', *Theology Today*, 32/3 (1975): 234–42.

Williams, Robert R., *Schleiermacher the Theologian: The Constructions of the Doctrine of God* (Philadelphia: Fortress Press, 1978).

Wren, Brian, *What Language Shall I Borrow? God Talk in Worship: A Male Response to Feminist Theology* (London: SCM, 1989).

Yocum, John, 'What's Interesting about Karl Barth? Barth as Polemical and Descriptive Theologian', *International Journal of Systematic Theology*, 4/1 (2002): 29–44.

Young, Pamela Dickey, *Feminist Theology/Christian Theology: In Search of Method* (Eugene, Oregon: Wipf & Stock, 1990).

Zizioulas, John D., 'On Being a Person: Towards an Ontology of Personhood', in Christoph Schwöbel and Colin E. Gunton (eds), *Persons, Divine and Humans: King's College essays in Theological Anthropology* (Edinburgh: T & T Clark, 1991), pp. 33–46.

——, 'The Doctrine of God and the Trinity Today: Suggestions for an Ecumenical Study', in Alasdair Heron (ed.), *The Forgotten Trinity: A Selection of Papers presented to the BCC Study Commission on Trinitarian Doctrine Today* (London: BCC/CCB, 1991), pp. 19–32.

——, *Being as Communion* (New York: St. Vladimir's Seminary Press, 1993).

——, 'The Doctrine of the Holy Trinity: The Significance of the Cappadocian Contribution', in C. Schwöbel (ed.), *Trinitarian Theology Today* (Edinburgh: T & T Clark, 1995), pp. 44–60.

Index

Lightning Source UK Ltd.
Milton Keynes UK
UKHW011209190519
342904UK00015B/193/P

9 780754 666738